Mini Farming

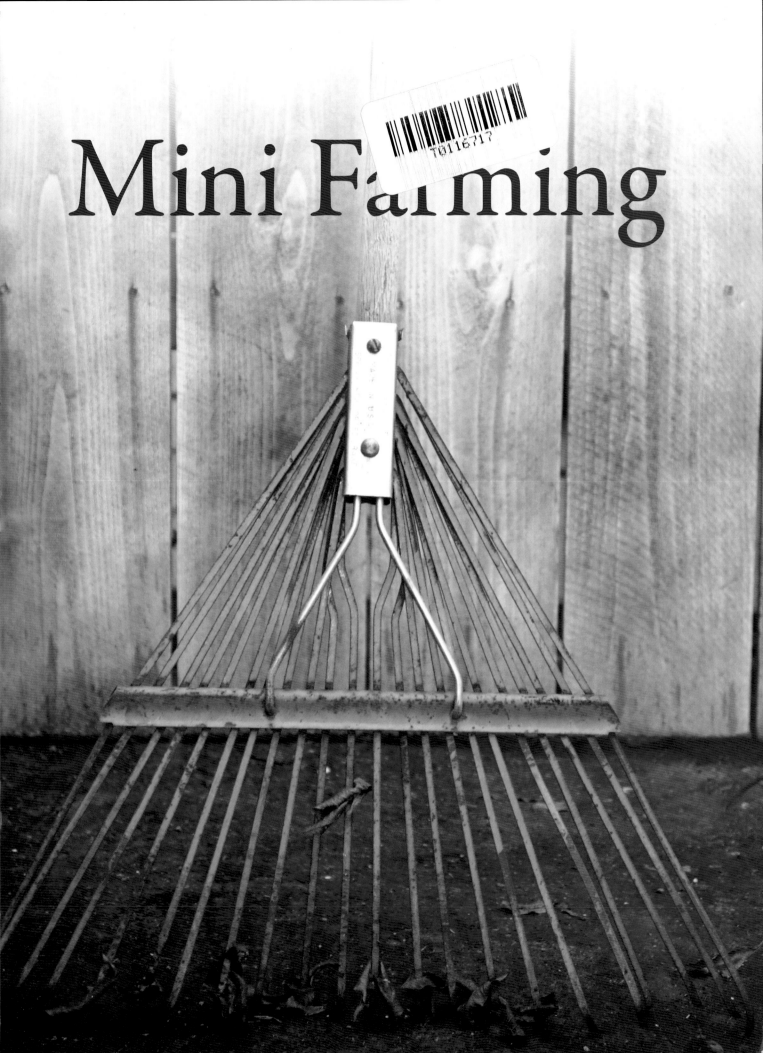

Mini Farming
Self-Sufficiency on ¼ Acre

Brett L. Markham

Skyhorse Publishing

Skyhorse Publishing books may be purchased in bulk at special discounts for sales promotion, corporate gifts, fund-raising, or educational purposes. Special editions can also be created to specifications. For details, contact the Special Sales Department, Skyhorse Publishing, 307 West 36th Street, 11th Floor, New York, NY 10018 or info@skyhorsepublishing.com.

Skyhorse® and Skyhorse Publishing® are registered trademarks of Skyhorse Publishing, Inc.®, a Delaware corporation.

www.skyhorsepublishing.com

24

Library of Congress Cataloging-in-Publication Data

Markham, Brett L.
  Mini farming : self sufficiency on 1/4 acre / Brett L. Markham.
      p. cm.
  Includes bibliographical references and index.
  ISBN 978-1-60239-984-6
  1. Agriculture--Handbooks, manuals, etc. 2. Farms, Small--Handbooks, manuals, etc. 3. Self-reliant living--Handbooks, manuals, etc. I. Title.
  S501.2.M37 2010
  635'.048--dc22
                              2009041561

Printed in China

Contents

Dedicated to my father, Thomas J. Markham,
the man I most admire and whose tenacity, resourcefulness, and
optimism have always been a beacon in my life.
His courage, moral leadership, boundless intellect, and helpfulness
have aided uncountable people for decades and have undoubtedly
changed the course of history.

Acknowledgments

I would like to thank my wife, Francine, for putting up with my idiosyncrasies and our ever-expanding mini-farm and for both proofreading and editing this book.

I would also like to thank my daughter, Hannah, a child of endless joy and keen insight whose well-being inspired me to develop the ideas and conclusions in this work.

Finally, albeit posthumously, I need to acknowledge the influence of my paternal grandfather, Gilbert Garfield Markham. My grandfather was a first-generation farmer who spent a lot of time with me on his farm, both instructing and answering my endless questions. He conveyed a lot of wisdom that I was too young to appreciate at the time but have since grown to appreciate greatly.

The sacred chain continues.

Introduction

Home food production is an important proficiency that contributes positively to the physical and financial health of the family. Along with this, it provides an important psychological and spiritual boost by reaffirming our connection with nature and nature's laws, reconnecting us with our ancestral roots, and providing the feeling of competence that comes from ensuring the supply of a basic necessity—food.

Just as important, the quality of food produced at home is superior to that available in the supermarket for a number of reasons. The demands of business drive many factors that decrease the nutritional value of commercial foods. Because very little food is produced near its point of use, fruit and vegetable varieties are selected on the basis of suitability for machine picking, long-distance shipping, and cold storage so that they still look good when they reach the supermarket. This results in homogeneous and visually appealing products that look better than they taste and have considerably less nutritional value than homegrown equivalents.

Spinach is a good example. With proper care and refrigeration, fresh spinach can be kept from spoiling for three weeks or more. But even when kept in the dark at 39 degrees, it loses about half of its B vitamin content in only a week. So the appealing bag of baby spinach under the brightly lit cooler in the supermarket actually has fewer nutrients than homegrown spinach that is blanched and frozen on the same day as harvest.

The same situation applies to other fruits and vegetables. Considering the time spent in packaging, shipment, and storage, homegrown produce that is canned, frozen, or dehydrated quickly after harvesting will pack more nutritional punch than even so-called fresh produce at the supermarket.

Nutrient density is not the only factor favoring home food production. Pesticide residue is another important consideration.

Corporate farms and orchards use a variety of pesticides to protect the quantity and visual appeal of their harvests. According to a 1999 Consumer's Union report based on U.S. government data, "An apple grown in the U.S. typically contains four pesticides, and some have as many as 10 different residues."[1] The same report listed several common vegetables, including winter squash and spinach, as typically containing residues of multiple pesticides, some with as many as 14. The report goes on to cite data indicating both widespread illegal pesticide usage and persistence of carcinogenic chemicals that were banned decades ago in present-day corporate harvests.

In addition, small home gardens are ideally suited to the use of organic or semiorganic materials and methods that can significantly reduce, and even eliminate, the need for synthetic pesticides. Regardless, if a home gardener decides to use commonly available over-the-counter pesticides, proper usage and scheduling is personally ensured by the gardener to make sure that the amount of residue remaining in the food is far less than in typical commercially grown produce.

Superior taste is a major benefit to home-grown foods. The two major factors influencing taste are freshness and the actual variety grown. With a backyard garden, it is not unusual to serve vine-ripened tomatoes within minutes of picking

them from the vine, whereas supermarket tomatoes are harvested while green and allowed to ripen during shipment. It is really impossible for any sort of food store to exceed the degree of freshness found in a backyard garden.

In addition, because the vegetable varieties used in corporate agriculture (a.k.a. "agribusiness") are selected for toughness in shipping, simultaneous ripening, and ease of mechanical harvesting, some of the best-tasting varieties of numerous fruits and vegetables are not even available in supermarkets because they aren't suitable for machine picking or bruise too easily. Conversely, the home gardener is free to choose from literally thousands of common and/or heirloom varieties on the basis of personal taste.

Commercial growers are in business. As a result, the dollar is their standard of value. Your health—to the extent it even crosses their minds—is a far secondary concern. Their primary aim is the production of goods with the lowest possible cost and selling them at the highest possible price consistent with the greatest profit. There is nothing automatically evil about this process, but it is obvious that the effort you can invest in making sure your food is safe, tasty, and healthful is far superior to that of a corporation half a continent away.

Finally, economy is an important reason to produce and preserve foods at home. The mini-farming methods covered in this book yield fresh produce at mere percentages of the cost of purchasing similar foods at the supermarket. This means that growing your own food can add precious dollars to the family budget, while preserving your own food can guarantee a supply of healthful food during lean times. Moving from vegetable gardening into full-scale mini-farming

[1] Benbrook, C. M., Groth III, E., Lutz, K. (1999) *Do You Know What You're Eating?* Retrieved Dec 31, 2005, from http://www.consumersunion.org/food/do_you_know2.htm

using intensive techniques can conceivably provide over 80% of a family's food, reducing cash needs by many thousands of dollars yearly.

I have met many people who used to grow gardens but have since abandoned the practice. While the details vary, in all of these cases the former gardeners had encountered conditions that made the realization of their gardening goals either impossible or impractical. Many had moved to homes with very small yards, so a traditional garden wouldn't fit. Some had experienced injuries that limited mobility. Others had encountered bad insect or other pest problems. Finally, many just gave up because gardening was too much time and trouble when compared to the benefits they derived. The lesson I have learned is that people need to have a reasonable prospect of achieving their goals in gardening, or they won't bother.

The goals of the mini-farmer are similar to those of the home gardener but with an added emphasis on economics. The mini-farmer's aim is to reduce the amount of income needed by providing a substantial portion of the household's food needs. This can allow a parent to stay at home with children, make homeschooling feasible, improve conditions under a fixed income, or act as a buffer against uncertain economic conditions.

In the chapters ahead, I intend to demonstrate how the goals of gardening and mini-farming can be achieved with greater enjoyment and much less time, effort, money, and equipment than you ever expected, in spite of whatever obstacles may arise.

The approaches adopted in this book are a combination of traditional, Biodynamic, Grow Biointensive, French Intensive, Square Foot, and other approaches that use raised beds and that I call "intensive agriculture." It stands on the shoulders of many great and dedicated gardeners, thinkers, philosophers, and farmers, so I claim no unique credit for it, but the synthesis has been made based on my own experience and will hopefully save the reader a lot of trial and error.

The content of this book can be used at various levels. It can be used to allow efficient hobby gardening for improved nutrition and enjoyment, a more substantial commitment to gardening, and full-fledged mini-farming. My aim, then, is to help the reader get started on a path to growing more economical, nutritious, and safe food with minimal effort while simultaneously helping the reader reconnect with the cycles of nature and heritage in a way that will enhance the spirit.

Brett L. Markham
New Ipswich, New Hampshire
2009

1

Overview of Intensive Agriculture

Intensive agricultural techniques, and their productivity compared to traditional row gardening methods, have been well documented in the past several decades, and certain methods have been used for centuries. They all share a number of common characteristics.

All of the intensive methods use raised beds and grow vegetables much more closely than traditional row methods and therefore require less land—thus requiring less water and labor while reducing the need for weeding. Intensive gardens produce the same amount of food in 20% of the space or even less than that, leading to greatly reduced costs.

Traditional row gardening is one-dimensional—that is, a straight line. A small furrow is dug with a hoe, and seeds are sprinkled in from a packet. After the seeds germinate, the farmer goes back down the row and thins plants to the recommended spacing. Each row takes its own space, plus space for walking paths on either side, and the walking paths become compacted under foot traffic. The entire area—rows and paths—is watered and fertilized. Because the rows are exposed to the drying effects of sun and wind on both sides, mulching

 Row gardens adapted from commercial agriculture are wasteful of space and resources on a home scale.

is required to conserve water and prevent weeds. The typical 100-foot row takes up at least 300 square feet of space. As a basis of comparison, the expected yield of carrots for that row is about 100 pounds.

In contrast, intensive mini-farming is three-dimensional. Seeds are planted in the raised bed using within-row spacings in all directions, giving a two-dimensional space, and crops such as pole beans are grown on trellises, adding a third dimension. This vastly increases the quantity of a given crop that can be produced per unit area. In the case of carrots, a garden bed 4 feet wide and 6 feet long (24 square feet) will yield 100 pounds of carrots. That's the theoretical yield, but in practice I've found 32 square feet

are required to get a full 100 pounds. Still, that's an amazing increase in space efficiency! Using trellising and pole beans instead of bush beans and indeterminate (vining) tomatoes instead of determinate (bush) tomatoes will also increase the yield per plant.

Using row gardening, the farmer has to fertilize, mulch, weed, and water 300 square feet of space to get 100 pounds of carrots. But by using raised beds and intensive gardening techniques that use close spacing, the farmer has to fertilize and water only 24 square feet—less than 1/10 the space and thus less than 1/10 the fertilizer and water. The cost savings are immense, and the intensive farmer can also dispense with mulching, because the plants are growing so closely together that they shade each other's stems and the ground, conserving moisture and shading out weeds. The shade provided by growing plants closely is also helpful in protecting beneficial soil microbes from the damaging effects of ultraviolet radiation from the sun. Last season I kept records of how much weeding was required per 100 square feet averaged across crops as diverse as broccoli and tomatoes, and because of the living mulch aspect of intensive gardening, less than 30 minutes *per season* were required per 100 square feet.

There are three schools of thought regarding the spacing of plants in intensively planted beds. The Grow Biointensive method recommends a hexagonal pattern using various sorts of hexagonal and triangular jigs. The Square Foot method recommends using a grid of squares dividing every square foot into a number of subsquares appropriate to the spacing of the crop being grown. My own method is to plant a properly spaced row, go up the distance within a row, and then plant seeds in parallel.

⊗ Carrots planted intensively in a raised bed yielded 100 pounds in just 32 square feet.

A little analysis yields a few facts. The Grow Biointensive method actually fits more vegetables into the same space compared to the other two, but for most vegetables the difference is 10% or less. Offsetting this advantage is the fact that the Grow Biointensive planting method is painstaking and that the average person interested in farming isn't about to envision a hexagon as being composed of a series of equilateral triangles. However, this process *will* increase yields for a farmer handy enough to set up the proper jigs to make the planting process easy. The jigs are plywood triangles composed of three 60-degree angles and with all three sides the same length as the planting distance between each plant of each different crop. A seed is planted at each of the three points.

The Square Foot method is about as simple as can be imagined geometrically: Everything is a square. Spacing can be figured easily based on within-row spacing of a given plant. The only downside is that you are subdividing individual square feet that need to be laid out within the beds. This works great on a small scale, but on a larger scale this can be problematic, especially when adding large-volume soil amendments to beds such as compost. Grids can be made that can be readily removed, but this again is more labor. For a 200-square-foot garden, the work is no big deal, but when the garden is scaled to 6,300 square feet to provide for the needs of a family plus marketable vegetables, the task of making and maintaining grids to set apart individual square feet becomes enormous. Thus the Square Foot method, where each square foot is individually marked off, is more suitable for hobby gardening than a mini-farm.

When I came up with my own way of intensive planting, I wanted something simple enough that my daughter would be able to do it.

First, look at the seed packet to determine the final distance between plants after thinning (circled in the illustration). Second, grab a small ruler and a blunt pencil. Third, use the ruler and pencil to put quarter-inch holes in the ground to mark off a square grid the size of the area you want to plant. The distance between holes is the final distance between plants after thinning. Put a seed in each hole, cover with dirt, and tamp it down—then water daily until the seeds sprout.

Note that all of these methods will eliminate the need to thin plantings. As a result, they conserve seed and thereby conserve money and save labor.

⊗ Use the final thinning distance as your initial planting distance for intensive agriculture.

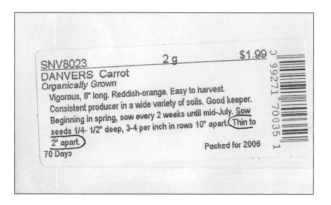

The yield differential for the carrots given in the example isn't atypical. A 100-foot row of lettuce spaced every six inches will fit into a 4-foot × 6-foot intensively planted bed with the same yield. Comparing the 24 square feet to the 300 square feet (including walking paths), and understanding that an acre contains 43,560 square feet, you will quickly see that a 3,500-square-foot intensive garden will produce the same output as an acre farmed conventionally.

Along with close spacing, intensive agriculture emphasizes vertically grown crops such as cucumbers, vining tomatoes, and pole beans. There are two reasons for this. First, using the third dimension of height allows you to get more production per unit area. Second, vining varieties produce more total food yield over the course of the season. Growing crops vertically on a trellis also makes harvesting easier, reduces diseases, and has the aesthetic advantage of growing consistently straight cucumbers.

So that crops grown on a trellis don't shade out other crops, trellises should be constructed on the north side of raised beds. The ultimate height of a trellis depends somewhat on what is being grown but also on your convenience. For most people, a trellis can be six or even seven feet high without causing inconvenience.

I use a variety of trellis structures including A-frames, boards screwed together, and electrical conduit. Anything will work as long as it is mechanically strong enough to handle winds while fully loaded with plants without falling over.

The approach to intensive agriculture called "mini-farming" in this book contains elements from many different systems that have been tested by the author at various times. While not

 Trellises maximize efficiency by allowing plant growth in three dimensions.

every approach can be listed, the most influential systems are described along with some references so that anyone who is interested can learn more about these ideas.

The French Intensive method of agriculture was originally developed to cope with the small yard sizes in France. It emphasizes a technique called "double-digging" to create the beds and depends on a considerable input of horse manure for fertilizer. The most comprehensive book on the topic is *Intensive Culture of Vegetables* by P. Aquatias.

The Biodynamic method was created by Rudolph Steiner in 1924 because of his observations of the detrimental effects of artificial fertilizers. It emphasizes the concept of the farm as a self-contained biological organism. The book *What Is Biodynamics?* includes seven lectures on the topic by Rudolph Steiner and gives a good overview of the method and its fundamentals.

The Grow Biointensive method is a combination of the French Intensive and Biodynamic methods first synthesized by Alan Chadwick and continued by Ecology Action, a nonprofit group focusing on sustainable agriculture. It keeps the double-dug raised beds of the French Intensive method and adds many aspects of the Biodynamic method. The book *How to Grow More Vegetables* by John Jeavons covers the method comprehensively.

Square Foot gardening was invented by Mel Bartholomew in the 1980s because of his observations of community gardens and his desire to improve the efficiency and enjoyability of gardening. The method emphasizes the use of raised beds using custom-made soil fertilized with organic amendments. The book *All New Square Foot Gardening* by Mel Bartholomew covers his methods in detail.

There are other approaches to intensive agriculture with a variety of names, but all of them are essentially composed of elements already incorporated in one of the four methods already listed. The methods of intensive agriculture advocated in this book are no different—they pull from the experiences of others and add the experience of the author. As a result, the approach that I present differs somewhat from earlier methods. I will explain the reasoning for the differences in the chapters ahead, but for now I think it would be worthwhile to point out the major differences.

My mini-farming technique differs from the Square Foot method in that I do not mark off individual square feet of bed or use the bed shape, special soil mix, or individual-plant hand-watering techniques advocated by that method.

Mini-farming differs from the Grow Biointensive method mainly in its lack of emphasis on growing grains, but it also dispenses with the seed-starting and plant-spacing methods, among others.

Mini-farming differs from the Biodynamic method in that it doesn't use special herbal preparations for preparing compost, plant seeds by moon phases, or consider the farm to be a self-contained entity. There are so many other differences, they can't all be listed.

My approach to mini-farming differs from the French Intensive method in that it doesn't rely on massive inputs of horse manure. In other respects the French method is similar to Grow Biointensive, so those differences apply as well.

Learning and Observation

Intensive agricultural practices are constantly being refined, extended, amended, and developed by well-known practitioners and by individual farmers. Agriculture is, at its heart, a biological rather than industrial process. As a result, it is subject to laws of nature that we humans are only beginning to understand. The path to success with intensive agriculture, as with any other endeavor, is through constantly expanding knowledge.

A constant input of new information is most easily and economically acquired through a library. Land-grant universities have a substantial selection of agricultural books and magazines available, and use of the facility is not limited to students. Likewise, the Internet has a wide array of resources available.

Experience is also an excellent teacher, and hands-on experience will provide insight unavailable in a book. Along with gaining experience, a mini-farmer should keep detailed records of events and observations.

I keep several journals for each year. One journal lists every plant variety to be grown that year, where the seed was acquired, and general information about that plant and its requirements. Following this are journal entries describing where, when, and how the seeds were started; transplantation information; and significant events that affected the crop up through harvest. Any pest problems are noted in the journal, along with the effectiveness of any remedies and especially information that might give a clue as to why some plants of a given crop may have been more or less affected.

Another important journal entry specific to intensive agriculture is plant spacing. A starting value for two-dimensional plant spacing is the within-row thinning distance specified on the seed package. This will give optimal yields in a row-type system and will often give optimal yields in a raised-bed intensive system, but a little experimentation is in order because yields relative to

⊗ Journals are an important tool for learning and improvement.

spacing will vary with soil and climate conditions. In the case of lettuce in my own garden, I have discovered that eight-inch spacings work better than six-inch spacings—but those results will be different for a different soil and climate.

All of this information helps to fine-tune the environment that I give the plant from year to year so that my reliance on fertilizers, horse manure, and other external inputs—even if organic—can be reduced from year to year.

A journal of crop-specific information also helps me to decide if I want to grow a particular crop variety the next year or perhaps grow it differently. In 2005, I grew a particular kind of carrot that tasted horrible raw but was fine when cooked. Since I grew it in the summer, I might decide to instead grow it as a winter or fall crop this upcoming year to see how that affects the taste. If my family usually eats carrots when raw, I might want to consider a different variety of carrot altogether. That carrot was also grown in soil that had received some composted horse manure. It would stand to reason that the carrot might taste better raw if grown in a different bed that has been fertilized with only vegetable-based compost. (And this *is* the case! Carrots shouldn't be grown in anything close to fresh manure, and I learned this through my journals!) With all of this information, I can fine-tune my carrots until they are the finest quality carrots available.

Another journal that I keep lists weather events, particularly abnormalities or anything that affects crops. Such a journal allows me to know that, in my area, I need to protect young spinach plants from hail when they are planted before the last frost date. Having this knowledge in hand allows my crops to be more productive and suffer less damage.

I also keep a calendar/planner that lets me lay out across the year when I need to perform various tasks—such as starting and transplanting seedlings or harvesting green manures. Such a calendar allows me to see and work around labor bottlenecks in advance. I note in the planner the date of first harvests for each crop based on published maturity dates for the crops, and I make note of instances where a particular crop matured earlier or later than I expected. Predicted harvest dates also allow me to see in advance when succession planting or starting a crop at a time when I ordinarily wouldn't will serve to reduce peak workloads for food preservation so the work can be spread out better.

My final journal lists practically everything I do related to soil fertility, including digging beds, compost contents, organic amendments added to soils, crop rotations, and so forth. This information is correlated with information about harvests of various crops and pest or disease problems.

The idea of all of this journaling is to put all of my experiences and observations into a context that allows me to use that information effectively to make better decisions each year than I made the year before. Working with biological systems is a process of constant learning, and a mini-farmer will ultimately benefit from keeping detailed notes.

Intensive agriculture, because it grows plants close together in a relatively small land area, is a field with a lot of room for experimentation and it makes the results of that experimentation more easily observable by the farmer. This gives mini-farmers an opportunity to make improvements in technique much more rapidly than those involved in industrial farming.

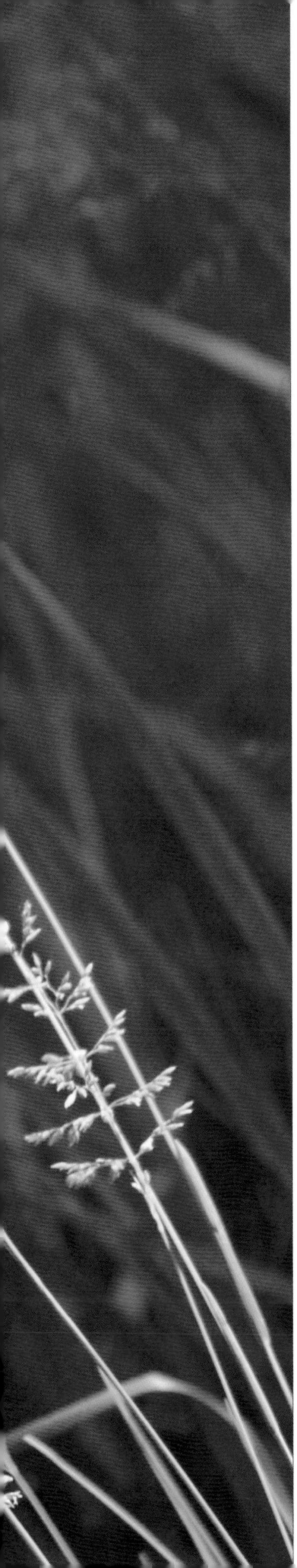

2

How Mini-Farming Works for You

Many homeowners undertake the task of gardening or small-scale farming as a hobby to get fresh-grown produce and possibly save money over buying food at the supermarket. Unfortunately, the most common gardening methods end up being so expensive that even some enthusiastic garden authors state outright that gardening should be considered, at best, a break-even affair.[2]

Looking at the most common gardening methods, such authors are absolutely correct. Common gardening methods are considerably more expensive than they need to be because they were originally designed to benefit from the economies of scale of corporate agribusiness. When home gardeners try to use these methods on a smaller scale, it's a miracle if they break even over a several-year period, and it is more likely they will lose money.

The cost of tillers, watering equipment, large quantities of water, transplants, seeds, fertilizers and insecticides adds up pretty quickly. Balanced against the fact that most home gardeners grow only vegetables,

---

[2] Bird, C. O. (2001) *Cubed Foot Gardening*

and vegetables make up only less than 10% of the calories an average person consumes,[3] it quickly becomes apparent that even if the cost of a vegetable garden were zero, the amount of actual money saved in the food bill would be negligible. For example, if the total economic value of the vegetables collected from the garden in a single season amounted to about $350,[4] and the vegetables could be produced for free, the economic benefit would amount to only $7 per week when divided over the year.

The solution to this problem is to both cut costs and increase the value of the end product. This can be accomplished by growing your own seedlings from open-pollinated plant varieties so you can save the seeds and avoid the expense of buying both transplants and seeds, using intensive gardening techniques that use less land, conscientiously composting to reduce the need for fertilizers, and growing calorie-dense crops that will supply a higher proportion of the household's caloric intake.

Using this combination, the economic equation will balance in favor of the gardener instead of the garden supply store, and it becomes quite possible to supply all of a family's food except meat from a relatively small garden. According to the USDA, the average annual per capita expenditure on food was $2,964 in 2001, with food costs increasing at a rate of 27.7% over the previous 10 years.[5] Understanding that food is purchased with after-tax dollars, it becomes clear that home agricultural methods that take a significant chunk out of that figure can make the difference, for example, between a parent being able to stay at

home with children and he or she having to work, or it could vastly improve the quality of life of a retiree on a fixed income.

The key to making a garden work to your economic benefit is to approach mini-farming as a business. No, it is not a business in the sense of incorporation and taxes unless some of its production is sold, but it *is* a business in that by reducing your food expenditures, it has the same net effect on finances as income from a small business. Like any small business, it could earn money or lose money depending on how it is managed.

Grow Your Own Seedlings

Garden centers are flooded every spring with home gardeners picking out seedlings for lettuce, broccoli, cucumbers, tomatoes, and so on. For those who grow gardens strictly as a hobby, this works out well because it allows them to get off to a quick start with minimal investment of time and planning. But for the mini-farmer who approaches gardening as a small business, it's a bad idea.

⊗ These broccoli plants grown from seed saved a lot of money in the long run.

[3] Jeavons, J. (2002) *How to Grow More Vegetables*
[4] Bartholomew, M. (2005) *Square Foot Gardening*
[5] USDA (2001) *Agriculture Factbook 2001–2002*

In my own garden this year, I plan to grow 48 broccoli plants. Seedlings from the garden center would cost $18 if discounted and possibly over $30. Even the most expensive organic broccoli seeds on the market cost less than a dollar for 48 seeds. If transplants are grown at home, their effective cost drops from $18 to $30 down to $1. Adding the cost of soil and containers, the cost is still only about $2 for 48 broccoli seedlings.

Considering that a mini-farm would likely require transplants for dozens of crops ranging from onion sets to tomatoes and lettuce, it quickly becomes apparent that even if all seed is purchased, growing transplants at home saves hundreds of dollars a year.

Prefer Open-Pollinated Varieties

There are two basic types of seed/plant varieties available: hybrid and open-pollinated. Open-pollinated plant varieties produce seeds that duplicate the plants that produced them. Hybrid plant varieties produce seeds that are at best unreliable and sometimes sterile and therefore often unusable.

Although hybrid plants have the disadvantage of not producing good seed, they often have advantages that make them worthwhile, including aspects of "hybrid vigor." Hybrid vigor refers to a poorly understood phenomenon in plants where a cross between two different varieties of broccoli can yield far more vigorous and productive offspring than either parent. Depending on genetic factors, it also allows the creation of plants that incorporate some of the best qualities of both parents while deemphasizing undesirable traits. Using hybridization, then, seed companies are able to deliver varieties of plants that incorporate disease resistance into a particularly good tasting vegetable variety.

So why not just use hybrid seeds? Because there's no such thing as a free lunch. For plants that normally self-pollinate, such as peppers and tomatoes, there is no measurable increase in the vigor of hybrids. The hybrids are just a proprietary marketing avenue. So buying hybrids in those cases just raises costs, and since the tomato seeds can't be saved, the mini-farmer has to buy seeds again the next year. The cost of seeds for a family-sized mini-farm that produces most of a family's food for the year can easily approach $200, a considerable sum! Beyond that, seed collected and saved at home can not only reduce costs but be resold if properly licensed. (Here in New Hampshire, a license to sell seeds costs only $100 annually.)

Another reason to save seeds from open-pollinated plant varieties is if each year you save seeds from the best performing plants, you will eventually create varieties with genetic characteristics that work best in your particular soil and climate. That's a degree of specialization that money can't buy.

Of course, there are cases where hybrid seeds and plants outperform open-pollinated varieties by the proverbial country mile. Corn is one such example. The solution? Use the hybrid seeds or, if you are so inclined, make your own! Hybridization of corn is quite easy. Carol Deppe's excellent book *Breed Your Own Vegetable Varieties* gives all of the details on how to create your own hybrids.

Hybrid seeds that manifest particular pest- or disease-resistant traits can also be a good choice when those pests or diseases cause ongoing problems. When using hybrid seeds eliminates the need for synthetic pesticides, they are a good choice.

Use Intensive Gardening Techniques

A number of intensive gardening methods have been well documented over the past century. What all of these have in common is growing plants much more closely spaced than traditional row methods. This closer spacing causes a significant decrease in the amount of land required to grow a given quantity of food, which in turn significantly reduces requirements for water, fertilizer, and mechanization. Because plants are grown close enough together to form a sort of "living mulch," the plants shade out weeds and retain moisture better, thus decreasing the amount of work required to raise the same amount of food.

Intensive gardening techniques make a big difference in the amount of space required to provide all of a person's food. Current agribusiness practices require 30,000 square feet per person or 3/4 acre. Intensive gardening practices can reduce the amount of space required for the same nutritional content to 700 square feet,[6] plus another 700 square feet for crops grown specifically for composting. That's only 1,400 square feet per person, so a family of three can be supplied in just 4,200 square feet. That's less than 1/10 of an acre. In many parts of the United States, land is extremely expensive, and lot sizes average a half acre or less. Using traditional farming practices, it isn't even possible to raise food for a single person in a half-acre lot, but using intensive gardening techniques allows only half of that lot—1/4 acre—to provide nearly all the food for a family of four, generate thousands of dollars in income besides, allow raising small

livestock plus leave space for home and recreation. Intensive gardening techniques are the key to self-sufficiency on a small lot.

Compost

Because growing so many plants in such little space puts heavy demand on the soil in which they are grown, all intensive agriculture methodologies pay particular attention to maintaining the fertility of the soil.

The law of conservation of matter indicates that if a farmer grows a plant, that plant took nutrients from the soil build itself. If the plant is then removed from the area, the nutrients in that plant are never returned to the soil, and the fertility of the soil is reduced. To make up for the loss of fertility, standard agribusiness practices apply commercial fertilizers from outside the farm.

The fertilizer costs money, of course. While there are other worthwhile reasons for avoiding the use of nonorganic fertilizers, including environmental damage, the biggest reason is a mini-farm with a properly managed soil fertility plan can drastically reduce the need to purchase fertilizer altogether, thereby reducing one of the biggest costs associated with farming and making the mini-farm more economically viable. In practice, a certain amount of fertilizer will always be required, especially at the beginning, but using organic fertilizers and creating compost can ultimately reduce fertilizer requirements to a bare minimum.

The practice of preserving soil fertility consists of growing crops specifically for compost value, growing crops to fix atmospheric nitrogen into the soil, and composting all crop residues possible (along with the specific compost crops)

---

[6] Duhon, D., Gebhard, C. (1984) *One Circle*

and practically anything else that isn't nailed down. (Chapter 5 covers composting in detail.)

A big part of soil fertility is the diversity of microbial life in the soil, along with the presence of earthworms and other beneficial insects. There are approximately 4,000 pounds of bacteria in an acre of fertile topsoil. These organisms work together with soil nutrients to produce vigorous growth and limit the damage done by disease-causing microorganisms known as "pathogens."

Grow Calorie-Dense Crops

As already noted, vegetables provide about only 10% of the average American's calories. Because of this, a standard vegetable garden may supply excellent produce and rich vitamin content, but the economic value of the vegetables won't significantly reduce your food bill over the course of a year. The solution to this problem is to grow crops that provide a higher proportion of caloric needs such as fruits, dried beans, grains, and root crops such as potatoes and onions.

Raise Meat at Home

Most Americans are accustomed to obtaining at least a portion of their protein from eggs and meat. Agribusiness meats are often produced using practices and substances (such as growth hormones and antibiotics) that worry a lot of people. Certainly, factory-farmed meat is very high in the least healthy fats compared to free-range, grass-fed animals or animals harvested through hunting.

The problem with meat, in an economic sense, is that the feeding for one calorie of meat generally requires anywhere from two to four calories of feed. This sounds, at first blush, like a very inefficient use of resources, but it isn't as bad as it seems. Most livestock, even small livestock like poultry, gets a substantial portion of its diet from foraging around. Poultry will eat all of the ticks, fleas, spiders, beetles, and grasshoppers that can be found plus dispose of the farmer's table scraps. If meat is raised on premises, then the mini-farmer just has to raise enough extra food to make up the difference between the feed needs and what was obtained through scraps and foraging.

Plant Some Fruit

There are a number of fruits that can be grown in most parts of the country: apples, grapes, blackberries, pears, and cherries to name few. Newer dwarf fruit tree varieties often produce substantial amounts of fruit in only three years, and they take up comparatively little space. Grapes native to North America, such as the Concord grape, are hardy throughout the continental United States, and some varieties, like muscadine grapes, grow prolifically in the South and have recently been discovered to offer unique health benefits. Strawberries are easy to grow and attractive to youngsters. A number of new blackberry and raspberry varieties have been introduced, some without thorns, that are so productive you'll have more berries than you can imagine.

Fruits are nature's candy and can easily be preserved for apple sauce, apple butter, snacks, jellies, pie filling, and shortcake topping. Many fruits can also be stored whole for a few months using root cellaring. Fruits grown with minimal or no pesticide usage are expensive at the store, and growing your own will put even more money in the bank with minimal effort.

Grow Market Crops

Especially if you adopt organic growing methods, you can get top-wholesale-dollar for crops delivered to restaurants, organic food cooperatives, and so forth. If your property allows it, you can also set up a farm stand and sell homegrown produce at top retail dollar.

According to John Jeavon's 1986 research described in *The Complete 21-Bed Biointensive Mini-Farm*, a mini-farmer in the United States could expect to earn $2,079 in income from the space required to feed one person in addition to actually feeding the person. Assuming a family of three and correcting for USDA reported rises in the value of food, that amounts to $10,060 per year, using a six-month growing season.

Mel Bartholomew in his 1985 book *Ca$h from Square Foot Gardening* estimated $5,000 per year income during a six-month growing season from a mere 1,500 square feet of properly managed garden. This equates to $8,064 in today's market.

A mini-farm that sets aside only 2,100 square feet for market crops would gross an average of $11,289 per year.

It is worthwhile to notice that two very different authorities arrived at very closely the same numbers for expected income from general vegetable sales—about $5.00 per square foot.

Extend the Season

A lot of people don't realize that most of Europe, where greenhouses, cold frames, and other season extenders have been used for generations, lies north of most of the United States. Maine, for example, is at the same latitude as southern France. The reason for the difference in climate has to do with ocean currents, not latitude, and latitude is the biggest factor in determining the success of growing protected plants because it determines the amount of sunlight available. In essence, anything that can be done in southern France can be done throughout the continental United States.

The secret to making season extension economically feasible lies in working with nature rather than against it. Any attempt to build a

super insulated and heated tropical environment suitable for growing bananas in Minnesota in January is going to be prohibitively expensive. A simple unheated hoop house covered with plastic is fairly inexpensive and will work extremely well with crops selected for the climate.

Extending the season brings two big advantages. First, it lets you harvest fresh greens and seasonal fare throughout the year including held-over potatoes, carrots, and onions, thus keeping the family's food costs low. Second, it allows for earlier starts and later endings to the main growing season, netting more total food for the family and more food for market. It also provides a happy diversion from dreary winters when the mini-farmer can walk out to a hoop house for fresh salad greens in the middle of a snowstorm.

Understand Your Market

As a mini-farmer you may produce food for two markets: the family and the community. The family is the easiest market to understand because the preferences of the family can be easily discovered by looking in the fridge and cabinets. The community is a tougher nut to crack, and if you decide to market your excess crops, you will need to assess your community's needs.

Food is a commodity, meaning that the overwhelming majority of food is produced and sold in gargantuan quantities at tiny profit margins that are outside the reach of a mini-farmer. The proportion of crops that are grown for market cannot hope to compare with the wholesale costs of large commercial enterprises. Therefore the only way the mini-farmer can actually derive a profit is to sell at retail direct to the community or high-markup organics at wholesale.

Direct agricultural products can work, as can value-added products such as pickles, salsas, and gourmet vinegars.

Your products can appeal to the community in a number of ways, but the exact approaches that will work in a given case depend on the farmer's analysis of the needs of that community. You should keep careful records to make sure that the right crops are being grown.

The Economic Equation

According to the Federal Bureau of Labor Statistics, as of October 2005, the average nonfarm wage earner in the United States earns $557.54 per week or $28,990 per year for working 40.7 hours every week, or 2,116 hours a year. According to the Tax Foundation, the average employee works 84 out of 260 days a year just to pay taxes deducted from the paycheck, leaving the average employee $19,620.

According to the 2001 Kenosha County Commuter Study, conducted in Wisconsin before our most recent increases in fuel costs, the average employee spent $30 per week on gas just getting back and forth to work, or $1,500 per year, and spent $45 per week on lunches and coffee on the way to work, or $2,340 per year. Nationwide, the cost of child care for children under age 5 was estimated at $297 per month for children under age 5 and $224 per month for children aged 5 to 12. This estimate is from an Urban League study in 1997, so the expense has undoubtedly increased in the meantime. Assuming a school-age child though, the expenses of all this add up so that the average worker has only $13,092 remaining that can be used to pay the mortgage or rent, the electric bill, and so forth.

Though there can be other justifications for adopting mini-farming, including quality-of-life issues such as the ability to homeschool children, it makes economic sense for one spouse in a working couple to become a mini-farmer if the net economic impact of the mini-farm can replace the income from the job. Obviously, for doctors, lawyers, media moguls, and those in other highly paid careers, mini-farming may not be a good economic decision. But mini-farming can have a sufficient net economic impact that most occupations can be replaced if the other spouse works in a standard occupation. Mini-farming is also sufficiently time efficient that it could be used to remove the need for a second job. It could also be done part-time in the evenings as a substitute for TV time.

The economics of mini-farming look like this. According to Census Bureau statistics from 2003, the average household size in the United States is 2.61 people. Let's round that up to 3 for ease of multiplication. According to statistics given earlier, accounting for the rise in food prices, the cost of feeding a family of 3 now amounts to $3,210 per person, or $9,630 per year. A mini-farm that supplied 85% of those needs would produce a yearly economic benefit of $8,185 per year—the same as a pretax income of $12,200, except it can't be taxed.

That would require 2,100 square feet of space, and 10 hours a week from April through September—a total of 240 hours. This works out to the equivalent of nearly $51 per hour.

If the farm also dedicated 2,100 square feet to market crops, you could also earn $10,060 during a standard growing season, plus spend an additional five hours a week from April through September. This works out to nearly $84 per hour.

When the cash income is added to the economic benefit of drastically slashing food bills, the minimum net economic benefit of $14,920 exceeds the net economic benefit of the average job by nearly $2,000 per year.

This assumes a lot of worst-case conditions. It assumes that the mini-farmer doesn't employ any sort of season extension, which would increase the value generated, and it assumes that the mini-farmer deducts none of the expenses from the income to reduce tax liability. In addition, once automatic irrigation is set up, the mini-farmer needs to work only three to four hours a day from April through November. Instead of working 2,116 hours per year to net $13,092 after taxes and commuting like the average wage earner, the mini-farmer has worked only 360 to 440 hours per year to net $14,920. At the end of the workday, the mini-farmer doesn't have to commute home—because home is where the farm is, and the workday has ended pretty early.

In this manner, the mini-farmer gains back more than 1,500 hours a year that can be used to improve quality of life in many ways, gains a much healthier diet, gets regular exercise, and gains a measure of independence from the normal employment system. It's impossible to attach a dollar value to that.

For families who want to have a parent stay at home with a child or who want to homeschool their children, mini-farming may make it possible—and make money in the process, by having whichever parent who earns the least money from regular employment go into mini-farming. For healthy people on a fixed income, it's a no-brainer.

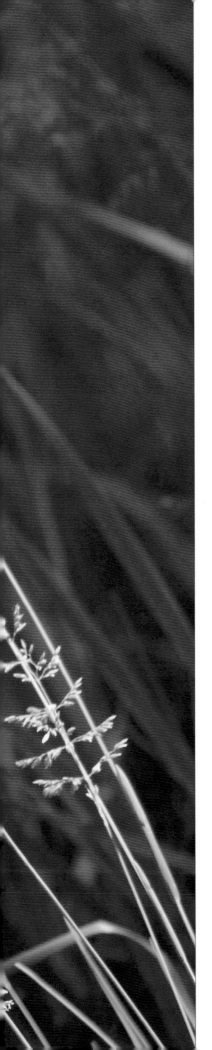

3

Raised Beds

Raised beds and properly constituted soil make mini-farming practical. Modern people in the industrialized world have a lot less spare time and a lot less available land than their ancestors.

Raised beds offer so many advantages over row gardening that it is hard to imagine why everyone except big agribusiness cartels isn't using them. Especially in northern climates, raised beds can help gardeners lengthen their growing season because they can raise soil temperature by 8 to 13 degrees compared to ground soil temperatures.

By raising the level of the soil, farmers and gardeners can start their crops earlier because excess moisture drains easily so the cold spring rains won't overwhelm new crops. Raised beds are also easily fitted with attachments, such as cold frames.

A raised bed is essentially a bottomless and topless box laid on the ground and filled with soil. The boxes can be built from wood, plastic boards, cement, and other materials. Raised beds can be made from mounded earth, but surrounding them with a box structure limits erosion of the carefully prepared soil of the bed.

⊗ Raised beds extend the season and reduce problems related to excess water.

Material Choices

The frames of raised beds are in constant contact with damp earth and can be subject to rotting. Ordinary lumber will last two or three years before replacement is needed. This can be delayed by carefully painting all exposed surfaces of the frames with a water-based exterior latex paint and allowing them to dry thoroughly before putting them to use. Do not use oil-based paints or paints containing antimildew ingredients or else you'll poison the soil in your beds. Because of the weight of the soil, boards used should be at least 1.5 inches thick to avoid bowing, and opposite sides of long runs should be tied together every eight feet or so. The biggest benefits of lumber lie in its easy availability and easy workability.

Ordinary concrete blocks are inexpensive and easy to use. They are readily available, durable, and heavy enough to hold the soil in a raised bed without need for mortar. They can be picked up and moved around to relocate or expand beds, and they can be reused almost indefinitely. The only downside is their weight—45 pounds for each. That means that in spite of their compact size, only 22 at a time can be hauled in a pickup truck rated to haul a half ton. Since each block is eighteen inches long, a pickup-sized load gives only 33 linear feet.

Boards made from recycled plastic used for decks and other outdoor structures have become more available in recent years and combine the assets of the easy handling of traditional lumber with the durability of concrete block. Several raised-bed kits are on the market that use plastic boards, and these may be a good idea if you plan on doing a small amount of gardening, but because of the expense of the kits, they don't make sense on the scale needed to feed a family. For a mini-farm, save expense by buying the plastic boards at the lumber store and cutting them to the right size yourself.

It is true that more modern pressure-treated lumber uses less toxic components than it used

⊗ Raised beds can be made from a variety of materials. This one is made with cinder blocks and landscape timbers.

to, but the components are still toxic, and they can leach into the soil of the growing bed, so they are best avoided.

Many other materials can be used, ranging from landscaping timbers to poured concrete forms. Just let imagination, cost, durability, and the potential toxicity of anything you might use guide the decision. Keep in mind that using materials that leach poisons into the growing beds completely defeats the purpose of the home garden or mini-farm because consuming the products grown in those beds can be extremely hazardous. (The arsenic in pressure-treated wood, for example, is both directly toxic and highly carcinogenic.)

Shape and Orientation of Raised Beds

The most common and useful shape for raised beds is rectangular. Certain planters for flowers are circular, and this works fine as long as the diameter is not so great that the gardener has to step into the bed. Another common shape is a 4-foot square. This works well for casual vegetable-only gardening on a small scale, but at the scale of providing all the needs of a family, it becomes wasteful of space and material.

I recommend a rectangular shape because it makes maximum use of space and minimal material while making it easy to add standardized structures like hoop houses.

Any rectangular bed is going to be longer than it is wide. To give maximum sun to crops and avoid shading, ensure that the long sides face north and south. Any trellising for vining crops should be established along the north edge to get the advantage of sunshine without shading other crops.

Size of Raised Beds: Width

Everyone has an opinion on the proper size of raised beds. The Grow Biointensive method favors a width of 5 feet and a length of 20 feet to establish a "microclimate" for intensive agriculture. Square Foot enthusiasts advocate a maximum width of 4 feet, because it is easy to reach into a bed that is 4 feet wide from either side and get to whatever is in the middle. Many experienced organic farmers use even narrower raised beds.

The five-foot width advocated by Ecology Action requires, for many people, stepping into the bed onto a board intended to more widely distribute the weight and minimize damage to the soil structure. But stepping into the garden bed at all, even using a board, defeats the purpose of careful management of the soil structure by compacting the soil. The board would need to be set up so it can be laid across the sides of the bed structure and be rigid enough that it won't bend when someone is standing on it. (This would be impossible using the complete Grow Biointensive method since, in that method, the raised beds are only mounded soil without structural sides. My method uses structural sides instead.)

The 4-foot width is narrow enough that most people can reach into the garden from both sides since only a 2-foot reach is needed. This will not work, however, when trellised crops that grow food on both sides of the trellis are grown against one of the long sides of the bed. In that case, picking pole beans, for example, requires a 4-foot reach, which most people don't have. My wife and I did this with a 4-foot-wide bed one year, and watching my wife balance on one of the frame boards while reaching for the beans with one hand and holding on to me with the other was a sure sign that I would need to make some changes the following year!

For reasons of experience and convenience, then, I recommend that beds should be four feet wide if they aren't going to be used for tall vines like pole beans. They should be three to three and a half feet wide otherwise.

Size of Raised Beds: Length

We already know that beds need to be rectangular for economic reasons and three to four feet wide for convenience—but how long can they be? Technically, they can be as long as the farmer wants, but there are some aspects of length worth considering.

One of the biggest causes of insect and disease problems is growing the same plants in the same space year after year. Bacterial, fungal, and viral diseases often have preferred host plants—and sometimes won't even grow in plants of an unrelated genus. Since these pathogens are competing against more beneficial microbes in compost-enriched soil, they can survive for only a limited period of time—usually three years or less—in soil that doesn't provide a suitable host.

Insect pests (some of which spread diseases) are quite similar. They have a particular appetite—a particular niche—such as cabbage. Such pests not only eat cabbage and infect it with diseases but also lay their eggs in the soil around the cabbage so that their offspring will emerge right next to their favorite food. One important way of foiling such pests is to make sure that when their offspring awaken in spring, they find plants that aren't appetizing.

Limiting the length of raised beds so that you have more room to create several of them makes it easy to practice crop rotation because the soil in one bed is isolated from the soil in the others. Making sure the same crop isn't grown in the same bed for three years solves a lot of problems in advance. In my own mini-farm, beds range in length from 8 to 24 feet.

Start at the Right Time and Grow Slowly

The time between when the soil can first be worked in the spring and when the early spring crops need to be planted is about three weeks. This is simply not enough time to create enough raised beds.

Ultimately, for total food self-sufficiency, you will need about 700 square feet per person. If you plan to raise market crops, you'll need even more. That will require a lot of beds. The number will depend on the length you choose.

Assuming the creation of beds that are 4-feet × 25-feet, that means you'll need at least seven beds per person or 21 beds for a family of three. Using 4-feet × 8-feet beds, that would be 22 beds per person or 66 for a family of three. In practice, depending on dietary preferences, chosen crop varieties, climate, and other factors, a larger or smaller number of beds could actually be used.

Initial creation of raised beds takes a considerable amount of time and is very labor intensive, but once they've been created, they require very little work to maintain. Raised beds can be created in a number of ways, but even the most time-efficient methods will take a few hours per bed. If you have limited time, getting all the beds made in spring will be physically impossible.

Therefore the best time to embark upon mini-farming is *the summer or fall before* the first growing season. This way the beds can be prepared in a more leisurely fashion and then sowed with cover crops for overwintering. In the spring, you only have to cut the cover crops and put them into the compost pile, cultivate existing beds, and start planting. (Cover crops are explained in the next chapter.)

It may be best to start mini-farming slowly—say, by initially creating enough beds for just a single individual's food—and then keep adding beds as time and materials allow until the required number has been established. This is because of the trade-off between time and money. If the prospective farmer has the time to establish all of the required beds initially, that's great. But if time is lacking, the only way to shortcut the system is to pay for heavy equipment and truckloads of compost.

I don't want the fact that fall is the best time to get started to discourage you from starting in either the spring or summer if that is when you want to start. It is always better to start than to delay because even just a couple of raised beds can produce a lot of food. If you get started in the spring or summer, just keep in mind that you'll want to add new beds in the fall as well.

Creating the Beds

For reasons of economy and productivity, I recommend creating the beds initially by double-digging. Lay out the area to be dug using stakes and string, then once it is dug, surround that area with the material you have chosen to create the box for the bed. Because the process of double-digging will loosen the soil, the level of the dug area will be between four and six inches higher than the surrounding soil.

Double-digging has been a standard agricultural practice for soil improvement in various places around the world for untold generations, and it is what I recommend because it is the most effective for the money required. The idea behind double-digging is that plants send their roots deeply into the soil, and making sure there are nutrients and aerated soil two feet deep provides ideal growing conditions. Up where I live in New Hampshire, any attempt at digging, no matter how modest, can be difficult because of the large number of rocks encountered. Did you ever wonder where all those picturesque rock walls in New England came from? Yep—they came from farmers getting rocks out of their fields.

My grandfather never double-dug anything but his asparagus beds. But, then again, he had 96 acres of land, horse teams, plows, tractors, four sons, and three daughters, so he wasn't trying to squeeze every ounce of productivity out of every square foot like a modern mini-farmer either. Nevertheless, the asparagus grown in a double-dug bed was far superior to any other.

Although many plants, especially grasses, can send roots several feet deep, the majority of a plant's root system exists in the top six inches of the soil. That's why Mel Bartholomew's Square Foot gardening system, which uses only six inches of soil, works. But in spite of the fact that six inches of perfectly prepared soil can be adequate, there can be no doubt that two *feet* of soil will necessarily hold a greater reservoir of nutrients and water.

As my father would say, with my apologies to our beloved cat, Patrick, in advance, "there's more than one way to skin a cat." Meaning, of course, that double-digging is not the only suitable way to prepare soil for mini-farming. There are actually three ways of digging the beds.

Digging Methods

The old-timers where I grew up never used the term *double-digging*. In the United States and Great Britain, that practice has been historically known as "bastard trenching" to differentiate it from full or "true" trenching. Most modern texts don't mention it, but there are actually three sorts of trenching that are useful under different circumstances. All three types of trenching are brutally hard work, particularly in areas with a lot of large rocks or with soils composed mainly of clay, but they offer benefits worth the effort. These three types of trenching are *plain digging*, *bastard trenching*, and *trenching*.

Plain digging relies on using a garden spade to dig into and turn over the soil to the depth of a single spade. The area to be dug is laid out using string or other marking, and a garden spade is used to remove the soil one-spade wide and a single-spade deep across the width of the bed, and that soil is placed into a wheelbarrow. Then a couple of inches of compost is added to the bottom of the first trench, and the soil from the next parallel trench is added on top of the compost in the first trench. This process continues until the last trench is dug and compost added to the bottom, and then the soil saved from the first trench is added to the hole left by the last trench.

The only difference between plain digging and double-digging (a.k.a. bastard trenching) is that in the latter, after a trench is dug a single-spade deep and before the compost is added, a digging fork is worked into the soil at the bottom of the trench to lift and break up the soil. Finally, more compost is added on top and mixed with the top six inches of soil. I perform this last step after I've built the form around the dug area.

Both plain digging and double-digging can be useful for newly created beds and can be

⊗ The garden fork and digging spade are indispensable tools for double-digging.

especially useful for an area that is covered with grass as the spits of dirt (the dirt that makes up a spade-full is known as a "spit") can be turned grass-side down in the adjacent trench as they are dug. It is extremely useful in either case, where the land to be used for farming was previously weeds or lawn, to sift through the soil to remove wireworms and grubs as you go along. When I use either of these trenching methods, I not only put compost in the bottom of the trenches but add some across the top of the finished bed and mix it in as well.

True or full trenching is serious work, but it is appropriate for regenerating soil in beds that have been previously double-dug or where the soil can be worked deeply without using a backhoe. A properly maintained bed should never need regeneration, but true trenching can be useful when dealing with land that was previously overfarmed using conventional methods since it exchanges the subsoil with the top soil. In true trenching, the first trench is dug a single-spade deep and the soil from that set aside, and then the same trench is dug another spade deep and that soil is set aside as well, separately from the soil from the top of the trench. Then a digging fork is used to break up the soil in the bottom as deep as the tines will go, and compost is added.

When the second adjacent trench is dug, the spits from the top are added to the bottom of the first trench, then the spits from the bottom are added to the top of that. In this way, the topsoil is buried, and the subsoil is brought to the top. Continue in this way until the last trench is dug, at which time the top spits from the first trench are put into the bottom of the last trench, and then those spits are topped with those that remain.

Because true trenching exchanges the topsoil with the subsoil, and subsoil tends to have far less organic matter, generous amounts of aged compost should be added to the top layer, worked in thoroughly, and allowed to sit for a couple of weeks before putting the new bed to use.

In any of the three trenching methods, you will be using hand tools to move, literally, thousands of pounds of soil for each bed. This can be grueling work, and you should always use spades and digging forks that have been either bought or modified to accommodate your height. The correct height of a spade or fork (plus handle) can be judged by standing the tool vertically next to you, then seeing how high it reaches on your body. The top of the handle should fall somewhere between your elbow and the middle of your breastbone.

Digging forks and spades can be purchased with either straight or "D" handles. You should get the "D"-handled versions, as they will lessen the amount of required back twisting. When using the tools, keep your back straight, and avoid both twisting and jerky movements. Work at a comfortable pace, and take breaks when needed. This way you get an excellent and safe aerobic workout that improves your strength and flexibility while improving the soil.

What about "No-Dig" Beds?

In my experience, I have found nothing that competes, in terms of sheer productivity, with properly double-dug raised beds. However, this can be a lot of work, and folks without a lot of time or with physical disabilities might not want to undertake the effort. You can still get very good results, though, using a no-dig method that I've tested.

Illustrated Double-Dig

Every year I expand my mini-farm a little by adding a few raised beds. The beds in my farm vary in size depending on the materials I had available at the time of construction, but most of them are 3-1/2 feet wide and 8 feet long. In the spring of 2006, I added a few beds and had my wife take pictures of the process so I could include them for your reference.

1 Mark off the area to be dug. In my case, I just laid out the boards where I would be digging. Notice a completed bed in the foreground and boards marking where the new bed will be in the background.

2 Dig the first row across the width of the bed one-spade deep, and put the dirt from that row in a wheelbarrow.

3 Loosen the soil in the bottom of the trench with a digging fork.

4 Add compost to the bottom of the trench.

5 Dig the second trench parallel and adjacent to the first one.

6 Because, in this instance, I am digging an area that was covered with grass, I turn the

⊗ Boards are used to mark off the new bed. You could just as easily use string or chalk.

⊗ Loosening the soil.

⊗ First row dug.

⊗ Adding compost.

⊗ Digging the second trench. Beware the author's stylish footwear!

⊗ Putting spits in the trench upside down.

⊗ Working compost into the top few inches of the new bed.

spits from the second trench upside down in the first trench.

7   Work some additional compost into the top few inches of the finished bed.

As you can see from the photo tutorial, preparing raised beds by double-digging is a pretty straightforward and very physical process. It is great exercise and loosens the soil to a depth of two feet, placing organic material throughout the entire depth. The yields from beds that I work like this are phenomenal!

Save up old newspapers—just the black-and-white portions, not the glossy parts. In the fall, build your frame out of 2 × 4 lumber right on the ground. Lay down the newspaper several layers thick, and then fill the bed completely with finished compost. Don't skip the newspapers because their purpose is to smother the grass underneath. If the grass isn't smothered, and if you are using only 2 × 4 lumber, you'll end up with a lot of grass growing in the bed.

When spring rolls around and the ground thaws, just use the digging fork to fluff it up a little; then plant, and you are done.

For no-dig beds it is particularly important to keep them planted with cover crops when fallow during the off-season because you are depending on the action of plant roots to mix the soil and keep it loose.

Because seeds don't always germinate well in compost, I'd recommend using the bed for transplanted crops for the first year, and then a good soil builder like beans the next year. In all other respects, you can treat this just like a regular raised bed. If fresh compost is added yearly, after three years the productivity will be the same as for a double-dug bed.

Trellising for Raised Beds: Flexible Trellising System

Trellises are necessary for certain crops and can be a valuable adjunct for others. Because raised beds don't provide much room for sprawling plants such as cucumbers or pole beans, adding a trellis makes growing these crops more practical and space efficient.

Many crops are more productive in vining versions than bush versions. This includes beans, peas, cucumbers, tomatoes, and more. Pole beans, for example, can yield almost twice as much product per square foot as bush beans. This means that a row of pole beans grown on a trellis along the north side of an 8-foot bed using only 8 square feet of space can produce nearly as many beans as 16 square feet of bush beans. This same calculation applies to other vegetables.

Electrical conduit makes a sturdy and versatile trellis.

As mentioned earlier in the chapter, beds will ideally be located with the long sides facing north and south. Trellises should be established on the north side. If, for some reason, this orientation isn't convenient, the second-best choice is to have the long side upon which trellises will be established on the north west or, in the worst case, west side. Don't establish trellises on the south or east sides of a bed or they will shade crops during the times of day that are most sunny.

There are as many ways to erect trellises as there are farmers, and I've used many different methods over the years. In the past few years, my preferred method of trellising uses rebar, electrical conduit, and conduit fittings. Electrical conduit comes in lengths 10 feet long. By cutting it to strategic lengths and using appropriate fittings, you can vary its height and length. By fitting it over rebar driven into the ground, you can lift it off the rebar easily in the fall for storage, and moving it to a different bed is a snap.

Because lumber used to create the beds is eight feet long, the longest you need the conduit to be is eight feet. This is for the horizontal piece on top. Meanwhile, trellis heights can range all the way from two feet for peas to four feet for tomatoes to even six feet for pole beans. A trellis height of more than six feet isn't a good idea, as reaching the top would be tiring or—even worse if a stool is required—dangerous.

The easy way to get a flexible system is to buy 10-foot lengths of conduit six pieces at a time. Three are cut into an 8-foot and a 2-foot piece, two are cut into a 6-foot and a 4-foot piece, and the final length of conduit is cut into two 4-foot pieces and one 2-foot piece. When done, you have three 8-foot horizontals, two 6-foot verticals, four 4-foot verticals, and four 2-foot verticals. In addition to these, for every six pieces of conduit, you will need six 90-degree elbows, four screw couplings, and six pieces of 2-foot rebar. (You can find rebar already cut to length and bundled at Home Depot and similar stores.)

Once the rebar is hammered into the ground on either end of the beds, you can completely assemble or disassemble a trellis of any height from 2-foot to 8-foot in two-foot increments using only a screwdriver.

⊗ Driving the rebar into the ground.

⊗ Placing an upright over the rebar.

Complete Trellis Creation, Step-by-Step

1   Hammer 2-foot pieces of rebar into the ground at either end of the raised bed, leaving 6 inches protruding above the ground.

⊗ Attaching the horizontal to the bend.

⊗ Deck screws drilled into the edge and protruding 3/8 inch.

Deck Screws

4 Put deck screws into the side of the raised bed along the trellis every 6 to 12 inches. Leave them protruding about a quarter of an inch.

5 Run string between the horizontal bar on top and the deck screws in the side of the raised bed.

6 Now you have a completed trellis!

❰❰ Run string between the horizontal and the deck screws.

2 Slip your vertical piece of conduit over the rebar. Repeat for the other side.

3 Attach a 90-degree elbow to each vertical piece of conduit, and then secure the horizontal conduit to the elbows.

Completed trellis. ❱❱

4

Soil Composition and Maintenance

The productivity and fertility of the farm and plant resistance to pests and disease depend on the quality of the soil. Soil quality can be enhanced and outside inputs reduced through proper tillage, compost, cover cropping, and crop rotation. These are crucial to maintaining the high level of fertility required for the close plant spacing in a mini-farm without spending a lot of money on fertilizer.

When French Intensive gardening was developed, horses were the standard mode of transportation, and horse manure was plentiful and essentially free. This explains the reliance on horse manure as a source of soil fertility. According to the Colorado State University Cooperative Extension Service, the average 1,000-pound horse generates 9 tons—18,000 pounds—of manure occupying nearly 730 cubic feet per year.[7] The sheer volume, smell, and mess of such quantities of manure often mean that places that board horses will give it away for the asking to anyone willing to haul it away.

---

[7] Davis, J. G., Swinker, A. M. (2004) *Horse Manure Management* Retrieved Jan 29, 2006, from http://www.ext.colostate.edu/pubs/livestk/01219.html

⊗ Horse manure should be composted and not added directly to the bed.

Horse manure is good food for crops as well. According to the same source, horse manure contains 19 pounds of nitrogen per ton, 14 pounds of phosphate, and 36 pounds of potassium. This works out to about 1% nitrogen, 0.7% phosphate, and 1.8% potassium.

There's no such thing as a free lunch, and horse manure is no exception. Raw horse manure can spread a parasitic protozoan called giardia and E.coli as well as contaminate water sources and streams with coliform bacteria. Raw manure can also contain worm eggs that are easily transmitted to humans, including pinworms and various species of ascarid worms. Horse manure is high in salts, and if used excessively, it can cause plants grown in it to suffer water stress, even if well watered. The highest permissible rate of application of horse manure assuming the least measurable salinity is between two and three pounds of manure per square foot per year.[8] In addition to the above objections, horse manure doesn't have a balanced level of phosphorus, meaning that it

should be supplemented with a source of phosphorus when used.

Straight horse manure is also in the process of composting. That is, the process has not yet finished. Unfinished compost often contains phytotoxic chemicals that inhibit plant growth. For horse manure to be directly usable as a planting medium, it must first be well rotted, meaning it either should be composted in a pile mixed with other compost materials such as plant debris or should at least sit by itself rotting for a year before use. The former method is preferable since that will conserve more of the manure's valuable nitrogen content. The potential problems posed by horse manure are eliminated through composting the manure with other materials first and then liberally applying the resulting compost to beds. The composting process will kill any parasites, dilute the salinity, and break down phytotoxins.

Making perfect soil from scratch, on a small scale, works quite well. The Square Foot gardening method gives a formula of 1/3 coarse vermiculite, 1/3 peat moss, and 1/3 compost by volume plus a mix of organic fertilizers to create a "perfect soil mix."[9] My own testing on a 120-square-foot raised bed confirms that the method works beautifully. For small beds, the price of the components is reasonable. A six-inch-deep 4-foot × 6-foot bed would require only four cubic feet of each of the components. Coarse vermiculite and peat moss currently sell for about $18 for a four-cubic-foot bale. Assuming free compost, the cost of making perfect soil mix comes to $1.50 per square foot of growing area. This works quite well on a small scale, but when even 700 square feet are put into

[8] Ibid

[9] Bartholomew, M. (2000) Ca$h from Square Foot Gardening

agricultural production, the cost can become prohibitive.

Double-digging was covered in the previous chapter, and it is what I recommend for mini-farming. Although it is more difficult in the beginning, it affords the best opportunity to prepare the best possible soil for the money invested. No-dig beds, also described in the previous chapter, are a second option.

Water-Holding Capacity and pH

Few soils start out ideal for intensive agriculture or even any sort of agriculture. Some are too sandy, and some are too rich in clay. Some are too acidic, and others are too alkaline. Many lack one or more primary nutrients and any number of trace minerals.

Soil for agricultural use needs to hold water without becoming waterlogged. Sandy soils are seldom waterlogged, but they dry out so quickly that constant watering is required. They make root growth easy but don't hold on to nutrients very well and are low in organic content or humus. (There is some dispute among experts on the exact definition of *humus*. For our purposes, it can be defined as organic matter in the soil that has reached a point of being sufficiently stable that it won't easily decompose further. Thus, finished compost and humus are identical for our purposes.) Clay soils will be waterlogged in the winter and will remain waterlogged as long as water comes to them. As soon as the water stops, they bake and crack, putting stress on root systems. Clay soil is clingy, sticky, and nearly impenetrable to roots. Loam soil is closest to the ideal, as it consists of a mix of sand and clay with a good amount of humus that helps it retain water and nutrients in proportions suitable for agriculture.

Both sandy and clay soils can be improved with vermiculite. Vermiculite is manufactured by heating mica rock in an oven until it pops like popcorn. The result is a durable substance that holds and releases water like a sponge and improves the water-holding characteristics of practically any kind of soil. Because it is an insoluble mineral, it will last for decades and possibly forever. If the soil in your bed isn't loamy to start with, adding coarse or medium vermiculite at the rate of four to eight cubic feet per 100 square feet of raised bed will be very beneficial. (Vermiculite costs $4 per cubic foot in four-cubic-foot bags at the time of this writing.)

If you can't find vermiculite, look instead for bails of peat moss. Peat moss is an organic material made from compressed prehistoric plants at the bottom of bogs and swamps, and it has the same characteristic as vermiculite in terms of acting as a water reservoir. It costs about the same and can also be found in large bales. It should be

❯ Vermiculite enhances the water-holding capacity of the soil.

added at the same rate as vermiculite—anywhere from four to eight cubic feet per 100 square feet of raised bed. Keep in mind that peat moss raises the soil's pH slightly over time and decomposes, so it must be renewed.

The term *pH* refers to how acidic or alkaline the soil is and is referenced on a scale from 0 to 14, with 0 corresponding to highly acidic battery acid, 14 to highly alkaline drain cleaner, and 7 to neutral distilled water. As you might imagine, most plants grown in a garden will perform well with a pH between 6 and 7. (There are a few exceptions, such as blueberries, that prefer a highly acidic soil.) pH affects a lot of things indirectly, including whether nutrients already in the soil are available for plants to use and the prevalence of certain plant disease organisms such as "club foot" in cabbage.

On the basis of a pH test, you can amend your soil to near neutral or just slightly acid, a pH of 6.5 or so, with commonly available lime and sulfur products. To adjust the pH up 1 point, add dolomitic limestone at the rate of 5 pounds per 100 square feet of raised bed and work it into the top two inches of soil. To adjust the pH down 1 point, add iron sulfate at the rate of 1.5 pounds per 100 square feet of raised bed and work it into the soil. To adjust the pH by half a point, say from 6 to 6.5, cut the amount per 100 square feet in half.

pH amendments don't work quickly. Wait 40 to 60 days after adding the amendments, and then retest the soil before adding any more. If amendments are added too quickly, they can build up in the soil and make it inhospitable for growing things.

Fertilizers

The fertility of soil is measured by its content of nitrogen, phosphorus, and potassium, and fertilizers are rated the same way, using a series of numbers called "NPK." The N in NPK stands for nitrogen, the P for phosphate, and the K for potassium. A bag of fertilizer will be marked with the NPK in a format that lists the percentage content of each nutrient, separated by dashes. So, for example, a bag of fertilizer labeled "5-10-5" is 5% nitrogen, 10% phosphate, and 5% potassium.

A completely depleted garden soil with no detectable levels of NPK requires only 4.6 ounces of N, 5 ounces of P, and 5.4 ounces of K per 100 square feet to yield a "sufficient" soil. In the case of root crops, less than 3 ounces of N are needed.

Inexpensive soil tests are available to test the pH, nitrogen, phosphorus, and potassium content of soil. A couple of weeks after the soil in the bed has been prepared and compost and/or manure have been worked in, you should test the soil's nutrient content and amend it properly. The most important factor in the long-range viability of your soil is organic matter provided by compost and manures, so always make sure that there is plenty of organic matter first, and then test to see what kind of fertilization is needed.

You can buy a soil test kit at most garden centers, and most give results for each nutrient as being depleted, deficient, adequate, or sufficient. The latter two descriptions can be confusing because in ordinary English, they have identical meaning. For the purposes of interpreting soil tests, consider "adequate" to mean that there is enough of the measured nutrient for plants to survive but not necessarily thrive. If the soil test indicates the amount to be "sufficient," then there is enough of the nutrient to support optimal growth.

The Rapitest soil test kit is commonly available, costs less than $20, and comes with enough components to make 10 tests. The LaMotte soil test kit is one of the most accurate available and can currently be purchased via mail order for less than $55. When preparing a bed, I recommend adding enough organic fertilizers to make all three major nutrients "sufficient."

Organic fertilizers are a better choice than synthetic ones for several reasons. Organic fertilizers break down more slowly so they stay in the soil longer and help build the organic content of your soil as they break down. Synthetics can certainly get the job done in the short term, but they also carry the potential to harm important microbial diversity in the soil that helps to prevent plant diseases, and they also hurt earthworms and other benefi-

cial soil inhabitants. For these reasons, I strongly discourage the use of synthetic fertilizers.

Organic fertilizers, like synthetics, are rated by NPK, but because they are made from plant, animal, and mineral substances, they contain a wide array of trace minerals that plants also need. Probably the biggest argument in favor of using organic fertilizers is taste. The hydroponic hothouse tomatoes at the grocery store are grown using exclusively synthetics mixed with water. Compare the taste of a hydroponic hothouse tomato with the taste of an organic garden tomato, and the answer will be clear.

There is one thing to keep in mind with organic fertilizers: Many of them are quite appetizing to rodents! One spring, I discovered that the fertilizer in my garage had been torn open by red squirrels and eaten almost entirely! Ever since,

The LaMotte soil test kit is very accurate.

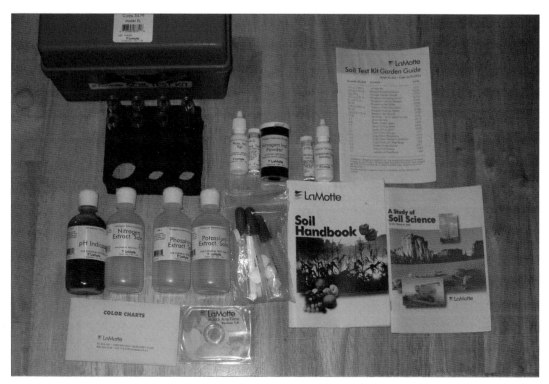

I store organic fertilizers in five-gallon buckets with lids.

There are a number of available sources for organic fertilizers. Some come premixed, or you can make them yourself from individual components.

Making your own premixed fertilizer is easy. For N, you can use alfalfa meal, soybean meal, or blood meal. For P, bone meal and rock phosphate work well. For K, wood ashes, greensand, and seaweed will work. The foregoing list is far from exhaustive, but the materials are readily available from most garden or agricultural stores.

Table 1 contains two numbers notated as either "leaf" or "root" because root crops don't need as much nitrogen as leafy vegetable crops. In fact, too much nitrogen can hurt the productivity of root crops. There's also no reason to formulate a fertilizer for depleted soil since that shouldn't happen after the first year, and maybe not even then if adequate compost has been added. If it does, just add triple or quadruple the amount used for adequate soil. Looking at these tables, it should be pretty easy to formulate a couple of ready-made fertilizers.

A "high nitrogen" fertilizer for vegetative crops like spinach could consist of a mix of 10 ounces of blood meal, 6 ounces of bone meal, and 21 ounces of wood ashes.

As long as you keep the proportions the same, you can mix up as much of it as you like to keep handy, and you know that 37 ounces of the mix-

Table 1: **Nitrogen Sources**

Nitrogen Source	%N	Ounces per 100 sq. ft. for depleted soil	Ounces per 100 sq. ft. for adequate soil
Alfalfa meal	2.50	184 leaf/120 root	52 leaf/34 root
Soybean meal	6.00	76 leaf/50 root	21 leaf/14 leaf
Blood meal	12.00	38 leaf/25 root	10 leaf/7 r oot

Table 2: **Phosphorus Sources**

Phosphorus Source	%P	Ounces per 100 sq. ft. for depleted soil	Ounces per 100 sq. ft. for adequate soil
Bone meal	21.00	23	6
Rock phosphate	39.00	13	4

Table 3: **Potassium Sources**

Potassium Source	%K	Ounces per 100 sq. ft. for depleted soil	Ounces per 100 sq. ft. for adequate soil
Wood ashes	7.00	77	21
Greensand	5.00	108	30
Seaweed	5.00	108	30

ture are required for each 100 square feet. Just a tad over two pounds.

A "low nitrogen" fertilizer for root crops like parsnips could consist of a mix of 34 ounces of alfalfa meal, 4 ounces of rock phosphate, and 30 ounces of greensand.

Just as with the first formulation, as long as you keep the proportions the same, you can mix up as much as you'd like, and you know that 68 ounces are required for each 100 square feet—a hair over four pounds.

Your actual choice of fertilizers and blends will depend on availability and price of materials, but using a variety of components guarantees that at some point practically every known nutrient—and every unknown nutrient—finds its way into your garden beds. Wood ashes should be used no more often than once every three years because of the salts they can put into the soil and because they can raise the soil pH.

Fertilizers should be added to the soil a couple of weeks before planting and worked into the garden bed; any additional fertilizer should then be added on top of the ground as a side dressing, perhaps diluted 50/50 with some dried compost.

The reason for dilution is that some organic fertilizers, such as blood meal, are pretty powerful—as powerful as synthetics—and if they touch crop foliage directly, they can damage plants.

Liquid fertilizers are worth mentioning, particularly those intended for application directly to leaves. These tend to be extremely dilute so that they won't hurt the plants, and they are a good choice for reducing transplant shock.

In some cases, liquid fertilizers can be a lifesaver. One year, I planted out cabbage well before last frost in a newly prepared bed. Having added one-third of the bed's volume in compost of every

⊗ Popular organic liquid fertilizers.

sort imaginable, I made the mistake of assuming the bed had adequate nutrients. What I had forgotten is that plants can't use nitrogen when the soil is too cold. A couple of days after the cabbage plants were planted, they turned yellow, starting from the oldest leaves first, which is a classic symptom of severe nitrogen deficiency.

As an experiment, I added a heavy side-dressing of mixed blood meal, bone meal, and wood ashes and watered it in on all the cabbage plants, but for half of them, I also watered the leaves with a watering can containing liquid fertilizer mixed according to package directions. The result was that all of the plants watered with the liquid fertilizer survived and eventually thrived, while a full half of the plants that received only a side-dressing died.

Now, I use liquid fertilizer—specifically Neptune's Harvest—whenever I transplant, especially in early spring.

Soil Maintenance

Believe it or not, soil is a delicate substance. More than merely delicate, it is quite literally alive. It is the life of the soil, not its sand and clay, that makes it fertile and productive. A single teaspoon of good garden soil contains millions of microbes, almost every one of which contributes something positive to the garden. The organic matter serves as a pH buffer, detoxifies pollutants, holds moisture, and serves to hold nutrients in a fixed form to keep them from leaching out of the soil. Some microbes, like actinomycetes, send out delicate microscopic webs that stretch for miles, giving soil its structure.

The structure of soil for intensive agriculture is maintained through

- cover crops (explained later in this chapter) to maintain fertility and prevent erosion;
- regularly adding organic matter in the form of left over roots, compost, and manures;
- crop rotation; and
- protecting the soil from erosion, compaction, and loosening.

Once the soil in a bed has been prepared initially, as long as it hasn't been compacted, it shouldn't need more than a fluffing with a broad fork or digging fork yearly and stirring of the top few inches with a three-tined cultivator. Digging subsequent to bed establishment is much easier and faster than the initial double-dig.

It was noted earlier that you shouldn't walk on the garden beds. An occasional unavoidable footprint won't end life on earth, but an effort should be made to avoid it because that footprint compacts the soil, makes that area of soil less able to hold water, decreases the oxygen that can be held in the soil in that area, and damages the structure of the soil, including the structure established by old roots and delicate microbial webs. Almost all species of actinomycetes are aerobic—meaning that they require oxygen. Compacting the soil can deprive them of needed oxygen.

The microbial webs in soil are extremely important in that they work in symbiosis with root systems to extend their reach and ability to assimilate nutrients.[10] Damaging these microbial webs—which can stretch for several feet in each direction from a plant—reduces the plant's ability to obtain nutrients from the soil.

My wife thought I was overreaching on this point and insisted on occasionally walking in the beds to harvest early beans, so I did an experiment. I planted bunching onions from the same packet of seeds in places where she had walked in the beds and in places where she hadn't. The results? Total yield per square foot, measured in pounds, was 20% lower in the places where my wife had walked. She only weighs 115 pounds! The lesson is plain: Maximum productivity from a raised bed requires avoiding soil compression.

Some gardeners favor heavy duty tilling of agricultural land at least yearly and often at both the beginning and end of a season. The problem with such practices lies in the fact that the very same aspects of soil life and structure that are disrupted by compaction are also disrupted by tilling, particularly deep tilling.

---

[10] Howard, D. (2003) Building fertile soil *Mother Earth News*, Issue 198, June/July 2003

Soil amendments, such as compost and organic fertilizers, should be mixed with the soil—no doubt. But this doesn't require a rototiller. A simple three-tined cultivator (looks like a claw), operated by hand, is sufficient to incorporate amendments into the top couple of inches of soil. Earthworms and other soil inhabitants will do the job of spreading the compost into deep soil layers.

The Amazing Power of Biochar

Most of us are used to thinking of charcoal as an indispensable aid to grilling, and that it certainly is! But less well-known is its equally beneficial effect when added to ordinary garden soil. The standard charcoal you buy at the grocery store may be impregnated with everything from saltpeter to volatile organic compounds intended to aid burning, so it may not be a good choice. There are some "all natural" or even organic charcoals out there that can be used, such as Cowboy Brand Charcoal, though. In addition, some companies make charcoal specifically intended for agricultural use, such as Troposphere Energy.

Of course, if you have access to hardwood, making your own charcoal isn't terribly difficult. In fact, for agricultural use, you don't even need hardwood—just any old vegetable matter—and you can make the charcoal that is trendy nowadays to call "biochar."

The benefits of biochar mixed in the soil are many and were first discovered by the peoples inhabiting the Amazon basin in pre-Columbian times. They discovered that turning their vegetable matter into charcoal, pulverizing it, and adding it to the soil enhanced the soil's productivity. Soil scientists have now discovered that charcoal, previously thought to be inert in soil, lowers the soil's acidity; creates a haven for the beneficial bacteria that live in symbiosis with the root hairs of crops; helps to keep fertilizers in the soil instead of letting them be washed out, thus decreasing the need for fertilizer; and helps to loosen tight soils. In addition, it helps to sequester carbon from the atmosphere, thereby reducing global warming. More benefits are being discovered all the time.

⊗ The three-tined cultivator is a workhorse for raised beds.

The easiest way to add this incredible fertilizer to your garden beds is to make it right where you want it used: in your beds. Use a hoe to make a couple of one-foot-wide and six- to nine-inch-deep trenches running the length of the bed. Place dried branches, leaves, and other vegetable matter neatly, but not too tightly packed, in the trenches. Then, light them on fire in several places. (Avoid using chemicals such as charcoal lighter or gasoline as these could seriously poison the soil.) Once the material is burning well and the smoke has turned gray, cover with the mounded-up soil on the sides of the trenches to deprive it of oxygen, and let it smolder until the pieces are no larger than a deck of cards. Then, douse the embers with plentiful quantities of water. If you do this every fall with garden refuse and other vegetable matter, you will soon have soil that, taken together with the other practices here, will have astonishing levels of productivity.

Cover Crops and Beneficial Microbes

Today we know a lot more than our great-grandparents did about the relationship between plants and microorganisms in the soil. It turns out that the microorganisms in soil are not merely useful for suppressing diseases but actually an integral part of a plant's root system.[11] Up to 40% of the carbohydrates that plants produce through photosynthesis are actually transported to the root system and out into the soil to feed microorganisms around the root system. In turn, these microorganisms extend the plant's root system and make necessary nutrients available.

Friendly microorganisms grow into the roots themselves, setting up a mutually beneficial cooperation (symbiosis) and respond with natural production of antibiotics when needed to protect their host. Planting cover crops will serve to keep these critters fed through the winter months and protected from environmental hazards such as sun and erosion. This way they are healthy and well fed for the next planting season.

For these reasons, harvesting should be considered a two-part process in which the task of harvesting is followed as soon as possible with the sowing of cover crops, which can also be known as green manures.

Green manures are plants grown specifically for the role they play in sustaining soil fertility, but they also reduce erosion and feed beneficial microbes outside the growing season. The benefits of green manures on crop yield are far from merely theoretical. In one study, for example, the use of hairy vetch (a common legume) as a green manure and mulch increased tomato yields by more than 100%.[12] Green manures are generally either grains or legumes; grains because of their ability to pull nutrients up into the topsoil from a depth of several feet,[13] and legumes because of their ability to take nitrogen out of the air and fix it in nodules in their roots, thereby fertilizing the soil. They are either tilled directly into the ground once grown or added to compost piles. Legumes use up their stored nitrogen to make seed, so when they are used as green manures, they need to be cut just before or during their flowering. During the summer growing season,

---

[11] Ibid.

[12] Abdul-Baki, A., Teasdale, J. (1993) A no tillage tomato production system using hairy vetch and subterranean clover mulches *Horticultural Science* 28(2) pp. 106–108

[13] Jeavons, J. (2002) *How to Grow More Vegetables*

Table 4: **Cover Crops/Green Manures and Nitrogen Yields**

Name	*Sow*	*Harvest*	*N Yield*	*Notes*
Hairy vetch	Spring or fall	Fall or spring	160 lbs/acre	Sow in August–September, can become a weed if followed by grains, don't follow with lettuce
Red clover	Spring or fall	Fall or spring	105 lbs/acre	Sow in August for winter cover, good choice under fruit trees, shade tolerant
Field peas	Spring	Summer	100 lbs/acre	Won't overwinter north of Maryland, good for interplanting with brassicas
Cereal rye	Fall	Spring	None	Sow in early fall, wait four weeks after cutting in spring before sowing subsequent crops because rye suppresses germination of other plants
Alfalfa	Spring	Summer	130 lbs/acre	Prefers well-drained soils, highest N fixation
Barley	Spring	Summer	None	Doesn't work in acid soils
Oats	Spring	Summer	None	Established quickly
Winter wheat	Fall	Spring	None	High in protein

green manures should be grown in beds that will be followed by heavy-feeding plants, such as cabbage, as part of a crop rotation plan.

An important aspect of making a mini-farm economically viable is the use of green manures to provide and enhance soil fertility and reduce dependence on purchased fertilizers. To that end, cover crops should be grown over the winter to start the spring compost pile and should also be planted in any bed not in use to prevent leaching of nutrients and promote higher fertility. The careful use of green manures as cover crops and as specific compost ingredients can entirely eliminate the need for outside nitrogen inputs. For example, alfalfa makes an excellent green manure during the growing season in that it leaves 42 percent of its nitrogen in the ground when cut plus provides biologically fixed nitrogen to the compost pile. I recommend that 25 to 35 percent of a mini-farm's growing area should be sown in green manures during the growing season, and all of it should be sown in green manures and/or cover crops during the winter.

Green manures interplanted with crops during the growing season can form a living mulch. Examples include sowing hairy vetch between corn stalks at the last cultivation before harvest or planting vegetables without tilling into a bed already growing subterranean clover.[14] On

---

[14] Sullivan, P. (2003) *Overview of Cover Crops and Green Manures*

⊘ Hairy vetch is an excellent cover crop.

my own mini-farm, I grow white clover between tomato plants.

Cover crops aren't a cure-all, and they can cause problems if used indiscriminately. For example, using a vetch cover crop before growing lettuce can cause problems with a lettuce disease called sclerotina.[15] Because the increased organic matter from a cover crop can cause a short-term increase in populations of certain pests such as cutworms, it is important to cut or till the cover crop three or four weeks before planting your crops.[16] Legume green manures, such as peas, beans, vetch, and clovers, also need to be covered with the correct type of bacterial inoculant (available through seed suppliers) before they are sown to ensure their health and productivity.

Given these complications, how does a farmer pick a cover crop? Cover crops need to be picked based on the climate, the crop that will be planted afterward, and specific factors about the cover crop—such as its tendency to turn into an invasive weed. Legumes and grains are often, though not always, sown together as a cover crop. Some cover crops, like oats and wheat, can also serve as

---

[15] Thomas, F. et al. (2002) *Cover Cropping in Row and Field Systems*
[16] Ibid

food. If this is anticipated, it might be worthwhile to investigate easily harvested grains like hull-less oats. However, keep in mind that the choice of green manures will be at least partially dictated by climate. Many crops that grow fine over the winter in South Carolina won't work in Vermont.

Crop Rotation

Crop rotation is one of the oldest and most important agricultural practices in existence and is still one of the most effective for controlling pest populations, assisting soil fertility, and controlling diseases.

The primary key to successful crop rotation lies in understanding that crops belong to a number of different botanical families and that members of each related family have common requirements and pest problems that differ from those of members of other botanical families. Cabbage and brussels sprouts, for example, are members of the same botanical family, so they can be expected to have similar soil requirements and be susceptible to the same pest and disease problems. Peas and beans are likewise part of the same botanical family; corn belongs to yet another family unrelated to the other two. A listing of the botanical names of most cultivated plant families with edible members follows:

Amaryllidaceae—leek, common onion, multiplier onion, bunching onion, shallot, garlic, chives

Brassicaceae—horseradish, mustards, turnip, rutabaga, kale, radish, broccoli, cauliflower, cabbage, collards, cress

Chenopodiaceae—beet, mangel, Swiss chard, lamb's quarters, quinoa, spinach

Compositae—endive, escarole, chicory, globe artichoke, jerusalem artichoke, lettuce, sunflower

Cucurbitaceae—cucumber, gherkin, melons, gourds, squashes

Leguminosae—peanut, pea, bean, lentil, cowpea

Solanaceae—pepper, tomato, tomatillo, ground cherry, potato, eggplant

Umbelliferae—celery, dill, carrot, fennel, parsnip, parsley

Gramineae—wheat, rye, oats, sorghum, corn

Amaranthaceae—grain and vegetable amaranth

Convolvulaceae—water spinach, sweet potato

Some plants will do better or worse depending on what was grown before them. Such effects can be partially canceled by the use of intervening cover crops between main crops. Thankfully, a large amount of research has been done on the matter, and while nobody is sure of all the factors involved, a few general rules have emerged from the research.

- Never follow a crop with another crop from the same botanical family (e.g., don't follow potatoes with tomatoes or squash with cucumbers).
- Alternate deep-rooted crops (like carrots) with shallow-rooted crops (such as lettuce).
- Alternate plants that inhibit germination (like rye and sunflowers) with vegetables that don't compete well against weeds (like peas and strawberries).
- Alternate crops that add organic matter (e.g., wheat) with crops that add little organic matter (e.g., soybeans).
- Alternate nitrogen fixers (such as alfalfa or vetch) with nitrogen consumers (such as grains or vegetables).

The most important rule with crop rotations is to experiment and keep careful records. Some families of plants have a detrimental effect on some families that may follow them in rotation but not on others. These effects will vary depending on cover cropping, manuring, and composting practices, so no hard and fast rules apply, but it is absolutely certain that an observant farmer will see a difference between cabbage that follows carrots as opposed to cabbage that follows potatoes. Keeping careful records and making small variations from year to year while observing the results will allow the farmer to fine-tune practices to optimize quality and yields.

A three-bed rotation applicable to where I live in New Hampshire might give you an idea of how crop rotation with cover cropping works. We'll start with the fall.

Table 5: **Example Three-Bed Rotation with Cover Cropping**

	Bed 1	*Bed 2*	*Bed 3*
Fall Year 1	Rye	Hairy vetch/rye	Hairy vetch/oats
Spring Year 2	Peas	Tomatoes	Corn
Midsummer Year 2	Broccoli/cabbage	White clover is sown between plants	Pole beans are sown between stalks
Fall Year 2	Hairy vetch/rye	Hairy vetch/oats	Rye
Spring Year 3	Tomatoes	Corn	Peas
Midsummer Year 3	White clover is sown between plants	Pole beans are sown between stalks	Broccoli/cabbage

5

Compost

Anytime you pass by a forest or a long-abandoned field, you see tons of vegetation even though it is pretty obvious nobody is fertilizing the wilderness. Forests and fields don't need fertilizer, because they exist within the framework of a sustainable nutrient cycle that returns nutrients to the soil via natural composting.

A tree takes elements from the earth and turns them into leaves that turn brown and fall to earth in the autumn, forming a layer on top of last year's leaves. Progressing down the layers, within just a few inches, the leaves have turned into a sweet-smelling, living compost. This gets mixed into the existing soil through the action of earthworms and other organisms. The same mechanism is at work when a squirrel eats an acorn and drops the shell to the forest floor and then relieves himself. It all combines in the forest floor so that everything goes back whence it came and becomes available for reuse.

This same is true even in death. The squirrel eaten by a hawk has all of its parts, in some form or another, returned to the earth; likewise, a huge tree hit by lightning decomposes into the earth for reuse.

Nature is already equipped to sustain itself, as it has for billions of years. Taking energy only from the sun, nature follows the Law of Conservation of Matter to recycle all of the elements that it takes from the earth. This cycle does not work within a given area of land when elements are removed from that area more quickly than they can be replaced without taking elements from somewhere else.

This is where conventional farming cartels find themselves. They export all of their fertility from their farms in the form of crops and then replenish that fertility with artificial chemicals or with manures brought in from several states away. Such a system can endure for a long time, but it is pretty expensive and geared best to large-scale operations. Smaller-scale home-sized operations work least expensively when every effort is made to maintain as much soil fertility as possible from sources within the operation. Conscientious attention to the nutrient cycles of the mini-farm can make a huge difference in crop yield and the amount of outside amendments and fertilizers that must be brought in—which in practical terms means reduced costs.

The nutrient cycles of the mini-farm encompass the life-death-rebirth of plants and animals as well as the grow-eat-excrete-grow of the plants and animals on the farm. The mini-farmer uses composting and fertilizer crops to accelerate the natural process of these cycles to maintain a high level of fertility in the soil.

The importance of compost in a mini-farm or even a small garden can't be overstated. Broadly, compost is the rotted remains of plant and animal products and by-products that have been aerobically decomposed so that the individual constituents cannot be distinguished. This is exactly what happens in nature, and the mini-farmer simply helps the process along. Once this has occurred, the resulting product becomes agriculturally indispensable.

Compost not only serves as a reservoir of fertility because of the individual elements and nutrients that it contains but also serves to destroy plant and animal diseases and toxins while improving the texture and moisture handling of the soil to which it is added. One commercial California vegetable grower was able to reduce pesticide use by 80% in just three years through applications of compost.[17]

The Composting Process

The core process of composting is simply this: The farmer stacks up a bunch of organic matter that, given time, air, and moisture, decomposes. Organic matter includes leftovers from the table, crop debris, grass clippings, leaves raked in the fall, and animal manure. In essence, anything that was either once alive or produced by something that was alive.

A combination of elements are responsible for organic decomposition but most notably microorganisms such as bacteria and fungi that are already present in soil, on plants, and even in the intestines of animals. When an environment hospitable to their growth and multiplication is created, the microorganisms digest the organic material. Along with this, a number of larger organisms such as earthworms get into the act of digesting the organic matter, thus creating an

---

[17] Hoitink, H. A. J., Fahy, P. C. (1986). Basis for the control of plant pathogens with compost *Annual Review of Phytopathology* 24 pp. 93–114

entirely different substance than what existed in the first place.

Microorganisms, like people, have different dietary and climate preferences. Some prefer to eat leaves, some prefer to eat straw, and others prefer to eat apples. As a result, the best level of decomposition and fertility occurs from adding a variety of organic substances to the pile.

Microorganisms are likewise competitive. Every species (and even variant of a given species) wants to make room for itself and its offspring. Because of this, many microorganisms have developed a variety of weapons that can be used against other microbes in the compost pile. The most widely understood is the production of antibiotics by a variety of organisms intended to inhibit the growth of other organisms. Heat-loving bacteria in a compost pile endeavor to heat up the pile to a high-enough temperature that other bacteria can't tolerate the heat and die off. But once they've finished their job, mesophilic bacteria move back into the pile and take over again, along with fungi and finally earthworms.

Composting to Destroy Pathogens

The microorganisms that create compost can be broadly classified as being either thermophilic—meaning "heat loving"—or mesophilic—meaning "intermediate loving"—both terms referring to the temperatures preferred and created by such microorganisms. A compost pile is called either thermophilic or mesophilic depending on the temperatures it achieves.

The most important aspect of the relative heat of a compost pile is pathogen death. Thermophilic composting will kill all known human pathogens—including parasitic worm eggs, bacteria, viruses, and protozoa—along with plant disease organisms and weed seeds. Using thermophilic composting, it is both possible and practical to recycle not just ordinary plant material such as leaves and grass clippings but also leftover fried chicken. In other words, thermophilic composting makes a much broader array of compost ingredients both practical and safe.

There are two factors affecting the death of plant or animal pathogens and weed seeds in compost. The temperature achieved by the compost, as mentioned, is a big factor. Another important factor is the time that the compost is held before being used. Microbial pathogens require particular hosts to complete their life cycles, and their spores can remain inert—and thus viable—only in a warm, moist compost pile for so long. Even if a compost pile isn't thermophilic, adequate holding time will still render the compost both safe and beneficial. Weed seeds can be killed by the high heat of a thermophilic compost pile, but they can also be killed by virtue of the fact that the warmth of even a mesophilic pile can induce premature germination, thus interrupting the life cycle of the weeds.

The holding time for mesophilic compost is two years if it contains, or is likely to contain, pathogens from infected crops, dead animals, or other ingredients. Thermophilic compost that contains any or all of these things need only be held for a year. Compost made from solely nondisease-infected vegetation can be used after six months, no matter the temperature of the pile.

Many books and articles on home composting contain long lists of things not to compost, and that list contains diseased crops, meat scraps, peanut butter, cooking oils, carnivore or omnivore feces, and so forth. Such a list of banned items makes perfect sense when dealing with mesophilic compost (or meeting organic certification standards), especially if it won't be held for a couple of years to ensure pathogen death—and most home composting is mesophilic. But by using thermophilic composting, the list of banned items can go into the compost pile,[18] and you can recycle all of your uneaten leftovers.

It is possible to compost human manure safely; however, the procedure isn't covered in this book. The proper procedures for recycling human manure are thoroughly covered with extensive documentation by Joseph Jenkins in *The Humanure Handbook*. (Mr. Jenkins has kindly made an electronic version of the book available on the Internet at no cost. Just look for it in a search engine.)

Thermophilic Composting

Four things are required to achieve thermophilic composting: adequate bulk, adequate aeration, adequate moisture, and a proper ratio of carbon to nitrogen, known as C/N ratio.

Composting methods are usually described as either batch methods or continuous methods. Batch methods add all of the ingredients at once, while continuous methods add to the pile progressively. Most mini-farmers and home gardeners are continuous composters by default. As a result the initial stages of a compost pile may not have enough bulk to retain the heat of thermophilic composting. This problem can be solved through timing: Start new compost piles in the spring, so that by the time cool weather arrives, the pile already has plenty of bulk to retain heat through the winter.

In the spring, you not only add the leaves that fell on the yard during the fall but also harvest green manures that were planted in the fall for a spring harvest and add those to the pile as well. You can also add livestock manure (if available) and any grass clippings or remaining crop debris. This gets the pile off to a good start with plenty of bulk. If leaves aren't available, straw or hay will work just as well. The various ingredients are added to the pile in alternating layers no more than two inches thick so that grass clippings or leaves don't get matted down to form a layer impermeable to air. If you wind up with a layer a little too thick, don't worry because the next time you turn the compost pile, the layers will all get mixed up.

Aeration is important because thermophilic composting is aerobic, requiring oxygen. There are two sorts of microorganisms involved in decomposing organic materials—aerobic microorganisms that work in the presence of oxygen, and anaerobic microorganisms that work in the absence of oxygen. Aerobic composting reduces or eliminates odors and allows for thermophilic microbes, whereas anaerobic composting smells like a septic tank and seldom develops much heat. Therefore, aeration is important to make good compost and maintain peace in the neighborhood. Aeration is achieved by regularly turning over and mixing compost piles. Practically every book or article written about composting advocates frequent turning of the pile to ensure adequate aeration. The idea of turning compost is so entrenched that a number of companies even

---

[18] Jenkins, J. (2005) *The Humanure Handbook*

⊗ Drilled PVC pipe used for compost aeration.

make fairly expensive gadgets for helping people turn and tumble their compost.

Too much turning of compost is unnecessary and can actually be counterproductive by causing a loss of both valuable nitrogen and organic matter.[19] Turning a compost pile will also serve to dissipate any heat. The solution to the problem is to build the compost pile in such a way that it is self-aerating.[20] This is accomplished by layering in straw as you go along—just keep a couple of

bales handy next to the compost pile. By adding a layer of straw and making sure that no layer in the pile of any given ingredient is more than a couple of inches thick without being broken up by either straw or another ingredient, a self-aerating pile is ensured. Or, you can try my method, in which large-diameter PVC pipes with holes drilled in them are buried vertically in the pile.

Not all piles can be constructed in a fashion that guarantees self-aeration, of course; in such cases turning the pile up to five times per year is absolutely necessary. In fact, if a pile is not self-aerating, it should be turned regularly. After prolonged heavy rains that can soak into the pile

[19] Brinton, W. F. Jr. (1997) Sustainability of modern composting–Intensification versus cost and quality *Biodynamics*, Summer 1997

[20] Jenkins, J. (2005) *The Humanure Handbook*, p. 50

⊗ Watering the pile as it is turned is important.

and force out the oxygen, turning is a good idea. In addition, the composting process uses a great deal of water, so when compost is turned, water should be added as needed.

Adequate moisture is another important factor in composting. Too much moisture in compost forces out the air, leading to anaerobic decomposition, which is not thermophilic and almost always smells bad. Too little moisture in compost causes the microorganisms to go dormant or work less effectively. Thankfully, the ideal range for compost is actually pretty tolerant and can be anywhere in the range of 40% to 60%,[21]

---

[21] Campbell, S. (1990) *Let It Rot* p. 95

and all that is required is for any dry layers added to the pile (such as leaves or sawdust) be dampened with a hose if rain isn't in the forecast. Any additional moisture needed will be supplied by rain in most of North America. Extremely rainy climates might require that the pile be covered with a tarp on occasion, and drought conditions will require that the pile be checked and water added if its moisture content isn't about that of a wrung-out sponge. Remember, again, that when turning compost, check to see if water is needed, and add it if necessary.

Just like humans require nutrients in given amounts to be most productive, microorganisms responsible for making compost have dietary needs. The most relevant dietary requirement of microbes in the manufacture of thermophilic compost is the ratio of carbon to nitrogen in the pile. Microbes need nitrogen to build proteins, and they need carbon for practically everything. A ratio of carbon to nitrogen of 30:1 will result in thermophilic compost.[22] This ratio need not be followed slavishly. Microbes are picky but not *that* picky. Anywhere from 35:1 to 25:1 will work fine.

The proper carbon/nitrogen ratio can be achieved by mixing ingredients with higher and lower C/N ratios in approximate proportions. For example, cow manure with a C/N ratio of 20:1 can be mixed with oak leaves with a C/N ratio of 50:1 to get the desired ratio of 30:1. Even more easily, green vegetable wastes mixed half and half with dry vegetable wastes will achieve the same result. A table listing the C/N ratios of common materials is below to use as a guide.

Table 6: Carbon to Nitrogen Ratios of Commonly Composted Materials

Material	Ratio
Vegetable wastes	12–20:1
Alfalfa hay	13:1
Cow manure	20:1
Leaves	40–80:1
Corn stalks	60:1
Oat straw	74:1
Wheat straw	80:1
Sawdust	100–500:1
Grass clippings	12–25:1
Coffee grounds	20:1
Poultry manure	10:1
Horse manure	25:1

If a compost pile is constructed, and it just won't seem to heat up, check the moisture and add water or drain as needed, then poke holes deep in it with a pole for aeration. If neither of these works, nitrogen needs to be added. Ideally, this would be done by mixing in green vegetation, but blood meal mixed with water and dumped into the aeration holes will work too. Blood meal is common and can be bought at garden stores and possibly the local Walmart. If my piles aren't heating up the way they should because of inadequate nitrogen, what I do is add a standard organic fertilizer containing nitrogen and a bit of compost activator every so often as I turn them.

A soil and/or compost thermometer can be purchased inexpensively so you can judge the performance of your pile. (I use a long laboratory thermometer because I have several already.) You want the pile to reach from 130 to 160 degrees for no less than 15 days total. In practice, your compost is unlikely to stay at such a temperature for 15 days in a row. By using a thermometer, you can see when the temperature is starting to drop. Mix the pile thoroughly every time you see the temperature drop, and within a couple of days, the pile will heat back up again if the moisture level is right. This way, you can be pretty certain of at least 15 days of thermophilic temperatures in your compost.

At thermophilic compost temperatures of 140 degrees, roundworm and other eggs are killed in two hours or less, and most other protozoans, bacteria, and viruses are killed within minutes. The most tenacious dangerous germ is salmonella, and it is killed in about 20 hours.[23] By

---

[22] Jeavons, J. (2002) *How to Grow More Vegetables* p. 39

[23] Feachem et al. (1980) *Appropriate Technology for Water Supply and Sanitation: Health Aspects of Excreta and Sullage Management*

providing 15 days at temperatures exceeding 130 degrees, you are creating compost that is absolutely safe to apply to crops that touch the soil, practically without regard to its ingredients.

Compost Aging

As noted earlier, both temperatures and retention time have an impact on pathogen destruction, along with the biochemistry of the compost pile. For a pile made from nondiseased plants and manures, an extensive retention time is not required to ensure that the compost is hygienic, but a minimum retention time is definitely required to make sure that the compost is *mature*. Immature compost can contain phytotoxins that retard germination and can use up the nutrients from any beds it is added to. The standards of the Canadian Council of Ministers of the Environment specify that six months is adequate retention time for compost,[24] and that works whether the composting has been mesophilic or thermophilic as long as diseased materials weren't used. If disease organisms were likely present (because debris from infected crops or meat products were added), then compost should be retained a year if thermophilically composted, and two years otherwise.

Proper aging of compost can be tested without a fancy laboratory using radish seeds, because radishes are extremely sensitive to the phytotoxins in immature compost.

Purchase some commercial seed-starter mix, dampen it, and put it in a seed-starting container. Put the compost to be tested in another container

---

[24] Composting Council of Canada (1999) *The Composting Process: Compost Maturity*

in the same environment as the first, then plant 20 radish seeds in each flat. Water both regularly, and keep at 70 degrees F.

Observe the germination. If the germination rate of the seeds in the compost is less than 80% of that in the commercial seed-starter mix, the compost needs to age some more.

Compost Activators

Almost every gardening magazine carries advertisements in the back for so-called compost activators. These products typically contain a mix of bacteria and fungi that help the composting process. While these products certainly won't hurt your compost, they aren't usually necessary either, because compost activators are all around you and free.

The two most useful compost activators are the prior year's compost and good garden soil. These contain a wealth of suitable bacterial and fungal spores that will seed your pile. Only a shovel or two of these mixed into the pile periodically is sufficient.

I have tried a couple of commercial compost activator products and found no difference between piles in which they had been used and piles in which they had not—except for cases where a pile has refused to heat up adequately because of lack of moisture. In these cases, adding the activator layered in with the additional water increases the rate at which the pile heats up.

The Grow Biointensive method of making compost—a mesophilic method—specifies that fully 1/3 of the final weight of your compost should be from garden soil. The reasoning for this is that it keeps the compost pile "cool" so that it will compost slowly. This has the benefit of preserving more organic matter and more nitrogen because a thermophilic phase is never reached.

I cannot deny this benefit, but I don't advocate this technique because the benefits of thermophilic composting—removing disease organisms and allowing a wider range of compost ingredients—outweigh the slightly greater loss of organic matter. So use a shovelful of garden soil or last year's compost as an activator, but don't get carried away or you'll end up with compost that won't reach high enough temperatures to kill disease organisms.

The Big Picture

Plant cover crops in the fall that are harvested in the spring and used to start a thermophilic compost pile when combined with leaves, straw, and other high-carbon materials. Add household organic wastes like food leftovers liberally to the pile, along with any animal manures available. Use straw or sawdust as a cover material when adding anything that would attract dogs or rodents or just bury it deeply in the pile. Add crop debris in the fall and then a good cover of hay or straw on top for the winter. In the spring, start a second pile, and let the first one sit for a year to cure, since uncured compost can hurt the soil's fertility; allowing a year to cure also ensures

⊗ The author's three-bin composting system.

hygienic compost. The following spring, the first pile is available for use.

If potentially pathogenic material has been composted or the compost never reached a thermophilic phase, it is best to hold the compost for a couple of years to be absolutely sure it is safe.

I have a three-bin system made out of chicken wire with a large bin in the center and bins half the size of the center one on either side. The larger center bin is used for current compost. By midsummer, the center pile has shrunk, and I shovel it into one of the two side bins. The next batch of compost from the center bin goes into the other side. By then, the compost in the first side is fully cured.

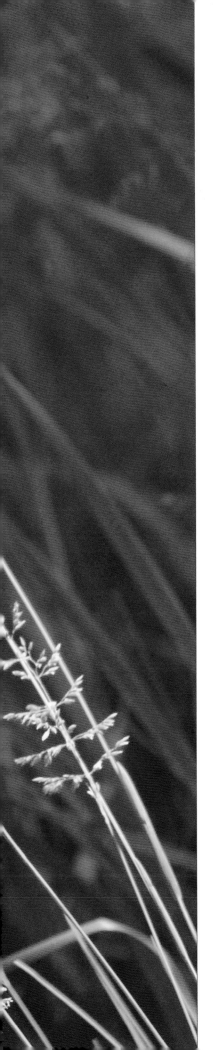

6

Plant Nutrients In-depth

In the past couple of chapters we have discussed the major macronutrients, soil structure, cover cropping, crop rotation, and other soil-building practices in a fair amount of detail. But this level of information is not sufficient in and of itself. It's a lot like saying that a human needs carbohydrates, fats, proteins, air, and exercise—but forgetting to mention vitamins.

Plants make their own vitamins, which is one reason why they are so nutritious. But to make them, or sometimes even survive at all, they need a wide array of both macronutrients and micronutrients. Most of the micronutrients take care of themselves between using various compost ingredients, specifically adding kelp or seaweed to compost once in awhile if available, and using commercial liquid kelp fertilizers such as Neptune's Harvest or Root Boost in the beds. In spite of this, deficiencies sometimes develop. In my garden, because I grow a lot of cabbage-family plants, boron can especially be an issue because with inadequate boron, broccoli grows with hollow stems. So I specifically add a teaspoon of borax (mixed with a cup of blood meal for easy dis-

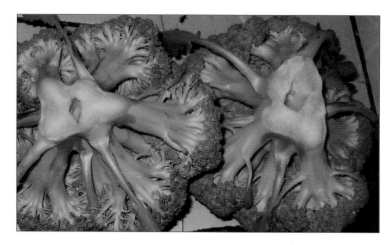

 These hollow stalks are the result of boron deficiency.

persal) to every garden bed at the beginning of each gardening season.

Macronutrients

Calcium: Calcium stimulates rhizobia bacteria, is critical for healthy cell walls, assists with movement of carbohydrates within plants, aids in the absorption of trace elements, and aids the activity of enzymes. Adequate calcium (or its even uptake) is necessary to prevent potato scab, blossom end rot, black lesions on carrots, and other diseases. Adding lime (which contains calcium) to the hole when transplanting brassicas can help prevent a fungal disease called "club foot." Bioavailable calcium is necessary for proper utilization of nitrogen.

Plants use large amounts of calcium, so it is important to ensure sufficient levels in the soil. Most often, this is done through adding lime of various sorts. Calcium can be added in the form of regular garden lime; dolomitic limestone, which also contains magnesium; and pulverized oyster shells. All of these take time to work and become bioavailable, so I generally recommend

adding them to beds in the fall so they have time to work before the garden season starts in spring. In general, you should add eight pounds of lime yearly to every 100 square feet of garden beds. I generally recommend using dolomitic lime as magnesium and calcium work in concert in a way that benefits the plants.

Nitrogen: Nitrogen is an essential element for life as, combined with carbon and hydrogen, it is a building block for amino acids, which combine to make proteins and even the basic data of life: RNA and DNA. Nitrogen is critical for every metabolic process in a plant and for the formation of important compounds such as chlorophyll. Predictably, plants need a lot of it. We covered nitrogen sources and quantities in a previous chapter.

Phosphorus: Phosphorus is an ingredient in the protoplasm within cells and is important for all cell division and growth. It is the single most important element for the germination and growth of plants, followed shortly by nitrogen. Almost all soils are deficient and need supplementation as described in a previous chapter. The most obvious place where phosphorus deficiency will become evident is in seedlings, because starting media is usually nutrient deficient. In these cases, the leaves will develop a purplish color on the underside. For seedlings, a complete liquid fertilizer containing phosphorus such as Neptune's Harvest (if growing organically) or Miracle Gro otherwise will head this off at the pass. Apply fertilizer to seedlings after the first set of leaves appear and every two weeks thereafter if using a nutrient-free growing medium. For crops in the ground, use the information from chapter 4.

Potassium: Plants require a large and continuous supply of potassium to help in the metabolism and movement of carbohydrates, protein synthesis, growth, and cell division. Adequate potassium supplies ensure better shape, color, and flavor of vegetables and fruits. The chief sign of deficiency can be seen in leaf edges that appear "scorched." Root crops, especially, require adequate potassium and perhaps even increased levels for best production. Chapter 4 contains information on the proper levels of potassium to maintain in your beds.

Micronutrients

Boron: Though classified as a micronutrient because of the small amount required, it is absolutely crucial to practically all life processes of plants including hormone activity, ion exchange, nutrient movement, and water metabolism. Every plant shows boron deficiency a bit differently, depending on the severity. In beans, the beans are deformed. In broccoli, the stems are hollow. Because deficiency symptoms can be easily confused with deficiencies in other elements, the best bet, short of a professional soil test, is to ensure adequate supply routinely. Because excess boron can be toxic to plants, and plants will absorb it in excess if too much is available, you have to be careful to only add what is needed. You can add three teaspoons of borax per 100 square feet of bed space once a year, and this will generally work out fine. You should mix it thoroughly with something like powdered lime or bone meal before broadcasting to ensure even distribution, and then work it into the top couple of inches of soil.

Copper: Copper plays an important role in root metabolism, photosynthesis, and enzyme activation, as well as protecting plants from adverse effects of excessive nitrogen. Copper, like boron, is required in only small amounts and is toxic in excess. It is available in the form of copper sulfate crystals and should be added to the beds yearly at the rate of 1-1/2 ounces (four tablespoons) per 100 square feet of bed. Because it is hard to distribute such a small quantity evenly over such a large space, it should be thoroughly mixed with something being added to beds in a larger quantity, such as lime, bone meal, or other fertilizer.

Iron: Though required in only small amounts, iron is essential for the chlorophyll cycle in plants. Without it, plants start to appear "bleached out" (called chlorosis) and suffer from stunted growth. Toxicity isn't a big issue with iron, as plants tend to self-regulate how much they take from the soil. Nevertheless, because it is required in only small amounts, excess shouldn't be supplied. Iron can be added incidentally through the use of blood meal as a nitrogen source. Because I use blood meal in my garden, iron deficiency has never been an issue. However, some may prefer not to use blood meal, in which case preventively adding six ounces of iron (or ferric) sulfate per 100 square feet of garden bed every year should do the trick. Another more organic alternative is to deliberately include nettle plants, which are very high in iron, in the compost pile.

Magnesium: Magnesium is an important element throughout the garden. It speeds up composting, makes nitrogen more readily available, stimulates rhizobia bacteria, assists in root development, and is necessary for carbohydrate motility within plants. It interacts in balance with calcium in a variety of ways and reduces the effects that could arise (however unlikely) from excess quantities of aluminum, manganese, or iron in the soil. Magnesium coexists with calcium in dolomitic lime, and you will have no problems from magnesium deficiency as long as you use dolomitic limestone as a source of calcium in your beds. Barring this, magnesium sulfate—also known as Epsom salt—is available at grocery stores or pharmacies and can be used at the rate of 24 ounces yearly per 100 square feet of garden bed.

Manganese: Though manganese is required only sparingly, its presence in adequate quantities can have an enormous positive effect on crop yields, especially for root crops. Deficiency is seen as a uniform yellowing in new leaves. This makes sense, because manganese is essential for the production of chlorophyll. Most soils have adequate naturally available manganese, but if the pH of the soil is higher than 6.5, supplementation may be needed. As well, overfarmed soils may be deficient. If you suspect deficiency, you can add 12 ounces of manganese sulfate per 100 square feet to your beds once every three years.

Molybdenum: Molybdenum is an essential catalyst for the formation of enzymes and synthesis of amino acids and proteins. Although it is essential, in excess it is extremely toxic to plants. If you accidentally add too much molybdenum to your beds, treat them with copper sulfate, which will reduce the bioavailability of the molybdenum so it will be less toxic. Most soils today, especially those in agricultural usage, are deficient in molybdenum. If you supplement with manganese when molybdenum is already deficient, that makes matters worse—so I recommend always using molybdenum and manganese together. Supplementation can be in the form of molybdic acid, ammonium molybdate, or sodium molybdate at the rate of 1-1/2 ounces per 100 square feet of garden bed mixed with something else to facilitate even application. Molybdenum disulfide, used as a lubricant, isn't suitable because it is so stable that it has no effective biological availability.

Sulfur: Sulfur is an important ingredient of essential amino acids required for building plant proteins. In essence, without sulfur, plants cease to exist. On the other hand, sulfur exists in many different forms, and some are more useful to plants than others while yet others are absolutely toxic. In general, the sulfate forms of sulfur are healthful to plants whereas the sulfide forms of sulfur are deleterious. Because sulfur compounds tend to acidify the soil a bit, you should keep an eye on the soil pH and add lime if needed to offset the effects of the sulfur in terms of pH. Sulfur is usually applied in the form of plain elemental sulfur, known as "flowers of sulfur." Evenly distribute over the beds at the rate of 24 ounces per 100 square feet once yearly.

Zinc: Zinc is crucial for seed production, metabolism, and regulation of the water and carbon dioxide equilibrium in plants. Zinc deficiency is not particularly common, but when it shows up, it can be identified in the form of chlorotic bands within the leaves of a plant. Zinc is much more available in acidic (pH less than 7) than in alkaline (pH greater than 7) soils. Thus, the 12 ounces of zinc sulfate per 100 square feet of bed that are needed to correct or prevent deficiency would need to be multiplied by five for a total of 60 ounces if the soil in the beds is alkaline.

Making a Micronutrient Mix

Once your mini-farm has been up and running for three years or so, this will probably be unnecessary for established beds because the soil fertility practices will conserve a lot of plant nutrients. But, when just getting started, it may be needed. For enough for 300 square feet, combine the following ingredients in a bucket, and dry mix thoroughly:

Borax: 1-1/2 ounces

Copper sulfate: 4-1/2 ounces

Ferric sulfate: 18 ounces

Magnesium sulfate: 72 ounces

Manganese sulfate: 12 ounces

Sodium molybdate: 4-1/2 ounces

Sulfur: 36 ounces

Zinc sulfate: 36 ounces

Nutrient Conservation

Other than boron, I've never had to supplement with a micronutrient on my farm. The primary reason is because the biochar in the soil holds nutrients so they don't leach, the use of cover crops keeps the nutrients from becoming mobile, and conscientious composting of all plant matter from the garden preserves the nutrients that have entered the plants from the soil so they can be returned to the soil.

The other reason is variety of inputs. When I use organic fertilizers, I use a variety. One time, I might use alfalfa meal for nitrogen, but another time I might use blood meal. For potassium I might use greensand at the beginning of a season but wood ashes at the end. And all throughout, the compost bin collects a wide array of materials ranging from crop debris and lawn clippings to stale eggs and the entrails of slaughtered animals. As a result, because the animals largely receive feed from off the farm, the compost contains more nutrients than were taken out of the soil in the first place, making it an incredible fertilizer.

This is important. Everything that you can't make yourself or conserve on your mini-farm becomes something that will eventually cost you money. Keeping costs down is the secret that makes mini-farming an economic activity that is more beneficial than simple gardening.

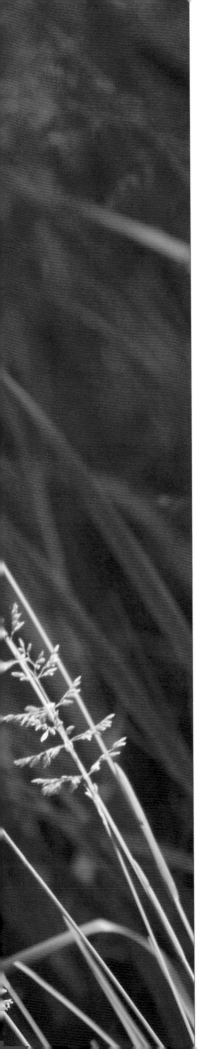

7

Time and Yield

Most of the United States, even the northern plains, has a growing season long enough to allow for multiple plantings of many crops. Moreover, well-orchestrated timing allows harvests to be timed either to allow a little at a time to be harvested for daily use or marketing—which is useful for crops like lettuce—or to allow multiple large harvests for the purpose of preservation and storage. Many crops are frost hardy, and second plantings will allow harvests to continue for as long as a month after the first fall frost, without using anything to extend the season. For example, two crops of broccoli or spinach can be raised in the same area as one crop, doubling production per unit area.

Succession Planting

This is a technique for maximizing productivity of garden space by having a new crop ready to plant as soon as an earlier crop is harvested. An example is planting a second crop of broccoli in the same space where a first crop of broccoli was harvested at midsummer. Another example is sowing spinach early and then planting beans where the spinach used to be as soon as the spinach is harvested.

Crops that work well for the early planting in a succession are anything from the cabbage family, spinach, peas, radishes, turnips, beets, and onions from sets. ("Sets" are the miniature onions for planting that you can buy in a mesh bag at the garden center. They aren't the same as supermarket onions.) The foregoing crops are usually harvested no later than the middle of July. Crops that can be planted in mid-July for a late summer or fall harvest include bush beans, lettuce, spinach, carrots, turnips, beets, parsnips, and anything in the cabbage family.

Timed Planting

Timed planting means spreading out harvests by staggering the planting dates for a particular crop across a few weeks rather than planting it all at once. The result is a steady supply of a particular crop for market or a continual harvest that can be frozen, eaten, or canned in small sessions.

The easiest way to do this is to take the total number of plants intended for a given crop and divide it by three. Sow the first third on the first sowing date for that crop, the second third a week later, and the final third two weeks later. This will give the same total harvest as planting the whole crop at once but will spread out the harvest over a two-week period.

The next aspect of timed planting is replanting. Take carrots, for example; if carrots were planted in four sessions, each two weeks apart, when the first planting is harvested, that area can be replanted with more carrots so the space never sits idle. By the time the final crop

of carrots is ready for harvest, you are only two weeks away from yet another first harvest.

Succession planting and timed planting both provide a little insurance so if serious weather hits early or late, there's still a harvest. All that you need to know to successfully use succession and/ or timed planting is the days to maturity for the crop under consideration and its frost hardiness.

Interplanting

Interplanting is used in two ways. It is used to give green manures a head start on the winter and to maximize the amount of food that can be harvested from a given area. Carefully chosen, interplanted crops can save on fertilizer as well, as when a nitrogen producer such as beans or clover is interplanted with a nitrogen consumer such as tomatoes or corn.

There are some practical considerations to interplanting, and chief among them are overcrowding and shade. Plants that require a lot of space or sunlight, such as tomatoes, could have difficulty if planted in an established stand of

⊗ Interplanting crops creates synergies.

corn. If planted before the corn has germinated, the tomatoes would shade the seedlings. On the other hand, white clover works well with most plants, as do beans.

Perhaps the most famous example of successful interplanting is the so-called Three Sisters of the Native Americans—corn, beans, and squash, which they grew together. In this case, the pole beans and squash vines used the corn stalks for support.

Fall Gardening

Frost hardy crops and biennials kept alive over the winter for seed production (called "overwintering") can be planted first in the spring, harvested in the summer, and then replanted for a second fall or early winter harvest. Late harvests can be achieved for many crops without going to the trouble of using season extension structures. Overwintering crops, so they can be used either as needed or for seed production, is more problematic. In the South or Pacific Northwest, it can be done outdoors. In the upper Midwest or Northeast, such plants have to be brought indoors for the winter or else protected with, at minimum, an unheated greenhouse or cold frame.

For purposes of fall gardening, crops can be divided into three categories: tender, semihardy, and hardy. Tender crops are damaged by a light frost. Semihardy crops will tolerate a light frost, and hardy crops will tolerate hard frosts.

The best bets for fall gardening are semihardy and hardy crops. Some hardy crops, like broccoli and spinach, often taste better when grown in the fall rather than in the spring. Semihardy crops should be timed for harvests within 28 days after the first frost, and hardy crops should be timed

within 56 days after the first frost. For this, the time to harvest needs to be known. Each variety of a given crop has slightly different dates of maturity, and those dates are indicated in seed catalogs and on seed packets. Because growth is slower in the fall, 10 days should be added to the maturity date, so plant 10 days earlier for fall harvests.

Table 7: **Crop Hardiness**

Tender	*Semihardy*	*Hardy*
Beans	Beets	Broccoli
Corn	Carrot	Brussels sprouts
Cucumber	Cauliflower	Cabbage
Eggplant	Celery	Kale
Melon	Chard	Onion
Okra	Lettuce	Parsley
Pepper	Parsnip	Peas
Squash	Potato	Spinach
Sweet potato		Turnip
Tomato		

Using Seedlings for a Head Start

Some crops, such as cucumbers, can be directly seeded in the garden or transplanted. Transplanting seedlings gives the plants a head start and can allow maximum production from the number of growing days in the season.

Winter squash, requiring 80 or more days to harvest, is a good candidate for transplanting seedlings, particularly in the northern half of the United States where there are often fewer than 90 frost-free days in a row in the growing season. Since squash shouldn't be direct seeded until 14 days after the last frost, leaving fewer than 80 remaining growing days, growing transplants instead will increase the amount of squash harvested without requiring the farmer to use season extension devices.

The same applies for crops in the fall garden. In the late season, broccoli can be direct seeded, but giving it a four-week head start by growing seedlings inside and then transplanting them will accelerate the harvest.

One place where I have used this technique to good effect is with a crop that most authors will tell you not to transplant: corn. Grown on the agribusiness scale, seed for sweet corn is usually coated with a fungicide to keep it from rotting in the ground. Seed corn is prone not just to rot but to being eaten by wire worms. In addition, it doesn't all germinate at the same time. On a very large scale, this all evens out. But on a small scale—say growing 48 plants in a 4-foot × 8-foot raised bed—it can be a problem. Transplanting seedlings is an ideal solution.

What I do is start 64 seedlings indoors about two weeks before the first frost-free date. It's important to not try any longer than two weeks because corn grows a taproot, and after that, transplant shock can be too great. After two weeks, some may not have germinated, and some will be taller than others. What I do is pick the 48 most uniform plants and transplant them into the bed. I keep the others handy for a week just in case cut worms or some similar pest strikes.

You can use this technique for most crops outside of root crops. By starting from seed indoors, you gain an advantage of anywhere from two to six weeks.

Example Timeline

The following table is part of the calendar for my own mini-farm in New Hampshire, so the exact dates may not work for you. Nevertheless, the examples given should be helpful.

Table 8: **Example Activity Schedule**

Date	Activity	Date	Activity
02/11/06	Start onion and leek seeds inside	05/06/06	Start cucumber, melon, and squash inside
02/18/06	Start broccoli, cabbage, and kale inside	05/07/06	Sow radish and salsify seeds outside
02/25/06	Start cauliflower inside	05/13/06	Sow 1/2 of carrots, beets, parsnips, and turnips; cut cover crops and add to compost pile
03/01/06	Start lettuce inside	05/27/06	Plant tomato and pepper transplants outside
04/01/06	Start tomatoes and peppers inside	05/28/06	Sow corn seed and second 1/2 of carrots, beets, parsnips, and turnips

Date	Activity	Date	Activity
04/15/06	Start marigold, nasturtium, pyrethrum, and dill seeds inside	06/03/06	Harvest radishes and plant cucumber, melon, and squash transplants where the radishes were
04/22/06	Transplant broccoli, cabbage, and kale outside	06/23/06	Harvest broccoli and kale and replant with new transplants for a second crop
04/23/06	Plant potatoes and peas outside, covered with hoop house	07/07/06	Harvest cauliflower and replant with new transplants for a second crop
04/29/06	Start new broccoli seedlings inside for second planting	07/20/06	Harvest potatoes and carrots, prepare potato area, and sow with carrots and spinach
05/06/06	Plant cauliflower transplants outside	07/24/06	Pull up pea plants and add to compost pile, sow area with lettuce

8

Watering and Irrigation

Making sure that crops have the proper amount of water without overwatering them is important. Properly watered crops are more resistant to pests, absorb nutrients more consistently, and are generally stronger and more productive.

While it is possible to water crops a little bit daily, such an approach presents problems. For one thing, if enough water isn't used to soak down deep into the soil, the roots of the plants will stay close to the surface, making it impossible for the farmer to skip watering for a couple of days.

A better approach is to water extremely thoroughly but less frequently. A "thorough" watering is the equivalent of one inch of rain, which equates to about five pints of water per square foot of garden bed. Under normal conditions, this much water will soak deeply into the soil so that plant roots will become better established, and watering will be required only once a week, or twice a week during extremely hot weather. (Later in this chapter I describe how to determine how much watering is required if it has rained.)

Garden soil, when dry, initially repels water. If water is simply dumped on top, the water will flow to the lowest spot it can find and pool there until it is absorbed. Get the soil a little damp first, and it will soak up water like a sponge.

There are as many approaches to watering gardens as there are gardeners. The Square Foot method waters each square foot of a raised bed individually using a ladle. The reasoning for this is not just water conservation but the fact that keeping foliage from being damp helps to prevent disease problems. This is true, but the problem lies in the fact that such a method of watering becomes burdensomely time-consuming when done on the scale of even a few hundred square feet.

The Grow Biointensive method imitates natural rainfall by using special watering attachments that make small droplets and let the water fall with only the force of gravity. By watering thoroughly each time, the frequency of watering is kept to about once a week. This is a lot less time-consuming than watering each square foot individually, and because it waters thoroughly rather than frequently, it is better than daily watering regimens in terms of disease, though not as good as the Square Foot method in that regard. Agriculture, like anything else, requires compromises! All things being equal, using a watering wand is the best technique for a mini-farmer in the first couple of years.

Use of a Watering Wand

A watering wand can be used to duplicate natural rainfall. This is worthwhile, as typical watering attachments can allow the water to be

❯❯ A watering wand allows delivery of water at the proper rate.

too forceful, causing erosion and disrupting seeds and seedlings.

Most watering wands, but not all, have a movable head that allows the use of different settings for water flow. If you get one like this, make sure to select the "shower" setting. Unfortunately, when watering by hand, it is difficult to know how much water is being delivered. Luckily, it is easy to figure out.

Take a garden hose with the shower watering attachment installed, place it in a five-gallon bucket, and turn it on. (The shower watering attachment is also known as a "watering wand." Use *nothing but* a watering wand if watering by hand or you'll damage your plants.) Use the sweep second hand on a watch to see how long it takes to fill up the bucket. If it takes two minutes to fill up the bucket, then you know that the flow rate of the hose and attachment is 2.5 gallons per minute. A 100-square-foot garden bed requires 62 gallons

❂ Use the "shower" setting to avoid damaging plants.

of water once a week. By dividing 62 by 2.5, you will discover that by watering the bed evenly for 25 minutes, you will add sufficient water. If your farm is anything like mine, most of the beds are roughly 4-foot × 8-foot, or 32 square feet. That's roughly 1/3 of 100 square feet, so if you divide the 62 gallons of water for a 100-square-foot bed by three, you get 20 to 21 gallons of water for a 32-square-foot bed. If your attachment waters at 4 gallons per minute, then that means watering the bed for five minutes.

This is obviously time-consuming. A three-person self-sufficient mini-farm will have more than a few beds, so hand watering would require a lot of time and be pretty boring. One way of avoiding monotony is to divide up the beds so that 1/5 of the beds are watered on each day of the week. Once you have expanded to a big enough mini-farm that watering chores are eating a lot of your time, you should arrange some sort of irrigation system (if possible) to optimize time usage.

Drip Irrigation

Probably the best approach in terms of time, efficiency, and disease prevention is drip irrigation in which tubes carry water to discrete areas of the garden at a predetermined rate of flow. It can be pretty expensive to install initially, but in the long run it pays for itself by freeing your time. One of the best aspects of drip irrigation systems is that they are modular and use standardized fittings, meaning that a farmer can start small and expand the system gradually as time and finances allow. Drip irrigation gives the benefits of watering each plant individually and keeping the foliage dry and thus discouraging diseases while saving considerable time.

Drip irrigation systems are rated in gallons per hour, either per foot or per emitter. (An emitter is a small device that delivers water from the system to the plants.) In the case of intensive agriculture, emitters should be spaced every 6 or 12 inches because the plants grow so closely together. Drip tape is ideal for intensive applications and should be run according to manufacturer's directions in such a way that there is at least one emitter per square foot of raised bed. An automatic timer can be installed so that if the flow rate of the emitters is known, the time can be set to allow precisely the right amount of water. Keep a rain gauge in the garden, and you will know that the garden needs to be watered only when the amount of rain in a week is less than one inch. When the amount of rain that fell is *less than one inch*, the amount of water (in gallons) needed per square foot can be calculated using the following formula: $0.62 \times (1 - z)$ where z is the number of inches of rain that fell that week.

Soaker Hoses

Not every mini-farmer will choose to install a drip irrigation or gray water recycling system. A good alternative is the use of soaker hoses. Soaker hoses can be laid lengthwise on top of the garden bed and snaked back and forth so that successive runs are no more than one foot apart.

⊗ Two popular styles of soaker hose.

Alternatively, they can be buried in the garden beds no more than four inches deep. I tried burying a soaker hose about eight inches deep in a bed, and since most of a plant's roots are in the top six inches of soil, it didn't work out so well. Soaker hoses need to be on top of the soil or buried no more than four inches deep.

The watering rates of soaker hoses will vary by manufacturer. One brand, made by Fiskars, waters at the rate of one gallon per hour per 10 linear feet of hose if connected to a 10-psi pressure regulator. Up to six lengths of soaker hose of up to 100 feet length each can be run from the same spigot/pressure regulator. Adding an automatic timer to the system makes watering effortless.

Calculating how long to leave the soaker turned on is straightforward. One inch of rain on a 100-square-foot garden bed is 62 gallons of water, and that is what is needed weekly for optimal plant health. If laid out properly, a 4-foot × 25-foot garden bed will use 100 feet of soaker hose. Since the hose waters at the rate of one gallon per hour per 10 linear feet, then 100 linear feet will put out 10 gallons of water an hour. So in six hours or so, 62 gallons will be delivered. When the automatic timer is set to water for six hours once a week, you are then free from watering chores except in the case of young seedlings that need to be watered by hand.

Gray Water Recycling

Gray water recycling is seldom considered as a means of watering crops. Household waste water is designated as either black water, meaning that it contains human waste, or gray water, which is everything else. If a home is equipped to handle gray water separately, then water that would otherwise go to waste can be used to water raised beds. The microbes in the raised beds and the plants themselves purify the gray water and derive nutrients from it. Such a system would contain a gray water holding tank and a pump, and the beds would contain embedded pipes with small holes drilled in them. (The Johnny Appleseed rest area in Massachusetts uses this technique.) Gray water can also be recycled using artificial wetlands that can double as a home for ducks or aquaculture of farm-raised fish. It stands to reason that toxic substances should never be dumped into a gray water system, so homes anticipating such a use need to "go green" in terms of the cleaning products they use.

Crop Proportions and Sizing

How much of each crop to grow depends on a number of factors but most importantly on your needs and the requirements of market outlets if you choose to grow enough to sell. Averages come in handy for general planning, but nobody is really average. What this means is nobody can make a chart telling you exactly what to grow.

Folks in the United States eat notoriously unhealthy diets. According to the USDA Center for Nutrition Policy and Promotion, only 10% of Americans have a healthy diet.[25] So before we get into crop proportions and sizing, let's take a brief look at nutritional requirements.

As of 2006, the USDA food pyramid specifies the servings per day of different food groups (see Table 9).

By examining what constitutes a "serving" in each case and doing a little multiplication, we can create target production suitable for a healthy diet, which can later be modified if necessary to match the family's food preferences and activity levels.

---

[25] Basiotis, P. et al. (2002) *Healthy Eating Index 1999–2000* published by U.S. Department of Agriculture Center for Nutrition Policy and Promotion

Table 9: **2006 USDA Food Pyramid**

Person	Grains	Vegetables	Fruits	Milk	Meat
Male, age 25–50	11	5	4	2	2.8
Female, age 25–50	9	4	3	2	2.4
Teenage male	11	5	4	3	2.8
Teenage female	9	4	3	3	2.4

For grains, a serving is a single slice of bread; 1/2 cup of rice, pasta, or cooked breakfast cereal; or one ounce of ready-to-eat breakfast cereal. Serving equivalents are computed on the basis of 1/2 ounce of flour per serving.

For vegetables, a serving is one cup of green leafy vegetables or a half cup of any other sort of vegetables, whether raw or cooked. Three-quarters of a cup of vegetable juice also constitutes a serving. Potatoes count as a vegetable, with half of a cup constituting a serving. Botany defines tomatoes as a fruit, but U.S. law defines tomatoes as a vegetable. For the purposes of the food pyramid, tomatoes are a vegetable.

With fruits, an average-sized whole fruit or 1/2 cup of fresh berries or canned/cooked fruit constitutes a serving. Three-quarters of a cup of fruit juice is also a serving of fruit.

All forms of meat but also dry beans, eggs, and nuts fall into the meat category. For red meat, poultry, and seafood, 2.5 ounces is a serving. One egg, half of a cup of tofu, half of a cup of cooked dried beans, and 1/4 of a cup of dried seeds each constitute a serving. One cup of milk or yogurt or 1.5 to 2 ounces of cheese constitutes a serving of milk.

Using food pyramid guidelines and serving sizes, we can determine the target production numbers for one person, as shown in Table 10.

Table 10: **Per-Person Yearly Food Requirements**

Crop	Per-Person Yearly Requirement
Vegetables	456 lbs
Fruit	365 lbs
Wheat, corn, oats, and rice	250 lbs
Total lean meats and eggs	159 lbs

What those numbers indicate is that the yearly diet for a family of two adults and one teenager requires 1,368 pounds of vegetables, 1,095 pounds of fruits, 750 pounds of grains, and 477 pounds of meat and eggs. This is, of course, subject to food preferences and allergies, so at the individual crop level, nobody can tell you what to grow. But at the level of gross nutrients, the USDA food pyramid can give you a good starting spot from which to customize.

Different crops give different yields per unit of space, and a mini farmer has to be aware of the expected yields to plan space allocation. Table 11 (page 82) gives approximate yield information for planning purposes based on a number of assumptions. Nonhybrid plant varieties in ordinary soil with sufficient water are assumed. Actual yield will depend on the variety of a given crop grown and individual growing conditions. And, it is quite possible (even likely) that a farmer with richly composted soil will exceed these yields.

Our hypothetical family of three (two adults and one teenager) requires 1,368 pounds of vegetables for the year. Averaging the yield of various vegetables, you get 220 pounds per 100 square feet of bed space, meaning that all of a family's vegetable needs can be provided easily in 700 square feet of bed space, assuming a variety of vegetables.

The same hypothetical family needs 1,095 pounds of fruit for the year. Muskmelons, cantaloupes, and watermelons all count as fruits. Unfortunately, in most cases, these don't keep very long past the growing season. Fruit trees and vines are best to produce fruit in significant quantities. These aren't grown in raised beds and are instead grown in the ground.

A dwarf apple tree can yield up to 160 pounds of fruit annually. Apples store pretty well in a root cellar and are easily made into applesauce, and dehydrated apples make a tasty addition to oatmeal. Another good source of fruit is sweet and sour cherries, which will yield 300 and 150 pounds of fruit per tree, respectively. Blackberry canes are easy and trouble free to grow and will yield up to 50 pounds of blackberries per 100 square feet. Strawberries will yield around 100 pounds per 100 square feet.

Any number of combinations of fruit could work, but one example that would yield the 1,095 pounds of fruit is as follows:

- 100 square feet of strawberries (100 lbs)
- 100 square feet of melons (200 lbs)
- 200 square feet of blackberries and raspberries (100 lbs)
- 2 sour cherry trees (300 lbs)
- 5 dwarf apple trees (800 lbs)

Knowing that the hypothetical family of three requires 750 pounds of grains, it is easy to calculate the space that would be needed for grain crops from the information in Table 11. Oats produce only 10 pounds per 100 square feet, but wheat can produce as much as 20 pounds in the same space. Even at that, dividing 750 by 20 and multiplying by 100 gives 3,750 square feet, which is an awful lot of space for a relatively small amount of food carbohydrates. On top of that, this small scale of growing grains isn't enough to justify buying a thresher, so the grain would have to be threshed by hand—an incredibly time-consuming chore. There is also the process of turning it into meal and/or flour by hand. I've done a lot of that over the years, and it is serious work.

Raising grains can become more practical if a suitable thresher is available at modest cost, and a number of public domain designs are available for folks who are mechanically proficient. Two of the most promising designs were cocreated by Allen Dong and Roger Edberg; these were donated into the public domain by the creators as a gift to humanity. These designs are included on pages 174 and 176.

In spite of the fact that the USDA counts potatoes as a vegetable, they can be substituted for a portion of the grains in the diet, and doing so may have positive effects on overall health, energy, and mood.[27] Three hundred and fifty pounds of potatoes can easily be grown in 200 square feet. Substituting that for a portion of the grain crops would leave only 360 pounds of grains still being needed.

---

[27] Desmaisons, K. (1998) *Potatoes Not Prozak*

The growing of grains for food purposes (as opposed to cover cropping) in a mini-farm needs to be carefully considered from an economic perspective. In 2006, the most expensive organic wheat sells for less than $15 for a 50-pound bag. Fifty pounds of the finest organic bread flour on the market currently costs $28. It would take 300 square feet of beds to grow that much wheat, and that same amount of space could grow over $1,400 worth of marketable crops instead. In addition, hand threshing wheat is time-consuming and must then be followed by grinding. Overall, within the United States, it really doesn't make sense for a mini-farmer to grow grains for their food value. This is why my approach to mini-farming, unlike the Grow Biointensive approach, doesn't emphasize growing grains at home.

Unless you can make a thresher economical and don't mind digging 3,800 square feet for growing grain, a much better approach is to learn how to use a bread machine. Purchasing bulk flour and whole grains, using a bread machine, and learning how to make grain-based products at home from scratch will ultimately be more economically beneficial and less time-consuming than growing grains for food unless you live in a remote region where such an otherwise economically unwise approach is necessary. Bread machines are the greatest thing since . . . sliced bread. Organic bread at the health food store routinely costs $4 per loaf as of this writing. By using a bread machine and buying the ingredients in bulk, you end up with chemical-free bread costing about $0.50 per loaf.

❷ If you grow grains at home, you'll need a grain grinder.

Table 11: **Average Crop Yields Planted Intensively**

Crop	Yield in Pounds per 100 Square Feet
Green beans (as a vegetable)	100
Green beans (dried, as a protein)	20
Beets (just the roots)	200
Beets (just the greens)	200
Broccoli	75
Cabbage	300
Cauliflower	200
Carrots	350
Chard	550
Corn (on the cob)	55
Corn (dried for cornmeal)	18

Crop	Yield in Pounds per 100 Square Feet
Cucumber	360
Eggplant	100
Kale	120
Leeks	500
Leaf lettuce	320
Head lettuce	180
Muskmelons	100
Onions	300
Peppers	120
Peas	100
Parsnips	290
Pumpkins	120
Spinach	130
Sunflower (shelled seeds)	6
Summer squash	250
Winter squash	200
Tomatoes	250
Watermelons	180
Barley	20
Oats	10
Rye	20
Wheat	20

Of all the dietary requirements, protein is the hardest to meet. Depending on your preferences, meat may need to be purchased, although it is feasible to produce meat and eggs at home by raising poultry. Larger livestock such as sheep and cattle are too big to be raised cost-effectively on smaller lots. The details of raising small livestock will be covered in a later chapter, so you may wish to consider space for a chicken coop in your farm plan.

But meat is not the only source of protein! Dried beans such as pinto, kidney, black turtle, soy, and others are rich in protein and easy to raise. I sow my dried beans in between my corn stalks, so they effectively require zero space. As noted earlier in this chapter, a mere half cup of cooked dried beans constitutes a serving of meat according to the USDA. That's only 1/4 cup of beans in their dried state. Vegetable proteins are seldom complete, meaning that they lack one or more amino acids, but this deficiency can be addressed by supplementing the beans with protein from grains such as wheat and corn. This way the entire mix of essential amino acids is available. I'm not jumping on the vegetarianism soapbox here. What I am saying instead is that if you can eat cooked dried beans and whole grain breads a couple of times per week, your health won't suffer, and you'll save a lot of money on meats.

In summary, assuming that whole grains and flours are purchased rather than raised at home, the core food needs of the family (other than meat) can be met by growing 700 square feet of vegetables and 200 square feet of potatoes or other tubers, purchasing flour in bulk, and growing a variety of fruit trees and vines. Protein can be acquired through purchasing meats, raising meat, and using beans and grains.

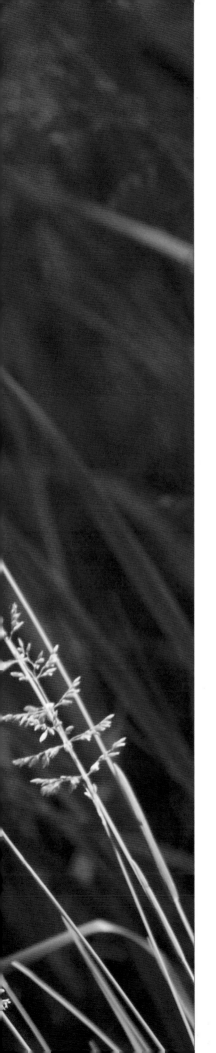

Pest and Disease Control

Pest and disease problems are an unavoidable fact of life for the mini-farmer. Sometimes, they are barely noticeable and cause no significant problems. But at other times they can cause major crop losses.

There are, unfortunately, hundreds of pests and diseases that affect vegetable crops. Going into the detail of identifying these is beyond the scope of this book, so instead I'll refer you to *The Organic Gardener's Handbook of Natural Insect and Disease Control,* published by Rodale and edited by Barbara Ellis and Fern Bradley. This 500-page book is loaded with color pictures and extensive explanation for every disease or pest you are likely to encounter, including specific details of organic methods for dealing with problems. What follows in this chapter is an overview that concentrates more on principles than details, along with my own unique passive-active-reactive pest management strategy developed specifically for the needs of mini-farms.

Since the old adage that "an ounce of prevention is worth a pound of cure" is true, mini-farming focuses automatically on passive prevention by giving plants what they need. Active prevention is used when experience or reliable data indicate that a particular pest or disease is likely to be a problem. Active reaction is employed when the value of likely crop damage will exceed the costs of active reaction methods.

Passive prevention is the application of good farming practices: well-composted and appropriately amended healthy soil, adequate sunshine, proper watering, crop rotation, and sufficient airflow. In essence, this simply means to give plants growing conditions that are as close to optimal as possible. This will make them healthier and thus less susceptible to diseases and less attractive to pests.

Active prevention uses active measures to prevent diseases or repel insect pests. Examples include applying repellent garlic or hot pepper sprays on plants to deter pests, installing physical barriers, putting out traps, or spraying the plants periodically with a fungus preventative. Sometimes, for certain types of pests, poisons that are usually used as a reactive measure may be required as active prevention.

Active reaction occurs when preventative measures fail and a problem already exists. Active reaction will often employ the same methods as active prevention, only with greater intensity, but it will also include, in most cases, the application of natural botanical or synthetic poisons or fungicides.

Pest management needs to be viewed holistically, as part of a bigger picture, to minimize crop damage while simultaneously protecting the long-range viability of the mini-farm. As part of this view, it is good to establish a threshold for what constitutes an acceptable level of damage before reactive, as opposed to preventative, measures need to be taken. This threshold is established economically, considering that the time, costs, and risks associated with active pest control measures will diminish the net grocery savings. So the threshold of acceptable damage for a given crop, in terms of percentage crop loss, is the

⊗ Potato beetles are a common garden pest.

level at which the value of the lost crop portion exceeds the cost of active control measures.

Passive Prevention

Passive prevention gives the biggest bang for both your time and money because the focus lies mainly in performing ordinary farming chores. Soil, water, sunshine, and crop rotations are the foundation of pest and disease control; all of these create an environment inhospitable to the persistence of pests and disease.

A healthy, living soil with plenty of nutrients allows for vigorous growth so that crops can outgrow problems. In addition, healthier plants are less attractive to pests and less susceptible to disease in most cases. Healthy soil plays host to various portions of the life cycles of many beneficial insect populations, along with beneficial microbes that compete with nasty pathogens for nutrients and generate antibiotics to eliminate them. It is no mistake that forests thrive independent of human intervention, and the more closely a farmer's garden approximates naturally optimal conditions for a crop, the less susceptible it will be to pest and disease problems.

An important aspect of healthy soil, particularly with intensive agriculture, is compost. As discussed in chapter 5, merely using compost in your soil can significantly reduce pest and disease problems.

Proper watering is another important aspect of disease control. Plant diseases spread most easily when plant tissues are wet; both excessive watering and overhead watering can increase the likelihood of disease problems. However, adequate moisture is also important because drought-stressed plants become more attractive to pests.

Crop rotation is impossible to over emphasize. Just like there are viruses and bacteria that affect some mammals but not others—such as feline leukemia—there are numerous plant diseases that affect one family of vegetables but not others. Since these microbes need a host hospitable to their reproduction to complete their life cycles, depriving them of the host they need through crop rotation is extremely effective at controlling many diseases. The same applies to insect pests, so the same crop should not be grown in the same bed two years in a row. Ideally, crop rotation will prevent crops of the same family from growing in the same bed any more often than once every three years.

Specific plant variety selection is another important preventative. Notwithstanding the

❷ Dill is a common attractant of beneficial insects.

economic benefits of using open-pollinated seeds (described in the next chapter), some hybrids carry disease- and pest-resistance genes that can make them a better choice if certain diseases or pests become a repetitive problem. On my farm, for example, I now grow hybrid cucumbers that are resistant to bacterial wilt disease.

Finally, never discount the power of the sun. The same UV rays that make excessive sunshine a risk factor for skin cancer also scramble the genetic code in bacteria and viruses, rendering them incapable of infection. Sunshine sanitizes.

Attracting beneficial insects is also useful. Most beneficial insects feed on or invade pest species at some point in their life cycle, but they also require certain plants for their well-being. Providing these plants in the garden will give beneficial insects a base of operations they can use to keep pest species controlled.

A small planting of early, intermediate season, and late-blooming beneficial insect attractors in each garden bed will help stack the deck in the farmer's favor. Ladybugs love to eat aphids; dandelion, marigold, and hairy vetch will attract them. Tachanid flies help keep cabbage worms and stink bugs in check; a planting of parsley or pennyroyal will give them a home. Beneficial insect attractors that bloom early include sweet alyssum, columbine, and creeping thyme. Intermediate bloomers include common yarrow, cilantro, edging lobelia, and mints. Late bloomers include dill, wild bergamot, and European goldenrod. An easy plan is to plant a few marigolds throughout the bed, a columbine plant, a bit of cilantro, and some dill.

You should familiarize yourself with the properties of beneficial plant attractors before planting them in your beds. Don't just run out

Table 12: **Preventative Plantings**

Beneficial Insect	Controlled Pests	Plants to Provide
Parasitic wasps	Moth, beetle, and fly larvae and eggs, including caterpillars	Dill, yarrow, tansy, Queen Anne's lace, parsley
Hoverflies (syrphid flies)	Mealybugs, aphids	As above, plus marigold
Lacewings	Aphids, mealybugs, other small insects	Dandelion, angelica, dill, yarrow
Ladybugs	Aphids	Dandelion, hairy vetch, buckwheat, marigold
Tachanid flies	Caterpillars, cabbage loopers, stink bugs, cabbage bugs, beetles	Parsley, tansy, pennyroyal, buckwheat

and plant mint in the garden bed directly, for example, because it will take over the entire bed. Instead, plant mint in a pot and then bury the pot in the garden soil so that the upper edge sticks out of the soil 1/2 inch or so.

You may also want to choose some plants that you will already use in some other way—such as mint for tea, dill for pickling, and cilantro for salsa. That way you are making maximum use of limited space. There is nothing wrong with growing goldenrods just because they are pretty!

Another valuable addition to the garden and yard, once the seeds have sprouted and the plants are growing well, would be chickens or guineas. Both types of birds, but guineas particularly, wreak havoc on bugs, especially bugs like ticks that nobody wants around anyway. Such livestock can effectively keep many sorts of garden pests from reaching the critical mass of population necessary to be threatening to crops.

Active Prevention

Active prevention is often necessary when a particular pest or disease problem is a practical certainty. In such cases, the active prevention is tailored to the expected problem and can often encompass methods used for both passive prevention and intervention. For example, you may notice your garden is regularly infested with earwigs. Once the bugs are noticed inside a cauliflower plant, they've already done a lot of damage. A weekly spraying with pyrethrin (a natural insecticide) or hot pepper wax (a repellent) will increase the usable harvest significantly.

The materials and techniques most often used for active prevention include traps, immune boosters, compost extracts, imported beneficial insects, and application of repellents, fungicides, and pesticides. (The latter is particularly important with certain fruit trees.)

Lures and Traps

Many insect pests can be caught in traps. In commercial operations, traps are usually used to monitor pest populations to determine the optimal timing for the application of pesticides. In a mini-farm, because of the smaller land area involved, it is often practical to employ enough traps to completely eradicate a particular pest (or one of the sexes of that pest) in the garden without resorting to poisons. Examples of pests easily trapped are codling moths, Japanese beetles, and apple maggots. Traps can also be employed for cucumber beetles, white flies, and a number of other pests, but they tend to be less effective. The time when various insects emerge varies from area to area. Because the lures used in traps often have limited lifespan, the timing of their deployment can be important. This is something you'll learn from keeping notes, and within a couple of years you'll have no trouble with the timing of traps.

Immunity Boosters and Growth Enhancers

One immune booster for plants on the market at the moment is marketed by Eden Bioscience in the form of harpin protein. Harpin protein, which is produced naturally by the bacterium that causes fire blight in apples and pears, elicits a broad immune response from vegetables that makes them more resistant to a wide array of pests and diseases while enhancing their growth. Eden Bioscience uses this discovery in a product called Messenger that is nontoxic and relatively inexpensive at my local agricultural supply store.

A company called Vitamin Institute sells a product called Superthrive that is advertised to improve the growth rate of plants and whose primary ingredient is thiamine. I have done some side-by-side testing, and the results have been ambiguous.

On the other hand, I have found a growth enhancer called Root Boost to live up to its advertising. It is not a fertilizer but rather an enhancer that is primarily based on kelp extract with the addition of humic acids. This product, when used as directed, really does enhance the soil and the plants that depend on it.

Compost Extract and Compost Tea

Compost extract is the most well-known and most widely studied homemade disease preventative. It is exactly what it sounds like: a shovel of properly aged compost in a water-permeable sack immersed in a bucket of water and steeped for 7 to 14 days.

As the chapter on composting pointed out, compost extract contains a cocktail of microbes and the chemicals that they produce. Compost extract contains a mix of beneficial bacteria and fungi that, when sprayed onto plants, eats the food substances that would otherwise be eaten by disease-causing organisms. As a result, the disease-causing organisms get starved out. A biweekly spray of compost extract is a good idea, and numerous studies attribute properties to the substance that are nothing short of miraculous. It can help prevent diseases such as black spot and powdery mildew. Best of all, it's free.

The next step up from compost extract is compost tea. Compost tea differs from an extract in that it is the result of an active attempt to increase the amount of fungi and bacteria in the solution through aeration. Still water (as used in compost extract) doesn't have much dissolved oxygen in it, and the beneficial microbes in compost require oxygen. So, actively aerating the water in which the compost is steeped will serve to boost populations of beneficial microbes from the compost. This can be done inexpensively by putting a fish tank aerator and air pump in the bottom of a container containing the water and compost. Some reasonably priced and favorably reviewed commercial options are also available through Keep It Simple, Inc. (www.simplici-tea .com) or Alaska Giant (www.alaskagiant.com).

Importing Beneficial Insects and Nematodes

Imported beneficial insects have their greatest applicability in greenhouses because, being quite mobile, when applied outdoors they are prone to fly away. Even outside they can be useful though, particularly when applied to crops infested with their favorite pest species and also provided with their favorite plants. Table 12 (earlier in this chapter) lists which beneficial insects to use for what problem and what sorts of plants should be established in advance of their arrival so they will stay in the garden.

Beneficial nematodes are extremely small worms that wait underground for a chance to work their way into pest insects and kill them. Beneficial nematodes are harmless to plants and pollinators and shouldn't be confused with pest nematodes such as root knot nematodes. Once inside the host, the nematodes release their gut bacteria, *Xenorhabdus luminescens*, into the insect's interior, where the bacteria multiply and the nematodes feed on them. The pest species eventually dies from infection. There are two commonly used species of nematodes, listed in Table 13. Beneficial nematode products often contain both species to be as broadly useful as possible.

Beneficial nematodes require extreme care in their handling and are usually shipped by over-night courier in a refrigerated package. They are stored in the refrigerator until they are used. It is

Table 13: **Beneficial Nematodes**

Species	Pests Controlled	Notes
Steinernema spp	Webworms, cutworms, vine borers	Not effective against grubs
Heterorhabditis spp	White grubs, vine weevils, root weevils	

best to wait until ground temperatures are above 50 degrees, the ground is damp, and a light rain is falling. Then put the nematodes in a pump-style sprayer and apply them to the ground where you want them. The reason for this is that beneficial nematodes are very prone to dehydration, and the falling rain helps them get into the soil. If you live north of Maryland, you'll need to apply them yearly because they can't survive the winter. If you live in a more southerly clime, the nematodes will probably survive, so a second application may not be needed.

Pest Repellents

Organic repellent mixtures are not 100% effective, but they serve as a valuable part of an integrated strategy for pest management. One repellent mixture is simple hot pepper. Capsaicin, the active ingredient in hot peppers, repels onion, carrot, and cabbage maggots. Simply finely chop up a cup of hot peppers, and steep it for a day in a gallon of water to which a single drop of dish soap has been added. Another repellent mixture is garlic, manufactured the same way. One thing that I do, with great success, is make hot pepper and garlic mixtures in a coffee maker that has been set aside for agricultural use only. There are some commercial repellent preparations worth noting as well, including CropGuard and Hot Pepper Wax.

There is *some* evidence that certain plants can repel pest insects. According to numerous sources, for example, nasturtiums and radishes repel cucumber beetles. I have experimented extensively with this practice and found no difference in cucumber beetle populations between cucumber plants surrounded by radishes and intertwined with nasturtiums and cucumber plants grown on their own. On the other hand, I have found that onion family crops repel wireworms, so I interplant leeks with my parsnips. A number of sites on the Internet list repellent plants, so I encourage you to experiment with the reputed properties of repellent plants and keep notes to see what works best for your garden.

Active Reaction

Even the most conscientious farming practices and most vigilant preventive measures will often fail to prevent pest and disease problems. Once these problems become apparent, reactive measures are in order.

Reactive measures will often include some of the same materials and methods as passive and active prevention. For example, many fungal infections can be eradicated by the timely application of compost tea, neem oil, or garlic oil. (Neem oil is an oil extracted from a tree in India.) Most often, though, reactive measures will involve the use of fungicides and/or natural or synthetic pesticides. Because these reactive measures use substances with greater potential to harm people or the environment, I don't recommend their

application unless the farmer is certain that a likelihood exists that failure to apply them will result in an unacceptable level of crop loss.

Another tip to make active measures most effective is to take a cue from doctors treating HIV and tuberculosis: Never treat an insect or disease problem with only one active agent at a time. Using only one active agent increases the odds of survivors living to convey immunity to that agent in the next generation. When you mix two or more active agents, you increase the odds of success while decreasing the odds of creating resistant organisms. So, for example, I routinely apply pyrethrin and rotenone in tandem, neem oil mixed with a microbial insecticide, or garlic and hot pepper repellents mixed together.

When Disease Prevention Fails

Plant diseases fall into four broad categories: bacterial, viral, protozoan, and fungal. Usually, these are impossible to distinguish by the naked eye except through experience with their symptoms. (See also the Rodale book recommended earlier in this chapter.) All such diseases present the problem that once a plant is infected, it becomes a storehouse of infective particles that can be spread to other plants via insects, wind, or handling. The longer an affected plant remains in the garden, the greater the odds that it will infect other plants. Diseases caused by viruses, bacteria, and protozoans are seldom treatable, but sometimes you can save a plant by pruning out the affected portions. Many fungal diseases, though, *are* treatable through a combination of pruning and spraying.

When a plant infection of any sort is first noticed, you may be able to save the plant by applying compost tea and/or Messenger. These products can stimulate an immune response that helps the plant overcome the infection. Their usefulness in that regard varies depending on the plants and diseases involved, so try it and keep notes of the results. A number of spray fungicides can also be used. Common fungicides include copper sulfate, Bordeaux mix (a mixture of copper sulfate and lime), baking soda, garlic oil, and neem oil. Baking soda is mixed two tablespoons per gallon of water with one ounce of light horticultural oil added, and the others are mixed according to label directions.

Some less well-known antifungal agents can have surprising results. I had a problem with powdery mildew on my lawn last spring (we had an especially wet spring), and I eliminated the infection by spraying with a mix of neem oil and fixed copper.

If saving the plant is either unsuccessful or inadvisable, then the plant should be removed from the garden immediately. Removing an infectious plant can be problematic since it can be covered with microscopic spores that will spread all over the place if the plant is disturbed. The solution is to spray the plant with something that will hold any spores in place and inactivate as many as possible before attempting removal. A good spray for this is made of two tablespoons of castile soap, one tablespoon of copper sulfate, one tablespoon of lime, and one tablespoon of light horticultural oil all mixed together in a gallon of water. The soap and oil will make the plant sticky so that spores can't escape, while the copper sulfate and lime serve to actually kill many infectious organisms. Spray the plant thoroughly with this (though not until it is dripping), and then cut it out and remove it, being as careful as possible to avoid letting it touch any other plants.

When dealing with plant diseases, you should consider your hands and tools to be a mode of disease transmission. When handling known diseased plants, it makes sense to handle *only* the diseased plants before hand washing and also to immediately sterilize any tools used on the diseased plants with bleach. A suitable sanitizing solution is one tablespoon of bleach per quart of water.

Diseased plant materials can be thermophilically composted with minimal or no risk as long as proper retention times are observed. If the farmer uses mesophilic composting instead, then diseased plant debris should be burned or placed in the curbside trash. It is also very important not to grow the same family of plant in the same area the next year. If a variety of the plant that resists that disease can be found, it would be a good idea to switch to that variety for at least a year or two, if not permanently.

When Pest Prevention Fails

The best soil management and prevention mechanisms will not be 100% effective against insect pests. For example, naturally attracted beneficial insects exist in balance with pest insects. If the beneficial insects were to eat all of the pest species, then the beneficial insects would starve or move somewhere else, and the pest species would experience a resurgence in the absence of its natural enemies.

Reactive control measures include anything used in the preventive stages, along with importing beneficial insect populations, applying microbial insecticides, and using substances that actually kill insects directly, such as soaps, oils, and natural or synthetic insecticides. Synthetic insecticides should be reserved as a last resort since they would reduce the healthfulness of the crop (as described later in this chapter) and would make it impossible for you to sell your produce as organic for several years if you wish to do so.

Both natural and artificial insecticides can also harm beneficial helpers, such as necessary pollinators and earthworms, and disrupt the life of the soil and thus harm fertility in the long run, so they are best employed only when absolutely necessary. Because natural insecticides don't last as long in the garden, they have less potential to do unintended damage.

Microbial Insecticides

Microbial insecticides are microbes (or toxins produced by microbes) that are deadly to pest insects but harmless to beneficial insects and humans. They have the advantage of being relatively benign but the disadvantage of being fairly species specific. For example, *Bacillus popilliae* is deadly to Japanese beetle larvae but harmless to other white grubs that infest lawns. They aren't contact poisons, and they must be eaten by the insect to be effective. Microbial insecticides have become increasingly popular, even among conventional farmers, and are readily available at agricultural stores.

Soaps and Oils

Plain old soap (not detergent, but soap) kills a number of insects by dissolving a waxy coating that they need to breathe and preserve moisture. Specialized insecticidal soaps can be used, or else a pure castile soap (such as Dr. Bronner's), mixed two tablespoons per gallon of water. Insecticidal soap will effectively control aphids, white

Table 14: **Common Microbial Insecticides**

Microbe	Pests Controlled	Notes
Bacillus thuringiensis var. *kurstaki*	The caterpillar stage of a wide variety of moths	Will not control codling moths
Bacillus thuringiensis var. *israelensis*	Mosquito, black fly, fungus gnat	
Bacillus thuringiensis var. *san diego*	Colorado potato beetle	
Nosema locustae	Grasshoppers	Because of grasshopper mobility, may not work for small yards

flies, scale, spider mites, and thrips. It needs to be reapplied fairly frequently—about weekly—to interrupt the life cycle of the target pest.

Light horticultural oils are highly refined mineral oils that control the same insects as insecticidal soap by covering and smothering the pest and its eggs. Mix and apply according to label directions.

Both oils and soaps should be tested on a single plant first, then wait a day, because they can be toxic to certain plants. (Their degree of toxicity to plants varies with heat, sunshine, humidity, general plant health, and other factors. Most often, they won't cause a problem, but it never hurts to test first.)

Natural Insecticides

The fact that something is natural doesn't mean that it is harmless. Ebola, smallpox, and strychnine are all 100% natural, for example. Natural insecticides fall under the same category and thus require care in their use. Natural insecticides can be purchased, or they can be grown and made at home. From a cost standpoint, the latter approach is preferable, though certain natural insecticides aren't practical for home manufacture.

Pyrethrin is a contact insecticide that controls most aphids, cabbage loopers, stinkbugs, codling moths, and white flies among other pests. It does not affect flea beetles, imported cabbage worms, or tarnished plant bugs.

To make your own pyrethrin, grow pyrethrum daisies (*Tanacetum cinerarifolium*) somewhere in the garden. Cut the flowers when they are in full bloom for the highest concentration of poison, and hang them upside down in a cool, dry, dark place to dry. Once they are dried, take a quart jar of the dried flowers and grind them up using an old food processor or blender that you pick up at a yard sale and that *you will never use for food again.* Mix it with one gallon of water and two drops of dish liquid, and allow it to steep for three days, stirring every once in a while. When done, filter it through cheese cloth that you will throw away afterward, store in a tightly capped bottle in a cool dark place, and label it appropriately as a poison so nobody drinks it accidentally. You dilute this for use by mixing one quart of the poison with three quarts of water, shaking, and applying via a sprayer. (I cannot stress strongly enough that all bottles containing poisons of any sort be labeled appropriately. Not far from where I live, a child died tragically a couple of years ago because of an unlabeled container of insecticide.)

Other natural insecticides are widely available, including neem and rotenone. These can be purchased at most garden centers or via mail order and should be used with as much care and caution as synthetics, because they can be toxic to humans.

Synthetic Pesticides

While this book focuses on organic methods, synthetic pesticides available to home gardeners bear mentioning. Ideally, because of a combination of growing conditions, attraction of natural predators, and other factors, pests won't be a problem so no pesticides will be needed—synthetic or otherwise. But that's the ideal. Reality can be far different, especially when first beginning a mini-farm. Even the most careful planning won't completely eliminate pest problems.

As a mini-farmer, you are trying to put a lot of food on the table, and you are trying to put *safe* food on the table. Perhaps, like me, you are an organic purist. But what happens when the theory of being an organic purist runs into the reality of a pest problem that threatens an entire crop? In my case, since I sell my produce as organic at 200% higher rates than conventional produce, it is actually better for me to lose a crop entirely than use synthetic pesticides. But what if my operation were strictly oriented toward putting food on the table? In that case, *maybe* I would use them, albeit cautiously and as a last resort, because some research shows that the synthetic pesticides available at the hardware store can be just as safe as botanical insecticides—and more effective—when used properly.

Please note that I said "maybe," "cautiously," and "as a last resort" for a reason. First off, in a mini-farm established using the methods in this book, economically threatening insect problems should be rare, and insect problems that won't respond to natural remedies even more rare. In fact, I have had only *one* pest problem where synthetics would have possibly been the better short-term solution.

Second, the government agencies charged with ensuring the safety of foodstuffs, drugs, and insecticides have a poor track record. For example, an article in *USA Today* disclosed that in 55% of FDA meetings regarding drug approvals, over half of the participants had financial conflicts of interest serious enough to note.[27] According to the same article, committees approving such things are actually *required by law* to include officials representing the industry in question. This is not exactly a recipe that would inspire confidence in most objective observers and perhaps explains the dozens of chemicals (including various insecticides and drugs) approved by government agencies and subsequently recalled after people have been harmed or killed.

Finally, studies indicate that synthetic pesticides make food less healthful by reducing the ability of plants to create antioxidants.[28] This explains my caution regarding synthetic pesticides. If you are nice enough to buy my book, should I repay your kindness by giving you advice

that could hurt you without totally disclosing the facts as I know them? Government agencies have a poor track record, and research in universities is often funded by self-interested parties. The extent to which this affects the results and conclusions of research is impossible to tell. So I am going to give you information on two synthetic insecticides, understanding that the research I have available says they are safe but that it could be discovered later that you shouldn't touch them with the proverbial 10-foot pole.

The use of natural insecticides like pyrethrin and rotenone is perfectly acceptable under the National Organic Program, but in practical terms these substances are every bit as toxic as commonly available synthetics while being less effective in many instances. The main difference is that the natural insecticides break down into nontoxic compounds very quickly under the influence of heat, sunshine, wind, and rain so they won't make it into your food supply if used properly, whereas the synthetics are specifically formulated to be more persistent.

Let's take pyrethrin as an example. Pyrethrin is a natural neurotoxin that insects quickly absorb through the skin. Once it is absorbed, the race is on between the insect's enzymes that detoxify the pyrethrin and the pyrethrin's toxic effects. Many insects, if they receive a sublethal dose, will pick themselves up and dust themselves off less than an hour after apparently being killed! Synthetic pyrethrins approach this problem by mixing the product with a substance like piperonyl butoxide that delays the insect's ability to make the enzymes to detoxify the pyrethrin, thus lowering the threshold considerably for what would constitute a lethal dose. Moreover, semisynthetic pyrethrins, such as allethrin, are often more toxic

[27] Couchon, D. (2000) Number of drug experts available is limited *USA Today*, Sept 25, 2000
[28] Asami, D., Hong, Y., Barrett, D., Mitchell, A. (2003) Comparison of total phenolic and ascorbic acid content of freeze-dried and air-dried marionberry, strawberry and corn grown using conventional, organic and sustainable agricultural practices. *Journal of Agricultural Food Chemistry*, Feb 26, 2003

to insects while being less toxic to mammals (such as humans) than their natural counterparts.

So a semisynthetic pyrethrin spray combined with piperonyl butoxide would require less poison to be used and be more effective, and the type of pyrethrin being used would be less toxic to humans.[29]

According to a metabolic study, neither natural nor synthetic pyrethrins accumulate in the body or show up in breast milk because they are quickly detoxified in the human body.[30] Any allethrin consumed by a human is rapidly transformed into something less toxic and eliminated.[31] In addition, allethrin is broken down into nontoxic compounds through the action of air and sunlight within a few days,[32] though not as quickly as natural pyrethrin.

The piperonyl butoxide used to increase the effectiveness of pyrethrins is a semisynthetic derivative of safrole—an oil found in the bark of sassafras trees. It works by inhibiting enzymes that detoxify the pyrethrins in the insect's body. Safrole is a known carcinogen, but the status of piperonyl butoxide as a carcinogen is disputed. Unlike allethrin, piperonyl butoxide is stable in the environment and doesn't break down easily.[33]

Given current information, the allethrin doesn't worry me much, but I am sufficiently uneasy about the persistence of piperonyl butoxide in the environment that I wouldn't personally use it. Either way, synthetic pyrethrins and those containing piperonyl butoxide should be used according to label directions and never be used on crops within a week of harvest; even then harvested crops should be well washed.

Carbaryl (also known as "Sevin") is another common synthetic insecticide used in home gardens. There is no clear evidence that carbaryl is carcinogenic or causes birth defects, and 85% of carbaryl is excreted by humans within 24 hours.[34] Carbaryl has a half-life of 7 to 14 days in sandy loam soil, and the manufacturer (GardenTech) states that it is not absorbed by the plant.[35] Therefore, if used according to label directions, and produce is carefully washed, it should be safe. According to numerous studies, "Carbaryl breaks down readily and experience shows it readily decomposes on plants, in soil and water to less toxic byproducts. Accumulation in animal tissues and biomagnification of residues in food chains with carbaryl and its metabolites does not occur."[36]

Certainly, the preponderance of science says that carbaryl is perfectly safe when used according to label directions. It definitely takes care of cucumber beetles much more effectively than my organic approaches. Nevertheless, common sense and the fact that it is a neurotoxin that takes a lot longer than most botanical insecticides to break down would dictate that it be used only as a last resort. All in all, if I were to use a synthetic insecticide, I would use carbaryl in preference to

[29] Extoxnet (1994) *Pyrethrins* from http://pmep.cce.cornell.edu/profiles/extoxnet/ pyrethrins-ziram/pyrethrins-ext.html. Retrieved May 20, 2006,

[30] Elliot, M. et al. (1972) Metabolic fate of pyrethrin I, pyrethrin II and allethrin administered orally to rats *Journal of Agricultural Food Chemistry 20*

[31] Kidd, H., James, D. (eds) (1991) *The Agrochemicals Handbook, Third Edition*

[32] Napa County Mosquito Abatement District (2006) Retrieved June 12, 2006, from www.napamosquito.org/Pesticide/ pesticide.htm

[33] New York State Health Department (2000) Retrieved March 13, 2006, from http://www.health.state.ny.us/nysdoh/westnile/ final/c3/c3summry.htm

[34] Extoxnet (1996) (Extoxnet is a government-funded database of toxic substances located at http://extoxnet.orst.edu)

[35] GardenTech (2006) Retrieved July 5, 2006, from http://www .gardentech.com/sevin.asp

[36] Hock, W. *Sevin (Carbaryl): A Controversial Insecticide*

the others available. And, in fact, that is what I used before switching to organic gardening.

Animal Pests

So far, in this chapter, when discussing pests we've largely been talking about insects. But one ignores larger pests, such as raccoons, rabbits, and deer, at his or her farm's peril. For many years, my farm ran along just fine with only minor damage from moles who ate strawberries and ripe tomatoes, and raccoons who occasionally stole an ear of corn. But one year, my entire crop of beans, sweet potatoes, and Brussels sprouts was wiped out in just one night by a herd of hungry deer. And they kept coming back to nibble at the sad remains. Clearly, action was needed.

Moles can be a bit of a nuisance in my garden. They are there, primarily, to eat grubs. If you get rid of the grubs by applying Milky Spore or beneficial nematodes, you will dramatically reduce the mole population. For faster relief, there are a number of castor oil products on the market that put castor oil into the dirt. When the moles dig, they get the castor oil on their fur, and they lick it off. This gives them diarrhea, and they move on within a couple of weeks. I've found this quite effective. A number of companies sell a battery-powered spike that generates noise that is supposed to deter moles. These may work for you, but I've found them ineffective.

Rabbits are only an occasional problem and don't usually do much damage on the farm. What I do is mix a hot pepper product with anything else I happen to be spraying and use it to wet the leaves. This serves as sufficient deterrent.

⊗ Products for deterring furry pests.

Deer are another matter entirely. I tried all the standard tricks. Bars of soap, hair clippings, urinating around the property line, and similar homespun remedies did nothing. Spraying the plants with hot pepper wax was inadequate and only marginally effective. I have found only three things that really work. The first is quite expensive: an impenetrable physical barrier in the form of a fence eight-feet tall. The second is a product called Deer Scram, which is a deterrent scent that is sprinkled around the area to be protected. The third is the use of a baited electric fence.

A baited electric fence is a regular electric fence that has been baited with peanut butter wrapped in aluminum foil. Deer adore peanut butter, so they put their mouth right on the aluminum foil and get zapped. This works incredibly well and requires only a single strand of fencing about four feet off the ground where pets are safe. This same trick works for raccoons if you add another strand about 18 inches off the ground.

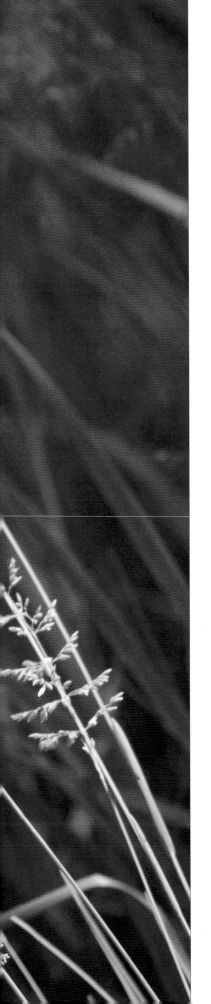

11

Seed Starting

It is a good idea to learn to start seedlings for three reasons. The first reason is economic: Starting seedlings at home saves money. The second reason is variety: Starting seedlings at home vastly increases the range of crop choices because certain varieties may not be available at your local garden center. Finally, since seedlings grown at home were never in a commercial greenhouse, you'll have a known-good product that is unlikely to be harboring pests.

Starting seeds is simple: Place seeds in a fertile starting medium in a suitable container; provide water, heat, and light; and that's it. Many seeds—such as grains and beets—are sowed directly in a garden bed, but others such as tomatoes, broccoli, and peppers, must be either started in advance or purchased as small plants ("seedlings") and then transplanted.

Timing

Seedlings need to be started indoors anywhere from 2 to 12 weeks before transplant time, depending on the particular crop. Transplant

Table 15: **Spring and Fall Planting Guide**

Crop	Start Spring and Summer Seedlings Relative to Last Spring Frost	Transplant Spring and Summer Seedlings Relative to Last Spring Frost	Start Fall Seedlings Relative to First Fall Frost	Transplant Fall Seedlings Relative to First Fall Frost
Broccoli	–12 weeks	–6 weeks	Transplant date –42 days	Frost date +32 days –days to maturity
Brussels sprouts	–12 weeks	–4 weeks		
Cabbage	–13 weeks	–5 weeks	Transplant date –56 days	Frost date +25 days –days to maturity
Cantaloupe	–2 weeks	+2 weeks	N/A	N/A
Cauliflower	–12 weeks	–4 weeks	Transplant date –56 days	Frost date +18 days –days to maturity
Celery	–13 weeks	–3 weeks	Transplant date –70 days	Frost date +11 days –days to maturity
Collards	–12 weeks	–4 weeks	Transplant date –56 days	Frost date +18 days –days to maturity
Cucumber	–3 weeks	+1 week	N/A	N/A
Eggplant	–8 weeks	+2 weeks	N/A	N/A
Kale	–13 weeks	–5 weeks	Transplant date –56 days	Frost date +25 days –days to maturity
Lettuce	–8 weeks	–2 weeks	Transplant date –42 days	Frost date +4 days –days to maturity
Okra	–4 weeks	+2 weeks	N/A	N/A
Onions	–12 weeks	–6 weeks	Transplant date –42 days	Frost date +32 days –days to maturity
Peppers	–6 weeks	+2 weeks	N/A	N/A
Pumpkins	–2 weeks	+2 weeks	N/A	N/A
Squash (summer)	–2 weeks	+2 weeks	N/A	N/A
Squash (winter)	–2 weeks	+2 weeks	N/A	N/A
Tomatoes	–7 weeks	+0 weeks	N/A	N/A
Watermelon	–2 weeks	+2 weeks	N/A	N/A

time is reckoned in weeks before or after the last predicted frost of the year for spring and summer crops and in weeks before the first predicted frost for fall and winter crops. The timing of transplanting is dictated by the hardiness of the particular crop. Broccoli is pretty hardy, so it is often planted 6 weeks before the last predicted frost, whereas cucumber is very tender, so it is planted 1 or 2 weeks after.

So the most important information that you will need for starting seeds is the date of the last frost for your geographic region. This can be found from the Cooperative Extension Service or from an Internet search in most cases. The National Climatic Data Center maintains comprehensive tables on the Internet that give the statistical likelihoods of frost on a given date along with the probabilities of the number of frost-free days, broken down by state and city. Weather.com also provides data relevant to gardening.

Once you've determined the average date of your last spring frost, determine the date for starting seeds and transplanting seedlings into the garden by adding or subtracting a certain number of weeks from the date of the last frost, depending on the crop (see Table 15).

If my average last spring frost is June 1st, then I would start my tomato plants seven weeks before June 1st and set them out on that date. Cabbage would be started 13 weeks before June 1st and set out in the garden 5 weeks before June 1st. Eggplant would be started 8 weeks before June 1st and set out 2 weeks after June 1st.

Anything that can be planted in the garden before the last spring frost can also be grown as a fall crop. For fall cabbage, if my average date of the first fall frost is on September 6th, and my cabbage requires 65 days to mature according to the seed package, then I would transplant my cabbage seedlings on July 28th. This is computed by adding 25 days (from the table) to September 6th then subtracting 65 days for the days to maturity (from the seed package). I can tell when to start my cabbage from seed by subtracting 56 days (from the table) from the transplant date. So I should start my cabbage seedlings for fall on June 2nd.

Starting Medium

Gardening experts have many varied opinions on the best starting medium. To confuse matters, seed catalogs try to sell all kinds of starting mediums for that purpose, and the number of choices can be confusing.

Whatever is used as a seed-starting medium should be light and easy for delicate roots to penetrate, and it should hold water well and not be infected with diseases. It should have some nutrients but not too heavy a concentration of them. Commercial seed-starting mixes are sold for this purpose and work fine, as do peat pellets of various shapes and sizes. At the time of writing, commercial seed-starting mixes cost about $3 for enough to start 150 plants, and peat pellets cost about $5 per 100.

Compared to the cost of buying transplants from a garden center, the price of seed-starting mixes or peat pellets is negligible. But for a farmer growing hundreds or even thousands of transplants, it may be economical to make seed-starting mixes at home. Most seed-starting mixes consist mainly of finely milled peat moss and vermiculite. The Territorial Seed Company recommends a simple 50/50 mix of vermiculite and peat moss,[37] but some authorities recommend adding compost to the mix because it can suppress diseases.[38] Some farmers also add a little clean sand. If these latter two ingredients are added, they shouldn't constitute more than 1/3 of the soil volume in aggregate. Don't use garden soil, and don't use potting soil. It is extremely important that any compost used to make seed-starting mix be well finished so that it contains no disease organisms or weed seeds. (Garden soil can be used as an ingredient if it is first sifted through a 1/4-inch mesh screen and then sterilized. Instructions for sterilizing are given later in this chapter. Potting soil can be used under the same conditions—if it is sifted then sterilized.)

A little compost or worm castings mixed into seed-starting mixes is fine and can be helpful in warding off diseases. But even organic fertilizer in too great a concentration will create an environment ideal for the growth of various fungi that will invade and harm the seedlings. An indoor seed-starting environment is not like the great outdoors. Wind movement, sunshine, and other elements that keep fungi at bay are greatly reduced in an indoor environment. As a result, the teaspoon of solid fertilizer that does so much good outdoors can be harmful to seedlings.

Another reason for keeping the nutrient content of seed-starting medium low is the lower nutrient concentrations cause more aggressive root growth. Improved root growth leads to a transplant that will suffer less shock when it is planted outdoors.

Here is my own recipe:

- Finely milled sphagnum peat moss, 4 quarts
- Medium vermiculite, 1 pint
- Well-finished compost passed through a 1/4-inch screen made from hardware cloth, 1 pint
- Worm castings (available at any agricultural store), 1 pint

Again, the simple 50/50 mix of peat moss and vermiculite recommended by the Territorial Seed Company and most commercial seed-starting mixes work perfectly fine. Feel free to experiment!

Because the starting medium used for seeds is deliberately nutritionally poor and provided in insufficient quantity to meet a seedling's nutritional needs, it will become necessary to fertilize seedlings periodically once their first "true" leaves appear. The first two leaves that appear, called the cotyledons, contain a storehouse of nutrients that will keep the plant well supplied until the first true leaves emerge. (Plants can be divided into two categories—those with two cotyledons, called "dicots," and those with one cotyledon, called "monocots." The first true leaves look like the leaves that are distinctive for that plant.) Adding solid fertilizer to the cells of a seedling tray would be both harmful and impractical, so liquid fertilizer will need to be used.

Seedlings are delicate, and full-strength fertilizer is both unneeded and potentially harmful. A good organic kelp, fish, or start-up fertilizer diluted to half strength and applied every two weeks after the first true leaves appear should work fine.

Containers

Mini-farming is not a small hobby operation. The average mini-farmer will grow hundreds

---

[37] http://www.territorial-seed.com/stores/1/March_2001_W133C449.cfm retrieved on 2/27/2006

[38] Coleman, E. (1999) *Four Season Harvest*

or perhaps thousands of seedlings. The best methods for starting seeds on this scale include cellular containers like those used by nurseries, peat pellets, and compressed soil blocks.

The use of undivided flats is advocated in the Grow Biointensive method. In this method, a rectangular wooden box of convenient size and about 2 inches deep is filled with starting medium, and seeds are planted at close intervals. The seeds are kept moist and warm, and once the cotyledons have appeared, the seedlings are carefully picked out and transplanted into a new flat with a greater distance between seedlings. This process is repeated again when the growth of the plant makes it necessary, and the final time the plant is transplanted, complete with a block of soil, it goes straight into the garden. The most obvious benefit of this method is that it is inexpensive. The largest detriment is that it is extremely time-consuming. Grow Biointensive publications also state that this method produces a beneficial microclimate and stronger transplants, but my own experiments have shown no appreciable difference between seedlings grown this way and seedlings grown exclusively in soil blocks or peat pellets. Certainly, this technique works well, and in a situation where the farmer is rich in time but poor in cash, it is a very good option.

The commercial growers who make the small six-packs of transplants for the garden center use plastic multicelled containers. These containers cost money, of course, but also save on labor costs and are easily transplanted. These units have a hole in the bottom of every cell, fit into rectangular plastic boxes that provide for bottom watering, and can be picked up at most agricultural stores for around $2 or $3 for a tray and eight 6-pack containers. The price of these works out to about

⊗ Broccoli seedlings destined for market.

$6 per 100 plants, which isn't expensive considering that the containers can be reused year to year as long as they are well washed between uses so they don't spread diseases. If you sell seedlings, as I do, you will want to take the cost of these containers (and labels) into account in setting your price. In practice, once acquired, the economics of using these is sound since the per-plant cost drops dramatically after the first year, and they save a lot of time compared to using undivided flats.

The disadvantage of multicelled containers is that each cell contains only two or three cubic inches of soil. This means that the soil can't hold enough nutrients to see the seedling through to transplanting time, so bottom watering with liquid fertilizer is required. Also, because of the small amount of space, roots grow to the sides of the cell and then wind around and around, contributing to transplant shock. Finally, because of the small soil volume, multicelled containers can't be left unattended for more than a couple of days because their water supply is depleted rapidly. Even with these disadvantages, they are the method of choice for producing seedlings for sale because of their convenience.

Peat pellets have a significant advantage over multicelled containers when it comes to transplant shock. Taking a transplant from a multicelled pack and putting it directly into garden soil can set the plant back for a few days as it acclimates to the new soil conditions. Peat pellets get around this problem because transplants are put into the garden without being disturbed, and roots can grow right through them into the soil. This allows for gradual acclimatization and virtually eliminates transplant shock.

Peat pellets cost about $5 per 100 and can be purchased at agricultural supply stores and occasionally at places like Walmart. They come as compressed dry wafers and are expanded by placing them in warm water. Once the pellets expand, the seeds are placed in the center and lightly covered, then the pellet is bottom watered as needed until time to plant in the garden. In the case of peat pellets, the seed-starting mix of a peat pellet is essentially devoid of nutrients altogether, making liquid fertilizer a must. If you use peat pellets, be sure to carefully slit and remove the webbing at transplanting time so it doesn't bind the roots.

Peat pots suffer from the same disadvantages that affect multicelled containers because of their small soil volume, plus they don't break down well, and they constrain root growth in many cases, so I don't recommend them. When I worked some compost into my beds last spring, I dug up perfectly intact peat pots that had been planted a year earlier.

Compressed soil blocks, while not aesthetically acceptable for commercial sale, are the best available choice for the farmer's own seedlings. That's because a compressed soil block contains 400% more soil volume than a peat pellet or multicelled container, meaning it will contain more nutrients and moisture. Seedlings raised in compressed soil blocks using a properly constituted soil mix may require no liquid fertilizer at all. Because roots grow right up to the edge of the block instead of twisting around, and the block is made of soil so decomposition isn't an issue, transplant shock all but disappears. They are also the least expensive option when used in volume.

Compressed soil blocks are made with a device called a "soil blocker" into which a soil mix is poured, and the mix is then compressed.

A standard mix for the soil used in the blocker contains 30% fine peat moss, 30% good finished compost, 30% sterilized garden soil and 10% fine sand.[40] A balanced organic fertilizer such as Cockadoodle DOO is added to the mix at the rate of 1/2 cup per four gallons of soil mix, and the pH is adjusted with lime if necessary to fall between 6.2 and 7.0. My own mix is 50% peat moss, 40% worm castings, and 10% coarse vermiculite with a bit of balanced fertilizer. (Garden soil can be sterilized by spreading

⊗ Peat pots often fail to break down quickly.

---

[40] Patry, S. (1993) *Soil Blocks Increase Space Utilization and Plant Survival* Retrieved March 7, 2006, from http://www.eap.mcgill.ca/MagRack/COG/COG_H_93_02.htm

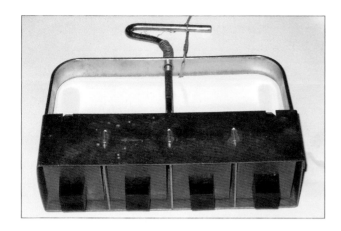

⊗ A standard 2-inch soil blocker with rectangular inserts.

it no more than 1-inch thick on a baking pan and baking in the oven at 200 degrees for 20 minutes. Don't use a good pan!) It is important that the ingredients used in a soil mix be sifted

⊗ Use 1/4-inch hardware cloth to screen out debris.

so large twigs don't interfere with the operation of the soil blocker.

Even though the devices for making soil blocks cost about $30 each, they are made of steel and will last many years, so they will save many times their cost compared to multicelled containers. I bought mine from Peaceful Valley Farm Supply over the Internet.

One particular technique for using soil blockers merits attention. An insert can be purchased for the 2-inch soil blocker that makes a 3/4-inch cubic indentation in the block to accept 3/4-inch soil blocks. This is a great idea because it allows germination to be accomplished in smaller soil blocks that are then transplanted into the larger ones. That way you aren't taking up a large soil block with seed that won't germinate.

◈ Soil blocks with sprouted lettuce seedlings.

Light

Plants evolved with needs for light intensity that match the output of the sun, which provides light that is so intense that merely looking at it can permanently damage the eye. Naturally, seedlings grown inside also need an intense light source that can provide enough light without also making so much heat that plants get burned.

With the exception of certain flowers, most plants do not need light to germinate. In fact some plants, like those in the brassica family, may have their germination inhibited by light. But once the first plant parts emerge above the ground, all plants need light to grow. In most of North America and Europe, there is not enough sunshine coming through even a south-facing window to adequately start seedlings during the winter months when most seed starting takes place, so a source of artificial light is required. Selecting an artificial light source should be based on an understanding of the plants' requirements.

Plants require light of various wavelengths or colors for various purposes. Red wavelengths, for example, regulate dormancy, seed production, and tuber formation, whereas blue wavelengths stimulate chlorophyll production and vegetative growth. Violet wavelengths affect plants' tendency to turn toward a light source. The best light sources for starting seedlings, then, should generate a wide spectrum of light wavelengths that encompass both the blue and the red ends of the spectrum.

There is a growing number of options for artificial lighting; unfortunately, most of these are quite expensive. Following is my particular approach that inexpensively meets the light needs for seedlings.

◈ A homemade rack for seedlings works great and costs little.

All sorts of special carts costing anywhere from $200 to $1,000 are sold for this purpose, but with a little ingenuity you can create a suitable contrivance, made like the one illustrated, at very low cost.

This device is made from a simple wire rack sold in the hardware department of Walmart for $50. Three racks hold up to four large seed trays each, and two 48-inch shop light fluorescent light fixtures are hung over each rack using simple adjustable chains from the hardware store. This way, the lights can be independently raised and lowered to keep them the right distance above the plants as they grow. The six lights (or fewer if you don't need them all) are plugged into an electric outlet strip that is plugged into a timer. Each light holds two 40-watt 48-inch fluorescent tubes.

The fluorescent tubes need to be selected with the needs of plants in mind. Cool white fluorescents put out more blue light, and warm white fluorescents put out more red light. Combining the two in the same fixture gives a perfectly acceptable mix of wavelengths. It's what I use, and a good many farmers use it successfully.[41] There are also special tubes for fluorescent light fixtures that are specifically designed for growing plants or duplicating the sun's wavelengths— and these work well too but at a cost roughly six times higher than regular tubes and at a reduced light output. The thing to watch for with fluorescent lighting generally is light output, because plants need a lot of it. Go with the highest light output tubes that will fit in a 48-inch shop light fixture. Because the lights are used approximately five months out of the year, the tubes need to be replaced only every other year. Replace them even

if they look and work fine, because after being used for two years, their measurable light output will have declined.

The intensity of light decreases in inverse proportion to the square of the distance from the source. In other words, the further away the lights are, the less light the plants will get. Fluorescent tubes need to be set up so that they are only an inch or two above the seedlings for them to get enough light. Because plants grow, either the height of the lights or the bottom of the plants needs to be adjustable.

Plants need a combination of both light and darkness to complete their metabolic processes, so too much of either can be a bad thing. Because even closely spaced florescent lights are an imperfect substitute for true sunshine, the lights should be put on an inexpensive timer so seedlings get 16 hours of light and 8 hours of darkness every day.

Don't forget: Once seeds sprout, shine the light on them!

Temperature

Many publications provide various tables with all sorts of data about the optimum temperatures for germination of different garden seeds. For starting seeds in the house, almost all seeds normally used to start garden seedlings will germinate just fine at ordinary room temperatures. The only time temperature could become an issue is if the area used for seed starting regularly falls below 60 degrees or goes above 80.

If seed-starting operations get banished to the basement or garage where temperatures are routinely below 60 degrees, germination could definitely become a problem. The easiest solution

---

[41] Murphy, W. (1978) *Gardening under Lights*

⊗ A heating mat is especially useful for peppers and tomatoes.

for this situation is to use a heat mat (available at any agricultural supply store) underneath your flats that will raise the soil temperature about 20 degrees higher than the surrounding air.

Water

Seedlings should be bottom watered by placing their containers (which contain holes in the bottom or absorb water directly) in water and allowing the starting medium to evenly water itself by pulling up whatever water is needed. Seedlings are delicate and their roots are shallow, so top watering can disrupt and uncover the vulnerable roots.

It is important that the starting medium be kept moist, but not soaking, for the entire germination period. Once the germination process has begun and before the seedling emerges, allowing the seed to dry out will kill it. Most containers used for seedlings are too small to retain an appreciable amount of water; for this reason seedlings should stay uniformly damp (though not soggy) until transplanted.

Unfortunately, dampness can cause problems with mold growth. Often, such mold is harmless, but sometimes it isn't, and telling the difference before damage is done is difficult. If gray fuzz or similar molds appear on top of the seedling container, cut back the water a bit, and place the container in direct sunlight in a south-facing window for a few hours a day for two or three days. This should take care of such a problem.

Another cause of mold is the use of domes over top of seedling flats. These domes are advertised to create an environment "just like a greenhouse." In reality, they create an environment extremely conducive to mold, even in moderately cool temperatures. No matter how clean and sterile the starting medium, anytime I have ever used a dome on top of a seed flat, mold has developed within two or three days. I recommend that you do not use domes.

Fertilizer

As mentioned earlier, once seedlings have their first set of true leaves, they should be bottom watered with a half-strength solution of organic liquid fertilizer once every two weeks in addition to regular watering. Since starting medium is nutritionally poor, some fertilizer will be a benefit to the seedlings, but anything too concentrated can hurt the delicate developing root system and cause problems with mold. The only exception to this is soil blocks, which can contain enough nutrients that liquid fertilizer isn't needed because of their greater soil volume.

Hardening Off

A week or two before the intended transplant date, you may wish to start the process of "hardening off" the transplants; that is, the process of gradually acclimating the plants to the outdoor environment.

This generally means bringing the seedlings outside and exposing them to sun and wind for an hour the first day, progressing to all day on the last day of the hardening-off period, which lasts about a week before transplanting. The process of hardening off serves to make the transplants more hardy.

In my experience, hardening off makes little difference with plants that are transplanted after the last frost, but it does have an effect on the hardiness of plants that are transplanted before the last frost. It should be done with all transplants anyway, because there is no way to know with absolute certainty if an unusual weather event will occur. I've seen no case in which hardening off transplants has been harmful and numerous cases in which it has helped so it is a good general policy for a mini-farm in which maximum yields are important.

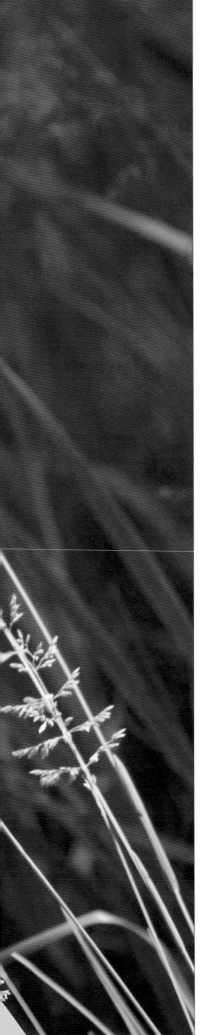

12

Selecting and Saving Seed

The selection of seeds can seem like an overwhelming task, especially if you are looking at a half dozen seed catalogs on a cold winter's day in January. When I look at seed catalogs, my eyes get bigger than my belly, and my mouth starts watering at each description of a different variety of each plant. Pretty soon, I have checked off enough different kinds of seeds that if I were to actually grow all of them, I would need a 600-acre farm and an impressive staff of workers.

Seeds are a very compact form of material wealth. A single packet of 30 tomato seeds that costs $2 can easily produce bushels and bushels of tomatoes—enough to make salsa and spaghetti sauce for the family for a year with leftovers to sell or give away. In addition, seeds, when properly selected and saved, are an insurance policy against hard times.

Anyone with limited space should be picky about seed selections in terms of climate preferences, productivity per unit area, disease resistance, and taste preferences. And if you save seed from plants grown the prior year, you will dramatically reduce the need to purchase seed.

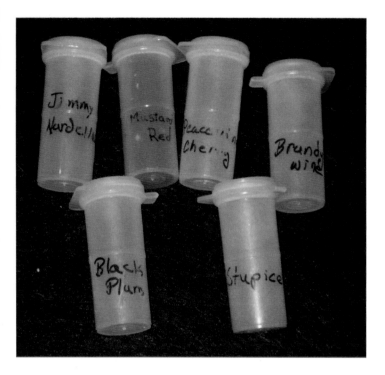

⊗ Home-saved seeds in airtight vials.

Also, raised-bed practices don't sow seeds in a row too closely together and then go back and thin out half the plants—thus wasting the seeds—as the directions on the seed packet instruct. In intensive agriculture, each seed is planted individually at the optimal spacing the first time around—so not a single seed is wasted.

Thus, the seed orders placed by a mini-farmer after the second year of farming will likely be a small number of hybrid vegetables selected for a particular reason, a few plants for which saving seed was either too difficult or unsuccessful, and a handful of new crop varieties that the farmer wants to try out. The full order for a mini-farm that will feed a family of three plus generate optional replacement income will probably amount to only $100 worth of seeds plus shipping after the second year if the farmer saves seeds from annual vegetables.

Explanation of Plant Varieties

There are two terms that will be used interchangeably in the remainder of this chapter and are used periodically throughout this book that need to be understood: *variety* and *cultivar*. In the sense in which I use the terms, they have the same meaning, but to explain what I mean, I have to get into a bit of biology.

Living things are categorized by biologists according to broad categories first and then into ever-finer categories. The broadest categories would be, for example, "plants" and "animals." The order of classification by plant scientists is kingdom, division, class, order, family, tribe, genus, and species. A variety is a subset of a species, and a cultivar is a cultivated variety.

The actual meaning of the word *species* is disputed even among scientists, but the generally accepted definition is that a species is made up of a population capable of interbreeding. Typically, two plants are considered to be members of the same species if they can interbreed and produce seeds that will grow plants that will also produce seeds. Thus cabbage, cauliflower, and broccoli are all members of the same species because they can interbreed with each other. However, there are certainly significant differences between these plants! The fact that two plants are members of the same species doesn't make them identical.

If you look through a seed catalog under "broccoli," you will find anywhere from 3 to 20 different types of broccoli. The sixth edition of the *Garden Seed Inventory* lists 32 different open-pollinated types of broccoli. These various types of broccoli have differences in taste, color, disease resistance, vitamin content, how long they take to produce a broccoli stalk, and a host of other important characteristics. Each of the different types of broccoli is its own *variety*. Some food crops, like broccoli, have a very small number of varieties in existence, but others, like tomato, have over a thousand different varieties.

You might select a particular variety of a given crop for any number of reasons—taste, pest resistance, short season, and so on. This is what I am referring to when I talk about a plant variety. In open-pollinated varieties, the traits that distinguish one variety from another are reliably inherited from one generation to the next.

Existing plant varieties are the culmination of untold thousands of years of careful selection for various traits; new varieties are created in the same fashion all the time. Since plant characteristics are heritable, as a mini-farmer, you will have the ability to select the best-growing plants of a given variety as parents for new seeds, and over time you can end up creating your own specifically adapted plant varieties.

Selecting Plant Varieties

A mini-farmer needs four types of information to select plant varieties: local climate, available varieties, personal tastes, and plant spacing/yields. To this basic information you will eventually add your own experiences.

Local climate information can be found from the local agricultural extension service or from the Web site of the National Climatic Weather Center. The Web site Weather.com also has a section specifically for gardens. The idea is to find out the length of the local growing season, so that plant varieties can be selected that have enough time to fully mature. A farmer in Virginia will have a much wider selection of appropriate corn and watermelon to choose from than a farmer in Vermont.

Because open-pollinated varieties of crops produce seeds that can be used to grow the same crop again the next year, they are a much better choice for mini-farmers. Seed can be saved from the most productive or hardy plants so that, over time, the open-pollinated variety that the farmer started with has been specifically adapted to that farm's climate and growing conditions. None of this is possible with interbred hybrids, which don't produce reusable seed, making open-pollinated seeds the better default choice of the farmer.

The matter of hybrids has been oversimplified a bit. Given a few years of careful selection and adequate space, it is possible with many (though not all) hybrids to convert them into a new true-to-type open-pollinated variety that preserves the desired traits of the hybrid but allows for saving seeds. For details on how to do this, see Carol Deppe's excellent book *How to Breed Your Own Vegetable Varieties*.

There are also some cases in which hybrids provide a significant advantage over otherwise equivalent open-pollinated varieties; corn is probably the best example. The difference in productivity between hybrid and open-pollinated corn can be huge, with the hybrid producing considerably more, and when a farmer is raising food in a very small area, differences in productivity make a difference. There are also instances in which hybrid plants incorporate traits such as disease resistance, and using a hybrid variety can save the farmer from needing to use fungicides on the crops. Outside of such cases, the overwhelming preponderance of a farmer's crops should be open-pollinated.

The good news about open-pollinated seeds is that they have become increasingly popular and are available from a number of companies at good prices. The Seed Saver's Exchange publishes a book called *Garden Seed Inventory* that describes and lists all of the open-pollinated varieties available for every garden plant along with commercial sources for every plant listed. The Seed Saver's Exchange is also a membership organization ($35/year) in which members make thousands of varieties of homegrown seeds available to each other at modest cost via two annually published compendiums provided to members.

A list of seed companies with whom I have had good experiences is provided at the end of this book, but use it as a starting place rather than a limitation. The open-pollinated seed business is very competitive, and excellent service is the rule rather than the exception. Most seed companies provide free written catalogs and Web sites containing a wealth of valuable information.

An important aspect of selecting seeds is the need for experimentation. There are hundreds of varieties of peas, beans, carrots, and other crops available, and each variety will perform differently because of climatic and soil differences as well as genetic variations that affect flavor. It is good to set aside a small area just for experimenting with new crop varieties and keep careful notes of the results.

Selecting Parents

Since many important characteristics of a plant variety are hereditary, it makes sense to save seeds from plants that do best in your own environment and to avoid saving seeds from plants that do poorly. This is most reliable when dealing with self-pollinating, plants, as both the mother and the father of the seed are known. For insect- or wind-pollinated plants, though, only the mother is known. Even so, it is better to know that at least one of the parent plants was superior.

The problem of unknown parentage can be dealt with by culling inferior-performing plants before they are mature enough to pollinate or by using hand pollination to ensure that both parents are known. Either way, by selecting parentage, the farmer constantly increases the seed pool in quality and productivity.

Saving Seeds

As previously noted, one of the advantages of open-pollinated seeds is that they can be saved so that the need to purchase seeds each year is reduced. Like anything else, there are costs and benefits that the farmer has to consider, and in all likelihood you will end up saving seeds from some crops but not others. A mini-farm exists as a way to produce food rather than an exercise in seed saving. Some seeds, like tomato and pepper, can be saved with minimal effort or inconvenience while others such as cauliflower will require significant efforts and land.

If the production and sale of seeds is something you are interested in, then extraordinary efforts to save seed are worthwhile. Outside of that, if buying a packet of seed for $1.50 saves hours of effort and tying up land that would otherwise be productive, it makes sense to buy the seeds. You will need to make that determination on the basis of your own circumstances and interests.

Saving seeds is a broad enough topic that entire books have been written on this subject alone. The gist, though, is straightforward: Nature mandates that plants reproduce themselves, and plants procreate by producing seeds. If these seeds are saved and replanted, they will re-create the original plant.

There are three major sets of plant attributes that affect seed saving. The first is whether the plant is annual, biennial, or perennial. Annual plants produce seed every year and are planted newly each year. Biennial plants require two years in the ground to produce seed. Perennial plants will continue to grow from year to year but often produce seed annually. Second is whether the plant is predominantly self-pollinating or predominantly cross-pollinating. Cross-pollinators require pollen from another plant to make seed, while strongly self-pollinating plants may fertilize their own flowers before the flowers even open! This attribute exists on a continuum with beans, for example, being almost exclusively self-pollinated and corn being exclusively cross-pollinated. Finally, the actual seeds will require either dry processing or wet processing, depending on the nature of the fruit. Spinach seeds are dry like grains and will be processed differently from tomato seeds immersed in fluid.

These attributes ultimately determine how much effort and land the farmer has to invest to produce seed. Biennials require overwintering and, especially north of Maryland, special attention so that they live through the winter. Plants that are predominantly cross-pollinating require a fairly large population, sometimes as many as 400 plants, to avoid a phenomenon known as "inbreeding depression" in which seed produced from an insufficient quantity of parent plants exhibits progressively decreased vigor and productivity. Seed processing generally, whether wet or dry, can require a fair amount of time. Table 16 lists the seed-saving characteristics of a number of common crops.

Saving seed from biennial plants presents difficulties for the mini-farmer whose every square foot of garden bed is important, and also because plants that are wintered-over in the garden complicate crop rotation schedules and the use of cover crops. Luckily, most biennial plants flower and set seed early in spring so they are out of the way in time for summer planting.

A good compromise for farmers who wish to raise their own biennial seeds is to set aside one or two beds for the specific purpose of producing seed. Such beds can be protected over the winter with a hoop tunnel such as the one described in chapter 13.

Inbreeding Depression and Genetic Diversity

In Table 16 is a column labeled "Min #." This signifies, for outbreeding/crossing plants, the minimum number of plants of that variety that must be grown together to avoid inbreeding depression.

For those plants that are self-pollinating, the number in that column (followed by an asterisk) represents the minimum number of plants from which seed should be saved to preserve a good cross-section of the gene pool for that particular variety. These numbers represent the plant populations used in commercial seed production. If the seed is being produced for home use, there is generally little harm in reducing the population by 25% or even 50%.

Isolation Distance

For seed production, it is important to observe the minimum isolation distances given in Table 16. These distances are for producing seed for home use. For commercial distribution, the distances would be greater in many cases. These isolation distances specify the minimum distance that a plant has to be from another plant of the same species but a different variety to keep the two from interbreeding and producing seeds that won't duplicate either plant. At first glance, this looks easier than it actually is for the following reason.

On a farm that occupies less than a quarter acre, all of the plants are within 100 feet of each other, meaning that for purposes of seed saving, there won't be enough isolation distance available to grow more than one variety of a given species without using isolation cages or other special seed-saving techniques to prevent interbreeding. This isn't a problem with self-pollinators like peas, beans, and tomatoes but can pose a real challenge with squash, spinach, or corn.

Isolation by Time

Some brassica family plants, like broccoli, are annual while others, like cauliflower, are biennial. This means that isolation between the two can be based on timing as broccoli will have long since made its seed before cauliflower flowers the following spring. The same technique can be used if the time of flowering is different for two varieties of the same species because of differences in maturation rates. Orchestrating this sort of isolation would be somewhat delicate but certainly possible.

Another method for the farmer dedicated to saving seeds is to make use of the fact that many seeds retain their viability (ability to sprout and grow a healthy plant) for a number of years and therefore don't need to be grown for seed each year. Cucumber seeds, for example, will remain viable for at least five years if stored properly. You could grow a different variety of cucumber each year for three years and save the seed from each variety. Then, on the fourth year, grow the same variety that you grew the first year. That way you are maintaining the seeds for three different varieties of cucumbers without having to do anything exotic to keep the varieties from interbreeding.

Barrier Isolation

Barrier isolation is the practice of using a physical barrier to keep flowers from one plant from pollinating another. The two methods most practiced are alternate-day caging and hand pollination.

Alternate-day caging is done by building cages out of fine window screen or floating row cover that will fit over the plants—two varieties of carrots, for example. On the first day, one variety is covered with a cage, and on the second day, the other variety is covered. This allows insects to pollinate both without cross-pollinating them.

Hand pollination is easiest on plants with large flowers—like cucumbers and squash—but can be done on many other plants given a sufficiently steady hand. Hand pollination is made easy with members of the squash and cucumber family because of the fact that they grow large male and female flowers separately. A bag is used to protect the female flower from undesirable pollen until it is hand pollinated using a male flower of the farmer's choosing. The female flower is protected with a bag again until it is no longer receptive to pollen, and that fruit is marked for seed usage. If female flowers are caught before they first open, hand pollination can be very successful at maintaining purity even in instances where multiple varieties of the same species are grown.

Dry Processing

Seeds that are naturally dry—such as those of spinach and wheat—are processed to separate the seeds from other plant materials by screening and winnowing. Screening is done with a screen selected for a mesh size that allows the seeds through but nothing larger. (Southern Exposure Seed Exchange sells screens that are presized for particular types of seeds.) This eliminates the larger debris. Debris smaller than the seeds is removed by winnowing. Winnowing can be accomplished by pouring the seeds from one container to another in front of a stiff breeze or a fan. Lighter materials get blown away, and seeds get preserved. (Getting good at this takes practice!)

Some dry seeds require threshing to be saved in appreciable quantities. Threshing is a technique that uses physical force to break away the pods surrounding the seeds and can be accomplished in a number of creative ways. Traditionally, farmers used a flail resembling a set of nunchakus for this task. The plants requiring threshing would be placed in a sturdy sack, and then the sack would be beaten with the flail and all the seeds would end up in the bottom of the bag. Another common technique is to place the plants to be threshed on a tarp, put another tarp on top so the plants are sandwiched in between, and then walk around on them.

Melons, winter squash, and green peppers are wet fruit, but their seeds can be saved like dry seeds by washing them in water to remove any traces of pulp and then drying before storage.

Wet Processing

For plants whose seeds are embedded in damp flesh, studies have shown that the viability of the seeds is highest if the fruit is allowed to become a bit more than fully ripe before harvesting.

Such wet seeds will also benefit from fermentation processing. In fermentation processing, the seeds and pulp are scraped into a glass container—a clean pint jar for example—and about half that volume of tap water is added to the jar. Swirl and mix, then cover the container and put it in a warm place. Three days later, the contents of the container have grown a rather disgusting mold, and the good seeds have sunk to the bottom. The seeds that have sunk to the bottom are removed, washed, and dried.

Fermentation is not strictly necessary, but studies indicate that this sort of processing mimics natural processes and has been demonstrated to reduce the incidence of diseases in the seeds.

Storing Seeds

The length of time that seeds are viable depends on how you store them, and this applies to both purchased seeds and homegrown seeds. The two most important factors affecting the longevity of seeds are heat and moisture.

Studies have demonstrated that between the temperatures of 32 degrees F and 112 degrees F, the time that a seed is viable *doubles* for every

Table 16: **Seed Characteristics**

Plant	Annual/ Biennial	Wet or Dry	Pollinator	Min #	Years Viable	Isolation Distance
Asparagus	Perennial	Dry	Insects	10		1,200'
Beans	Annual	Dry	Self	20*	2–3	150'
Beets	Biennial	Dry	Wind/cross	25	3–5	1,200'
Broccoli	Annual	Dry	Insects/cross	50	3–5	300'
Brussels sprouts	Biennial	Dry	Insects/cross	50	3–5	300'
Cabbage	Biennial	Dry	Insects/cross	50	3–5	300'
Carrots	Biennial	Dry	Insects/cross	75	2–3	1,200'
Cauliflower	Biennial	Dry	Insects/cross	100	3–5	300'
Celery	Biennial	Dry	Insects/cross	25	2–3	1,200'
Chives	Perennial	Dry	Insects/cross	20	1	1,200'
Corn	Annual	Dry	Wind/cross	200	2–3	500'
Cucumber	Annual	Wet	Insects/cross	25	5–10	500'
Eggplant	Annual	Wet	Self	20*	2–3	10'
Kale	Biennial	Dry	Insects/cross	50	3–5	300'
Leek	Biennial	Dry	Insects/cross	20	2	1,200'
Lettuce	Annual	Dry	Self	12	2–3	20'
Melons	Annual	Dry	Insects/cross	25	5–10	500'
Onion	Biennial	Dry	Insects/cross	30	1	1,200'
Parsley	Biennial	Dry	Insects/cross	25	2–3	1,200'
Parsnip	Biennial	Dry	Insects/cross	75	2–3	1,200'
Pea	Annual	Dry	Self	20*	2–3	20'
Peppers	Annual	Dry	Self/cross	10*	2–3	20'
Pumpkin	Annual	Dry	Insects/cross	25	2–5	500'
Radish	Annual	Dry	Insects/cross	75	3–5	500'
Soybean	Annual	Dry	Self	20*	2–3	200'
Spinach	Annual	Dry	Wind	75	2–3	1,200'
Squash	Annual	Wet	Insects/cross	25	2–5	500'
Tomato	Annual	Wet	Self	20*	5–10	10'
Turnip	Annual	Dry	Insects/cross	25	3–5	1,200'

9 degrees F that the temperature is lowered.[41] The moisture content of the seeds is also important, as similar studies have shown that an increase in seed moisture of as little as 5% to 10% can reduce seed viability more rapidly than increasing the temperature from 68 degrees F to 104 degrees F.[42] (Seed banks store seeds in chest freezers at below-freezing temperatures. For home seed

---

[41] Bubel, N. (1988) *The New Seed Starter's Handbook* p. 204

[42] Ibid p. 205

⊗ Tools for properly drying seeds for storage.

savers, storing seeds at temperatures below freezing is unusual because the moisture level of the seed must be carefully controlled to keep such cold temperatures from damaging the seed.)

Therefore, keep seeds cool and dry. This is easy to accomplish using moisture-indicating silica gel, small muslin bags like those used for spices, and mason jars with sealing tops. Moisture-indicating silica gel and the small muslin bags can be purchased from the Southern Exposure Seed Exchange. When dry, moisture-indicating silica gel is blue, and when damp it is pink. Once it becomes pink, put it on some aluminum foil on a pan in the oven on the lowest setting and gently heat it until it turns uniformly blue again. It can be reused indefinitely, so it's a good investment.

Place the seeds to be stored in a mason jar either within paper seed packets or not, because the seed packets pass moisture readily. (You might do this with commercial seed packets you received in the mail, just to make sure they are properly dehydrated before storage.) Put two or three tablespoons of moisture-indicating silica gel in a drawstring muslin bag and put it in the jar with the seeds and seal. A week later, remove the bag containing silica gel from the jar, reseal, and place the jar in a cool basement or a refrigerator. If you use this method, your seeds should remain viable for a long time, and your investment in either purchased seeds or the personal effort of saving seeds is protected.

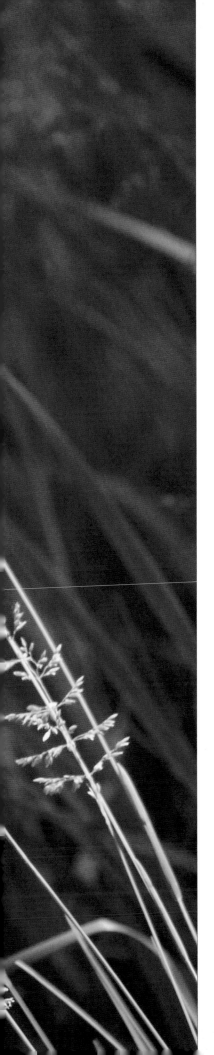

13

Season Extension

While season extension isn't an absolute necessity for the mini-farmer, it has some advantages. The most obvious is that season extension will allow you to grow warm season crops like sweet potatoes that require more growing days than available in your area, but there are other less obvious advantages.

A simple, unheated hoop house, constructed with two layers of plastic, will allow many crops, such as parsnips and carrots, to be stored in the ground rather than harvested in fall. It will also allow many biennial plants, such as cabbage, to successfully overwinter for purposes of seed production. Finally, it will allow you to grow many cold-hardy crops for sale or consumption, such as spinach and other salad greens. Along with these more practical benefits comes the psychological value (for us northeastern farmers) that such a structure will have in midwinter when the inviting growing foliage can be seen inside against a backdrop of dismal snow.

There are a lot of approaches to season extension ranging from simple cold frames to fancy heated greenhouses with specialized glass and framing. The approach to this, as with everything else in mini-farming, is economic.

Cold frames are simple, four-sided rectangles that are open on the bottom and sloped on the top and oriented so that the downward end of the slope faces the sun. Usually, they are covered with old windows, so they can be made cheaply. The only heat provided is that of the sun, so they can be placed just about anywhere. A cold frame will provide a temperature about 20 degrees warmer than the outside air during the day but will drop to within 5 degrees of outside temperature overnight unless it is well insulated or has provisions for heat retention. If raised beds are used, cold frames can easily be made to fit.

Hotbeds are cold frames that have a mechanism for heating built in. A couple of hundred years ago, hotbeds were made by digging a pit three feet deep, filling it to within six inches of the top with fresh horse manure that would provide heat as it composted and then covering that with six inches of regular garden soil in which crops were planted. More modern hotbeds use either buried heating cables underneath where the plants grow or pipes carrying warm water. Obviously, hotbeds keep crops warmer than cold frames, but the amount of warmth they provide varies with design.

⊗ A cold frame can extend the season by several weeks.

The unheated hoop house is a simple skeleton framework of hoops covered with the kind of plastic that folks in the northern parts of the United States use to cover their windows during the winter. Because it holds a far greater volume of air, it will tend to provide more warmth than a cold frame. There are a number of hoop house kits available from companies such as Hoop House Greenhouse Kits (www.hoophouse .com), and the most expensive of these cost less than $1,000. For farmers who are handy, there are also a number of free plans available on the Internet, including an easily built and inexpensive structure designed by Travis Saling viewable at westsidegardener.com. The pvcplans .com Web site has a number of free plans available describing how to make greenhouses from PVC pipe.

The idea of an unheated environment that gets all of its heat from the sun can be taken further to create a solar greenhouse. Unlike a hoop house, which is translucent on all sides, a solar greenhouse is translucent only on the side facing the sun, and the other sides are insulated to retain heat while drums of water painted black sit against the back wall creating a solar mass. Portions of the back wall are often reflective to put more light onto the plants. A solar greenhouse is certainly more expensive to construct than a hoop house, but it has the advantage of having smaller ongoing operational costs than a traditional greenhouse because it doesn't use supplemental heating.

Either a hoop house or a solar greenhouse can be made into a heated greenhouse by adding supplemental heat. Supplemental heat can be provided by a heating appliance of practically any type compatible with your budget.

What to Grow

The decision on what to grow decides the design of the season extension adopted, rather than the other way around. Miner's lettuce grows only a couple of inches tall, so it will work fine in a cold frame, but kale is so tall that a hoop house would be required. Winter-hardy crops like spinach and kale don't require supplemental heat, lettuce would require only a little, and tender crops like tomatoes would require a considerable amount. Especially with increasing fuel costs, it is important to consider whether growing frost-tender crops like tomatoes in the winter makes economic sense, and most often it does not.

I recommend growing hardy crops using no supplemental heat or semihardy crops using just enough supplemental heat to prevent freezing. Under such conditions, growth of crops is slow, and it is best to establish them late in the summer or early in the fall so that by the time winter hits, the season extender is serving mainly to extend the harvest rather than actively grow crops.

So what crops are suitable for this purpose? Carrots, parsnips, and parsley will do well in a hoop house or cold frame. Both parsnips and carrots started at midsummer will taste sweet come January. Salsify planted just at the first fall frost can be harvested a bit past Yule. Many leaf lettuces will grow, though their outer leaves may sustain some damage. (Try the Winter Density variety.) Beets will hold in the ground in a cold frame, and chard may grow if you are south of Pennsylvania. Kale will hold well and even grow, as will Brussels sprouts and green onions or leeks. (The American Flag variety of leek will work well.) Both Brunswick and January King cabbage can be harvested around New Year's if planted midsummer.

There are a few particularly cold-hardy crops ideal for season extension, including miner's lettuce, corn salad (a.k.a. "mache"), italian dandelion, wintercress, and purslane. While these are unusual, they are a real taste-treat that adds character to winter salads.

Besides winter crops, an unheated hoop house can also help the farmer get a head start on spring season crops and even extend the season long enough to grow crops or varieties that would otherwise be impossible, such as the aforementioned sweet potatoes in the Northeast. A hoop house also expands the possibilities for cover crops and green manures because of the change in environment.

Special Considerations

A hoop house, cold frame, or hotbed is inherently protected from precipitation. The good news is water is completely in the farmer's control. The bad news is the lack of rainfall will tend to concentrate salts in the soil in the protected area, which will hurt plant growth. It takes three or four years for this to happen, but it is still a problem. Another problem with a more permanent structure is that the space within it can accumulate pests and diseases. Especially since pests have nowhere to go, the enclosed area can cancel some of the benefits of crop rotation within that space.

The most space-efficient way to handle this is to make the structure easily erected and dismantled, and dismantle it late every spring. For more permanent greenhouse designs, the plastic can be removed during the late spring through early fall, which would have the same effect. For large structures, such as 90-foot-long greenhouses, it is obviously too time-consuming, but for structures of the size usually employed in a mini-farm, it is will be feasible if they are designed with easy maintenance in mind.

Larger farms in Europe and the United States have movable greenhouses on rails that are rolled from one location to another with each season to accommodate growing needs and diminish the problems of a permanent standing structure. This may be a bit beyond the needs of a mini-farmer, but it can be accomplished with a little ingenuity and moderate expense by a farmer who is so inclined.

Improving Greenhouse Efficiency

An unheated hoop house can do a great deal to extend the growing season, but a few simple modifications at very low cost can dramatically improve the light and heat utilization of such a structure.

In the winter when the sun is low in the sky, a good proportion of the light that hits a hoop house will enter the south side and exit the north side without ever touching a plant.

If a reflective sheet is installed along the entire north wall up to the ridge pole, light that would otherwise escape will get reflected back onto the plants, thus increasing the light available to the plants and raising the temperature. A good material for this purpose is reflective insulation, available inexpensively from most home improvement stores. Not only will the aluminum surface of the insulation reflect light, but it will also reflect 97% of radiant heat that would have escaped through the plastic back into the hoop house.

The next modification is to add a method of heat retention. A simple hoop house will lose tem-perature quickly after sunset, and one way to slow down the temperature drop is to line up a number of black-painted barrels against the north wall of the hoop house—though not actually touching the reflective insulation—and fill them with water. The drums of water will absorb the heat from the sunlight during the day and then radiate that heat back into the hoop house at night. The value of this approach is enhanced by the addition of the reflective insulation because the radiant heat gets reflected back into the enclosed space from all directions. Barrels can be emptied and moved anytime the greenhouse is moved, or they can be used for raising fish, with exchanged water being used as nitrogen-rich liquid fertilizer. (Yes, fish *can* be raised in a barrel using the technology of *aquaculture*, but aquaculture isn't covered in this book.)

So, what happens if there is no sun for a week and the water drums freeze? South of Connect-icut, this is unlikely to be a problem, but it is a pos-sibility further north. You may need to abandon using barrels or abandon the simple hoop house design altogether and build a solar greenhouse. There are a number of solar greenhouse designs available on the Internet. What they all have in common is significant insulation (R-30) every-where but in the windows that face south and reflective coating on all interior walls.

Portable Hoops for Raised Beds

Raised beds lend themselves to easily construct-ed and inexpensive attachments for season exten-sion, particularly if constructed with a width of four feet. The easiest attachments are cold frames mentioned earlier and portable hoops.

⊗ Loops on the frame of a raised bed.

Raised beds can be equipped to accept portable hoops by attaching 1-inch rings to the outside of the beds at the ends and every two feet.

The portable hoops are made from 10-foot-long pieces of 1/2-inch PVC pipe that have been cut in half for ease of storage. To build the hoops, the two 5-foot pieces of PVC are connected via a straight coupling, and then each end is inserted into one of the 1-inch rings on each side of the bed. The hoops are covered with translucent plastic sheeting 10 feet wide available at any hardware store. The plastic can be secured at the long edges by sandwiching it between 1-inch × 2-inch boards so it can be easily rolled up and deployed, or it can by secured with homemade snap clips made by slicing pieces of garden hose lengthwise. Which technique will work best depends on the strength of prevailing winds in your area.

⊗ Insert the PVC pipes into the loops.

⊗ Completed hoop house.

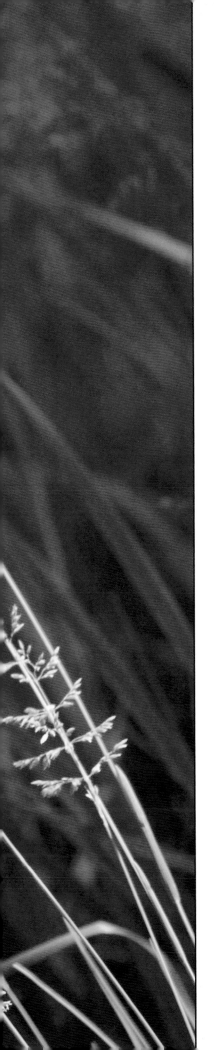

14

Fruit Trees and Vines

Fruit trees and vines can provide an enormous amount of food compared to the effort invested. Many fruit and nut trees produce, literally, bushels of fruits or nuts, and some blackberry variants produce gallons of berries per vine. Unfortunately, even though berries may even produce in their first or second season, full-sized fruit and nut trees take several years to come into production and may produce nothing at all for the first few years. Dwarf trees will normally produce fruit within three years, but the volume of fruit they produce is lower.

To offset this problem, diversify! If possible, in the year preceding the start of your mini-farm, plant a small section with berry and perhaps some grape vines for the next year's harvest. Along with these, plant dwarf fruit trees and some full-sized nut trees. In this way, the harvest starts modestly with berries the first year and expands to include dwarf cherries the next year, dwarf apples the year after that, and so on. Within seven years, the farmer is producing enough fruit and nuts for the family plus some surplus.

Fruits are full of idiosyncrasies in terms of disease and pest problems, pruning requirements, suitable climate, and so on. This is particularly true of vinifera grapes, apples, peaches, and other popular fruits. I recommend reading as widely as possible about the fruits you plan to grow and selecting hardy varieties specific to your area, using a reputable nursery, and trying to purchase varieties that are resistant to expected diseases.

I recommend St. Lawrence Nurseries in Potsdam, New York, but there are other reputable nurseries as well. An invaluable Internet resource at the time of this writing is Garden Watchdog, at www.davesgarden.com. Garden Watchdog has a listing for almost every company in the gardening business and a list of feedback from customers along with ratings. Check out any mail-order nurseries with Garden Watchdog before ordering.

In addition to ordering high-quality trees that are likely to be less susceptible to problems, you should work proactively to keep pest problems minimal by making sure plants that attract beneficial insects are already established where the trees will be planted. Most notably, this means clover. Clover attracts insects that feast on the most tenacious pests of apple-family trees and fruits such as codling moths, apple maggots, and plum curculios. The exact type of clover to be planted will vary with the condition of the soil, expected temperatures, and expected precipitation. A good resource for selecting the right variety of clover is a comprehensive organic gardening catalog like that from Peaceful Valley Farm Supply.

Plant trees in the spring, and spray them for the first time in the fall with dormant oil that smothers and controls overwintering insects. The following spring spray the trees with a lighter horticultural oil in spring when the buds have swelled but not yet blossomed. Also spray them with either a lime sulfur or organic copper-based fungicide according to label directions every spring after their first year. Traps for common problem insects such as codling moths or apple maggots should be set out and maintained at a high enough density to trap out all of the males of the species.

Fruits and nuts often have specific pollination requirements that make it necessary to plant more than one tree. Sometimes the trees have to be of slightly different variants because trees of the same variety were propagated by grafting and are therefore genetically identical and self-sterile. A few nurseries sell trees propagated from seed rather than grafting, and these trees will pollinate each other without issue even if the same variety. Be sure to pay attention to catalog information and ask questions of the nursery staff to avoid later disappointment!

Pruning will be necessary to maximize the productive potential of the trees. There are many schools of thought on the subject of pruning, and numerous weighty tomes have been written, but the basics are easily described.

Blackberries and Raspberries

Cane fruits, like raspberries and blackberries, grow long and heavy enough that the tips of the canes touch the ground—where they then set a new root and grow more new canes. This isn't necessarily desirable, as it leads to an ever-expanding impenetrable thorny mess, so it is best to trellis the canes to prevent this. The easiest trellising for cane fruits is a four-foot-tall "T" at each end of the row of canes with galvanized wire run from each end of the T along the length of the

⊗ Raspberries are nutritious and easy to grow.

row. The wire holds up the canes so they don't touch the ground, and new canes are trained to stay behind the wire. This makes the berries easy to pick as well.

Blackberries are pruned by distinguishing between *primocanes* and *floricanes*. Primocanes are canes in their first year that bear leaves but no flowers or fruit. Floricanes are those same canes in their second year, when they bear flowers and fruit. After a cane has fruited, it slowly dies, so fruiting canes should be cut out and removed once their fruiting season has passed. Primocanes

⊗ This sort of T-trellis is easily made and works well

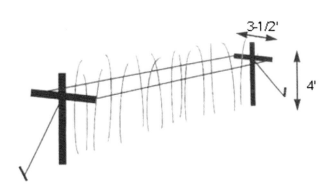

should be *topped* during their first year of growth, meaning they should have their tops cut off just about 4 inches above the trellis. This will cause them to send out lateral shoots so that when they bear fruit the next year, they will bear more abundantly.[43] The lateral shoots should be trimmed to 12 inches to 18 inches.

The same general technique applies to raspberries, with some minor changes. Yellow and red raspberries shouldn't be topped, and the laterals that form on purple and black raspberries should be trimmed to just 10 inches. Ever-bearing raspberry varieties fruit in the late summer of the primocane stage and then again in the early summer of the floricane stage. After the early summer fruiting, the floricanes should be removed. The easiest way to distinguish floricanes in ever-bearing raspberries is that the first-year fruit is on the top of the cane and the second-year fruit is at the bottom.[44]

Grapes

Grapes can be divided into three general varieties: European, American, and muscadine. European grape varieties (*Vitis vinifera*) are vulnerable to a nasty pest called phylloxera, which is a tiny louse-like insect that causes all sorts of problems, especially in the eastern United States. Muscadine grapes, native to the southern United States, can be successfully grown only south of Maryland because of their climate requirements. Other American grape varieties are naturally resistant to phylloxera and can be grown practically anywhere in

[43] Strik, B. (1993) *Growing Blackberries in Your Home Garden* Oregon State University

[44] Lockwood, D. (1999) *Pruning Raspberries and Blackberries in Home Gardens*

the continental United States. For varietal wine production, scion wood of European grape varieties is often grafted onto American variety root stocks to reduce their vulnerability to phylloxera.

Since grape vines are expensive and can last for decades, it is important to pick a grape variety appropriate for your local climate. Check a reputable vendor for recommendations. All grape varieties can be used to produce jams, jellies, raisins, and wines for home use. Grapes do best in *moderately* fertile soil because soil as fertile as that in a vegetable garden will cause the

❖ Properly pruned grape vines yield good crops.

leaves to grow so quickly and in such volume that the fruit will be shaded by the leaves, which will keep them damp and increase the likelihood of disease.

It is possible to start a grape vine in the fall, but odds of success are far greater if it is started in the spring because that gives the transplant more time to get established and store energy in its root system for overwintering.

When you first bring home a grape vine, it will likely have numerous shoots coming out of the root system. Cut off all of the shoots but the strongest one, then cut that one back to only three or four buds. Plant the vine in well-drained soil in a locale with plenty of sun, and water thoroughly. Pretty soon new shoots will emerge at the buds, plus some more from the roots. Cut off the ones that emerge from the roots, and once the new shoots from the buds have grown to about 12 inches, select the best and strongest of these and cut off the others. The best shoot will be pretty much upright. Drive a strong stake into the ground close to the plant, and throughout the summer keep the shoot tied nice and straight to that stake.

Meanwhile, set up your training and trellising system. There are many types, but about the easiest is the Kniffin system using two horizontal galvanized steel wires at three feet and six feet from the ground tied to two strong posts secured in the ground.

The first spring a year after planting, take the chosen shoot (which should have grown to a length somewhat taller than the bottom wire), and select the two strongest lateral shoots and tie those to the bottom wire while continuing to tie the growing trunk vertically to the stake.

Later in the season, once the growing trunk has grown to slightly below or slightly above the top wire, cut it off there and select the two strongest lateral shoots to tie to the top horizontal wires.

Occasionally, the chosen shoot that will serve as the trunk won't put out lateral shoots the first year. If that occurs—it's no big deal. Grape vines are vigorous and forgiving, so if a mistake is made in one year, it can always be corrected the next year. Just take the main shoot that serves as the trunk once it is slightly above the first wire, and tie it to one side of the wire and trim it back to three or four buds. These will form shoots. Select the two strongest of these—one of which will be run horizontally in the opposite direction on the wire, and the other of which will be run vertically up the stake and handled as detailed previously.

Ongoing pruning will be important to maintain fruit production because grapes produce on the shoots that come from one-year-old wood. So any shoots that arise from wood that is more than one year old won't bear fruit. That means that the horizontal shoots selected the first year should be removed for the second year and new shoots from the trunk trained along the wires.

⊗ The Kniffin system is one of the easiest for training grapes.

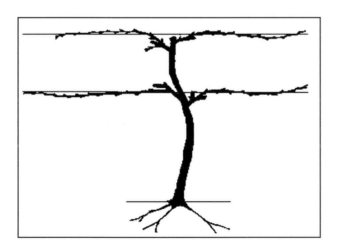

The foregoing is not the final word on grape pruning and training, as many other systems are available to those desiring more information—but this should be enough to get you started.

Grapes are prone to black rot and botrytis fungus, as well as birds and deer. Because of the rot and fungal problems, it is important to avoid sprinkler irrigation of grapes and practice good sanitation by consistently removing old fruit and leaves at the end of each season. A copper-based fungicide applied at bloom time is most effective against rot and fungus.[45]

On a small scale, birds and deer can be foiled with netting; on a larger scale, some creativity (such as noisemakers and fencing) will be required. I grow my grapes far away from everything else, and the birds and deer haven't found them so far!

Strawberries

Very few fruits are as prolific and easy to grow in limited space as strawberries. Moreover, because of their delicate nature, they are expensive to ship long distances, so they sell well in season if you decide to market them. Beds are easy to establish and require minimal maintenance on the scale of a mini-farm.

Strawberries come in three basic types: spring-bearing, ever-bearing, and day-neutral. The spring-bearing variety produces a single crop; the ever-bearing variety produces crops in spring, summer, and fall; and the day-neutral strawberry produces fruit throughout the season. Spring-bearing varieties can be early season, middle season, or late season, meaning that through

[45] Baugher, T. et al. (1990) *Growing Grapes in West Virginia*

⊗ Strawberries do extremely well in raised beds.

careful selection of more than one spring-bearing variety, it is possible to extend the length of harvest substantially. Consider the intended use of the strawberries—preservation or fresh eating—in selecting varieties for either a continuous small crop or one or more larger harvests.

Strawberry plants can be spread either through seeds or through plants and runners. The best bet in most cases is to buy strawberry plants of known characteristics and then let them spread by runners. Runners are a long stem that emerges from the crown of the strawberry plant and establishes a new crown and root system wherever it contacts suitable earth. Simply place the runners where they will fill in the gaps in your planting—no more than four strawberry plants per square foot.

Strawberries should be well fertilized with compost and any needed organic amendments and be mulched with straw or fallen leaves after the last frost. They occasionally fall prey to botyritis blight, a gray mold that can grow on the berries. To keep this controlled, keep the beds clear of debris, make sure strawberries are harvested when ripe or slightly underripe, and spray with an organic fixed-copper fungicide as needed.

Apples and Pears

Apples and pears are the quintessential home fruit trees and can be grown in almost any part of the United States. A wide selection of modern and heirloom varieties are available that are suitable for fresh eating, preservation, and pies.

Apples and pears offered in nurseries are usually produced by grafting the scion wood of the desired variety onto a more hardy compatible rootstock, such as that of flowering crab. The original rootstock can produce shoots below the graft (known as "suckers"), and these should be trimmed as soon as they are spotted.

Apples and pears should be pruned and trained when they are quite young or else they will become difficult to manage and produce inferior fruit. The objective of training the tree is to provide optimal air circulation and sunlight

⊗ Pears are a bit easier than apples to keep pest free.

while keeping the fruit low enough to the ground so that it can be picked without a crane.

It is easiest for a mini-farmer is to select dwarf or semidwarf trees from the beginning. This will reduce pruning requirements and make maintenance easier and safer. Ideally, the tree will be pruned so that the shape is similar to a Christmas tree, which will allow maximum penetration of sunlight and easiest spraying while keeping the greatest bulk of the fruit closest to the ground.

A large number of articles on the specifics of pruning and training pomme fruits are available, but it isn't hard to master if a few rules are followed. (Apples, pears, and quinces are collectively referred to as *pomme fruits*. The word *pomme* comes from the French word for *apple*.)

When the young tree is first planted, tie it to a straight, eight-foot-long stake driven at least three feet into the soil for strength, cut off any limbs that are larger than 50% of the diameter of the trunk, and trim the trunk back to a height of three feet. Branches are strongest when they leave the trunk at an angle between 60 and 75 degrees, so when the branches are young, it is easy to bring them back to that angle by tying them with string or inserting small pieces of wood between the branch and the trunk. The branches on trees will tend to grow toward the sun, so that tendency will have to be countered the same way because you want the tree to grow straight and well balanced.

Subsequent pruning is best done in late winter or very early spring. The first spring after planting, remove any limbs closer to the ground than two feet and any limbs that are larger than 50% of the diameter of the trunk. If the tree has developed more than seven limbs, select the seven best distributed around the tree to be saved, and prune the rest. It is important when a limb is pruned that it be pruned back all the way to the trunk, otherwise it will sprout a bunch of vertically growing wood and create troubles. Once the pruning is done, limbs that need it should be tied or fitted with spacers to get the right angle to the trunk.

Beware of cutting off just the tips of the remaining limbs, because this can delay fruiting. Once the tree has been fruiting for a couple of years, such cuts can be used sparingly for shaping, but it is better to solve shading problems by removing entire limbs.

For all following years use the same rules by aiming for a well-balanced upright tree without excessive shading.

Stone Fruits

Stone fruits include cherries, apricots, peaches, plums, and nectarines. Because most stone fruits are native to warm climates and are thus susceptible to problems from winter injury or frost killing the flowers in the spring, it is important to carefully select varieties suitable for your area by consulting with a knowledgeable seller with a good reputation. No matter what cultivar is selected, it should be planted in an area protected from wind and with good sunshine and drainage. It is best to select a one-year-old tree five or six feet tall with good root growth.

Like apples and pears, stone fruits can be grafted onto dwarfing rootstocks. Unfortunately, none of the dwarf varieties grow well north of Pennsylvania.[46] The good news is that a number of hardy stone fruit varieties native to North America are available. The bush cherry (*Prunus*

[46] Pennsylvania State University (2001) *Small Scale Fruit Production: A Comprehensive Guide* http://ssfruit.cas.psu.edu/chapter5/chapter5h.htm

⊗ Nectarines are easy to grow and easy to can or freeze.

besseyi), American wild plum (*Prunus americana*), and American beach plum (*Prunus maritima*) can be grown throughout the continental United States, and Indian blood peach (Prunus persica) can be grown south of Massachusetts. All of these are available in seed form from Bountiful Gardens (www.bountifulgardens.org) and are also available from a number of nurseries.

Almost all nursery stock is grafted rather than grown from seed for a number of reasons, but the effect of this is that if two trees of the same type and variety are selected, they may be genetically the same exact plant and thus incapable of pollinating each other, causing low fruit yields. More than one of any stone fruit should be selected to aid in pollination, and it is important to consult with knowledgeable nursery personnel about exactly what varieties need to be grown to ensure proper pollination. Space nectarines, peaches, plums, and apricots anywhere from 15 to 20 feet apart, and space cherries anywhere from 20 to 30 feet apart for best pollination and fruit yields.

Stone fruits should be planted in early spring by digging a hole big enough to accommodate the entire root system without bunching it up or looping it around and deep enough that the graft

union is about two inches above the ground. Once the soil is filled back into the hole, the area should be watered thoroughly to help the soil settle around the roots. Stone fruits should be fertilized in early spring only (using a balanced organic fertilizer) and never later in the summer. Fertilizing in late summer will cause vigorous growth that the root system hasn't grown enough to support so the tree could be harmed and have difficulty overwintering. By fertilizing in the early spring, the tree has a chance to grow in a balanced way across the entire growing season so it will overwinter properly.

A good fertilizer can be made by mixing together 1 pound of bone meal, 1/2 pound of dried blood, and 3 pounds of dried kelp or greensand. Apply 1/2 pound to the soil surface around the drip line of the tree (the "drip line" is the area on the ground just under the widest branches) by using a crowbar to make four to eight holes six inches deep in a circle around the plant and sprinkling some of the fertilizer in each hole. Use 1/2 pound the first year, then an additional half pound every year thereafter until, in the ninth and subsequent years, 5 pounds are being used each spring. Stone fruits prefer a pH of 6.0 to 6.5, and if a soil test shows amendment to be needed, that can be done in the spring as well. Keep in mind, however, that lime can take several months to work, so don't overlime and raise the pH above 6.5.

The following pruning directions are equally applicable to both dwarf and full-size trees. Because all stone fruits are susceptible to brown rot, they should be trained to an open center rather than a central leader (a single main trunk that reaches all the way to the top of the tree) like an apple tree. This will allow maximum light and air penetration to keep brown rot problems under control.

When the tree is first planted, cut off any branches closer than 18 inches to the ground, and cut the central leader at 30 inches above the ground. This will force branches to grow out at 18 to 30 inches above the ground, which will yield branches at the right height when the tree is mature. Select three or four good branches that are growing evenly spaced around the trunk, and prune back the others all the way to the trunk, then prune back the central leader to just above the topmost selected branch. These selected branches will be the main *scaffolds* of the tree, referring to their structural importance. Stone fruit branches are strongest when they leave the trunk at an angle between 60 and 90 degrees, so now is the time to establish those angles and the direction of growth using a combination of ropes and wooden spacers inserted between the branch and the trunk.

Stone fruits should not be pruned in winter because of susceptibility to winter injury and because of a disease called cytospora canker. Rather, they should be pruned between the time they bloom and the first week after the flower petals have fallen.

The first pruning after planting should occur just after blooming in the early spring of the next year. At that time, any branches that are broken and diseased should be removed, and the main scaffolds should be cut back half their length to an outward facing bud. Any vertically growing shoots should likewise be removed, and spacers or ties for maintaining branch angles should be checked and adjusted as necessary.

The second pruning after planting will occur at the same time the next year. By this time, the main scaffold branches will be developing new branches on them. Select three or four sublimbs on each main scaffold to be preserved. These should be on opposite sides of the scaffolds, not growing straight up or bending down, and be at least 18 inches away from the main trunk. The main scaffold branches should then be cut back by 1/3 to an outward-facing bud, and all limbs but the selected sublimbs should be cut back to the branch or to the trunk as appropriate.

Subsequent pruning simply needs to maintain the open center by removing vertical limbs and limbs that grow inward toward the center. Limbs and sublimbs should be headed back to an outward-facing bud each year to make sure new fruiting wood is growing each year, and limbs should be pruned as needed to maintain the desired shape and size of tree and to avoid broken limbs.

Nut Trees

Compared to fruit trees, nut trees are easier to prune and care for. The only downside is that, except for filberts, they grow to be quite large and thus require as much as 50 feet between trees. Walnuts and, to a lesser extent, pecans and hickories produce a chemical called juglone in their root systems that inhibits the germination of other plants, so they shouldn't be planted close to a garden. A number of trees are unaffected by juglone, including cherries, oaks, pears, and most cone-bearing trees, among others. The only vegetables unaffected by juglone are onions, beans, carrots, corn, melons, and squash.

Most nut trees aren't self-fruitful and therefore must be planted in pairs. The same caveat applies to nuts as to fruits in that many nut trees are made by grafting and thus are genetic clones. For this reason, two different varieties of the same

⊘ Chestnuts, walnuts, and other nuts are highly nutritious.

nut will need to be planted unless those trees were grown from seed, in which case two trees of the same variety will work fine.

Nut trees can be grown from seed as long as the requisite period of cold stratification is met to break dormancy. (Cold stratification means exposing the seed to a period of subfreezing temperature for a period of time. Many seeds for trees require this or they will never sprout.) If you plant the seed in the fall and protect it from rodents, it will sprout in the spring. Plant it about two feet deep and mulch with hay over the winter, then remove the mulch in early spring.

The tree should be transplanted into a hole big enough to handle the entire root system. About 2/3 of the soil should be carefully shoveled around the roots and then well watered and the remaining soil shoveled in and tamped down. The area around the tree should then be mulched to reduce competition with weeds and the trunk protected with a circular hardware cloth protector to keep deer and other critters from eating the bark. (Hardware cloth is available at any hardware store at minimal cost.)

Because nut trees have a long taproot that grows slowly, they need to have about half of their top growth pruned back during transplanting, leaving several buds. This balances the upper and lower portion of the tree to enhance survivability. New vertical-growing shoots should emerge from the buds left behind, and when they are 8 to 12 inches long, the most vigorous should be selected as the tree's new central leader, and the remainder cut off even with the trunk.

From that point forward, you are mainly aiming for a balanced tree, so prune to keep the tree balanced. Conduct all pruning in late winter or very early spring, and remove all dead or damaged branches. At the same time, progressively shorten the lowest limbs a little each year until the tree is about 20 feet high, at which point all limbs lower than 6 feet should be removed flush with the trunk. This preserves the food-making ability of the lower limbs until it is no longer needed.

Growing distance/productivity for such large trees can be troublesome on a small lot, but there are ways to get around the problem. Table 17 gives the ultimate distance that the trees should be from each other when fully grown.

Table 17: **Nut Tree Planting Distance**

Type of Nut Tree	Distance between Trees
Black walnut, hickory, pecan, and hican	50 feet in all directions
English and Persian walnut	35 feet in all directions

Type of Nut Tree	Distance between Trees
Chestnut (Chinese, most American chestnuts succumbed to the chestnut blight)	40 feet in all directions
Filberts	15 feet in all directions

Keep in mind that nut trees produce nuts long before reaching full size and that nut wood is some of the most expensive, so selling it could net a nice bundle. If you wish to do so, plant the nut trees about 10 feet apart and then selectively harvest them for wood as their branches come close to touching. In the end, you have properly spaced highly productive nut trees and hopefully a wad of cash.

Diseases and Pests

There's no such thing as a free lunch—or even free fruit! Fruit and nut trees are prone to numerous pest and disease problems. Thus, they require a regular schedule of sanitation and spraying to keep them healthy and productive, and they can pose a challenge to mini-farmers, particularly if they are committed to raising fruit without synthetic pesticides. This is more of a problem with fruits than with nuts, but it can be made manageable through advanced planning and a thorough understanding of the requirements. Pomme fruits such as apples and pears share common pests and diseases, as do stone fruits such as cherries, plums, and peaches. No matter what fruits you grow or what diseases are prevalent, meticulous cleanup of debris around the trees and vigilant pruning of diseased tissues will provide the proverbial "ounce of prevention."

The difficulties of raising apples and pears explain the high concentrations of toxic contaminants in nonorganic varieties. Therefore you should carefully consider if some other fruit might be more suitable given the amount of time you will need to spend if you wish to produce organic apples and pears. According to the Agricultural Sciences department at Pennsylvania State University, as many as 6 to 10 pesticide applications might be required yearly to produce reasonably appealing apples, though as few as 2 or 3 applications are feasible with scab-resistant varieties. Spraying is simplified, and pomme fruits are more practical if dwarf varieties are selected.

Scab is a fungal disease of apples and pears. The spores mature over a four- to six-week period of wet weather in the spring that corresponds with the wet weather required for the release of the spores. The spores take up residence on the leaves of the tree where they grow and produce more spores, starting a cycle of reinfection that infects the fruit as well, causing ugly, misshapen fruit. If all debris (apples/pears and leaves) is removed before the spores can be released, and a good antifungal agent (such as fixed copper or Bordeaux mix) is applied every 10 to 14 days starting in early spring and extending through early summer, scab infection can be controlled. A better solution, because antifungal agents can injure the tree, is to plant apple varieties that are naturally resistant to scab, such as Liberty. Carefully research the varieties you plan to grow.

There are a number of other apple or pear diseases, such as fire blight, that require comprehensive management programs to produce good fruit. Antibiotics are combined with pruning of diseased tissue for treatment of fire blight once it becomes established.

The most prevalent pest of pomme fruits is the apple maggot, a little white worm. Luckily, the apple maggot is one of the few insects that can discern—and are attracted to—the color red. They can be effectively controlled by hanging red-painted balls coated with a sticky coating (such as Tangletrap). The balls should be hung just after flowering and remain through harvest, being renewed periodically to keep them sticky. Several are required for each tree.

The codling moth is another serious pest. This nondescript gray and brown moth lays eggs on the fruit. The first eggs hatch when the fruit is slightly less than one inch in diameter, and the small worm burrows into the fruit where it eats until it reaches full size then burrows back out, becomes a moth, and starts the cycle again. Codling moths are conventionally controlled by spraying carbaryl or permethrin at least once every 14 days following petal fall. These poisons can be avoided by aggressive organic measures including "trapping out" the male moths by using up to four pheromone traps per full-sized tree, encircling the tree trunks with flexible cardboard covered with a sticky coating to trap the larvae, and spraying frequently with the botanical insecticide ryania.

Stone fruits, like pomme fruits, require constant spraying to deal with a number of diseases and pests. Chief diseases include powdery mildew, leaf spot, peach leaf curl, crown gall, cytospora canker, black knot, and brown spot. Japanese beetles, fruit moths, aphids, borers, and spider mites round out the threats.

A regular spraying schedule is required for stone fruits. If raising the fruit organically, this includes fungicides such as Bordeaux mix, lime sulfur, and fixed copper and insect controls such as neem oil, horticultural oil, and organic insecticides used according to label directions. The spraying should start when buds swell in the spring and continue with the frequency specified on the product label until the fruit has been harvested. All dropped fruit and leaves should be raked up and removed from the area in the fall.

Black knot of the plum can't be controlled this way and instead requires that any sections of wood evidencing this distinctive infection be completely removed from the tree and destroyed by incineration.

Most nut trees never show signs of disease, and the regular spraying required for fruit trees is not needed in most cases. Major nut tree diseases include chestnut blight, pecan scab, walnut anthracnose, and walnut blight.

Chestnut blight was introduced into the United States before 1900 through the importation of various Asian chestnut species that carry the causative fungus but are resistant to it themselves. The American chestnut, native to Eastern North America, has no resistance to this fungus; within a generation this majestic tree, soaring up to 100 feet and measuring up to 10 feet across, was reduced to little more than a shrub that struggles a few years before succumbing to the threat. To put the impact of chestnut blight into perspective, it is estimated that in 1900, 25% of all the trees in the Appalachians were American chestnuts.

There are four ways of dealing with chestnut blight: prompt removal of infected branches, treatment of cankers in existing trees for five years with injections of a hypovirulent strain of the fungus, planting resistant Asian chestnut varieties, and planting American varieties that have incorporated disease-resistant genes through repetitive backcrossing and selection to maximize native DNA content while retaining resistance genes.[47]

Mini-farmers interested in growing and preserving American chestnuts should seek guidance (and seeds!) from the American Chestnut Cooperators' Foundation (www.accf-online.org). Farmers interested in resistant Asian stocks can find suitable varieties at local nurseries.

Pecan scab, evidenced by sunken black spots on leaves, twigs, and nuts, is more of a problem in the southern than northern states. At the scale of a mini-farm, it is most easily controlled through meticulous sanitation—the raking and disposal of leaves and detritus through burning. Severe infestations require multiple fungicide sprays yearly.[48]

Walnut anthracnose, a disease characterized by small dark spots on the leaves that can grow to merge together and defoliate entire trees in severe cases, affects black walnuts but not Persian varieties. Meticulous sanitation is normally all that is required on the scale of a mini-farm, but springtime fungicide spraying may be needed in severe cases.

Walnut blight is just the opposite in that it affects the Persian walnut varieties but not American black walnuts. Walnut blight looks like small, water-filled sunken spots on leaves, shoots, and/or nuts. The disease doesn't travel back into old wood, so the tree and crop can be saved by spraying fixed copper during flowering and fruit set.

Pest insects in nut trees can be controlled through keeping the area mowed and free of tall grasses that would harbor stinkbugs, meticulous sanitation to control shuckworms, and regular insecticide spraying to control hunkflies, weevils, and casebearers. For a handful of nut trees (unless the mini-farm is in close proximity to a large number of similar nut species), pests are unlikely to become a major problem, and it is likely that spraying will never be necessary.

---

[47] Anagnostakis, S. (2000) *Revitalization of the Majestic Chestnut: Chestnut Blight Disease*
[48] Doll, C., McDaniel, J., Meador, D., Randall, R., Shurtleff, M. (1986) *Nut Growing in Illinois, Circular 1102*

15

Raising Chickens for Eggs

I wrote this book for the purpose of learning about self-sufficiency through mini-farming, and self-sufficiency, in my opinion, has no political agendas attached to it. If, for personal, health, or religious reasons you are opposed to consuming animal food products, then skip this chapter and the next one. If you are a meat eater but are understandably squeamish about eating homegrown eggs or turning animals into meat, I nevertheless encourage you to continue reading simply for your own knowledge.

Nothing says "farm" like the sound of a rooster crowing in the morning, and nothing is more aggravating to neighbors than a rooster that seems to crow all day, every day. Still, small livestock have a place on the mini-farm because of the high-quality protein that they provide. If you currently purchase meat and eggs, know that homegrown meat and eggs can be raised at a very low cost that will save you money.

For the purposes of a mini-farm occupying half an acre or less, cows, goats, and similar livestock will place too high a demand on the natural resources of such a small space and will end up costing more than the value of the food they provide. In such small spaces, the greatest

⊗ These chickens are so friendly they eat out of your hand.

practical benefit can be derived from chickens, guineas, some species of ducks, and aquaculture. Rabbits are also a possibility, but remember that children (and adults!) can get attached to them easily. But chickens, overall, are the most cost-effective choice on a small lot.

Overview

Chickens are foragers that will eat grass, weeds, insects, acorns, and many other things they happen to run across. They will virtually eliminate grasshoppers, slugs, and other pests in the yard, thus keeping them away from the garden. Many cover crops like alfalfa, vetch, and soybeans are delicacies for birds and since cover crops are recommended to be grown anyway, a small flock of 10 or 20 birds can be raised with minimal feed expenditures over the growing season.

Don't expect to get rich in the chicken and egg business because you would be competing at the wholesale level in a commodity market, so it's unlikely to be a direct money maker. But it *is* feasible to produce meat and eggs for yourself at costs that significantly undercut those of the supermarket while selling the odd dozen to friends and coworkers. On our own farm, the eggs we sell completely liquidate the cost of feed so that our own eggs are free, plus we get to keep the chickens valuable nitrogen-rich manure for our compost pile.

Chickens

A flock of 12 laying chickens costs about $6.00 per week to feed during the winter months when they can't be fed by foraging. They will earn their keep by producing about two to four dozen eggs weekly (more during the summer, fewer during the winter). Obviously, the family can't eat that many eggs, so a little negotiation with friends or coworkers who appreciate farm-fresh eggs will net you $2 to $3 per dozen. (Egg cartons cost about $0.20 each from a number of manufacturers. For more information, just type "egg cartons" into an Internet search engine. We get ours at a local get-together known as a "chicken swap.") To put the cost of chicken feed into perspective, a flock of 12 chickens costs less to feed than a house cat.

At the supermarket, a chicken is just a chicken, but eggs run the gamut from cheap generic eggs costing less than a dollar a dozen to organic eggs costing more than five dollars a carton. From the standpoint of raising chickens, there are numerous breeds available, each of which has its strengths and weaknesses. Many chickens are bred specifically for meat yield, and others are bred mainly for laying eggs. There are also dual-purpose varieties that split the difference.

For a mini-farm, I would recommend a hardy egg-laying variety such as the Rhode Island Red, which has the benefit of being good at hatching its own eggs over the more cultured Leghorn (pronounced "legern") varieties. Another good choice would be a dual-purpose breed like the New Hampshire or Orpington. In my experience, the laying productivity of hens diminishes over time, so these birds can be transitioned into the freezer and replaced with younger hens. (Old layers transitioned into the freezer are tough and best used for soups, stews, and chicken pot pies, so label them accordingly.) If you choose to hatch eggs from your chickens to supplement your flock, new roosters of the chosen breed should be brought in every couple of years to reduce inbreeding.

You'll find that hens and roosters are fun to watch and provide endless amusement. When the farmer steps outside, plate in hand, to deliver meal leftovers to the chickens, they'll come running! Then, the chicken that managed to retrieve an especially attractive piece of food will be chased all over the place by other members of the flock. The roosters will be vigilant and defend the rest of the flock against attack but otherwise just strut around looking proud and important. Chickens definitely establish a "pecking order" amongst themselves, so new chickens should be separated from the rest of the flock until they are large enough to defend themselves.

You need only one rooster for every 20 or fewer hens. In fact, you need *no* roosters at all unless you are planning for the hens to raise babies. Too many roosters is a bad idea since they are equipped with spurs on their legs and will fight each other unless the flock is large enough to accommodate the number of roosters. Roosters are not usually dangerous to humans, but there have been cases of attacks against small children, so it's good to keep an eye on kids who are playing in the same yard with roosters. In addition, if your flock has

⌄ With too few hens, roosters leave some bald spots.

fewer than 20 birds, the rooster will likely mount the chickens so often that they may develop bald spots.

I recommend the following breeds of general purpose chickens for a mini-farm: Rhode Island Red, New Hampshire, Wyandotte, Sussex, and Orpington. These breeds make good meat and eggs, will get broody and hatch their own eggs, and make good mothers. Especially important around kids or in suburbia, they have gentle dispositions. But don't be complacent, especially about roosters. If they feel that one of the hens is being endangered, they *will* attack, and once they do, breaking them of the habit is difficult.

Caring for Baby Chicks

All birds have requirements in common with any other livestock. They need special care during infancy, food, water, shelter, and protection from predators.

Chickens can be started as eggs in a commercial or home-built incubator. Most often, they are purchased as day-old chicks. They can be obtained at the local feed and seed store in the spring or ordered from a reputable firm such as McMurray Hatchery (www.mcmurrayhatchery.com), Fairview Hatchery (www.fairviewhatchery.com), or Stromberg's (www.strombergschickens.com). After hatching or arrival, baby birds should be provided with a brooder, food, and water. For a mini-farm-scaled operation, a brooder need be nothing more than an area enclosed on the sides free of drafts, an adjustable-height heat lamp, and a thermometer. (These products are available at agricultural supply stores.) The floor of the brooder should be smooth (like flat cardboard or newspapers) for the first few days until the chicks figure out

how to eat from the feeder, and then you can add some wood shavings. Make sure to clean all the droppings and replace the litter daily. Feeding and watering devices for baby birds are readily available.

When the baby chicks are first introduced to the brooder, duck their beaks briefly in the water so they recognize it as a water source. Just before hatching, chicks suck up the last of the yolk so they are all set for up to 24 hours without food after hatching, but you want them to have food and water as soon as possible.

Incubators and brooding areas must be thoroughly cleaned and disinfected before populating them in order to keep a disease called coccidiosis controlled. Coccidiosis is caused by a parasite that is spread through bird droppings and is more dangerous to baby birds than to adults. It is easy to tell if a baby bird has contracted the parasite because blood will appear in the droppings. Feed for baby birds is often formulated with an additive for conferring immunity to the parasite; some small-scale poultry farmers report that the disease can be controlled by adding one tablespoon of cider vinegar per quart to the birds' drinking water for

⊗ Baby chicks in a brooder made from plywood.

three days. Either way, the importance of cleanliness and disinfection in areas to be inhabited by baby birds can't be overemphasized.

Disinfection requires a thorough ordinary cleaning with soap and water to remove all organic matter followed by applying a suitable disinfectant for a sufficient period of time. A number of disinfectants are available including alcohols, phenolic compounds, quaternary ammonia disinfectants, and a large number of commercial products sold for that purpose. The most accessible suitable disinfectant is chlorine bleach diluted by adding 3/4 cup of bleach to one gallon of water. This requires a contact time of five minutes before being removed from the surface, then the area has to be well ventilated so it doesn't irritate the birds.

Baby chicks should be started on a type of feed called "starter crumbles" and kept on it for six to eight weeks or until fully feathered. Once fully feathered, they can go on layer rations and be put in the hen house. They don't usually start laying eggs until they are a little over 16 weeks old.

Vaccinations

You should check with the agricultural extension agent in your local area for vaccination recommendations. Poultry are prone to certain diseases, such as Newcastle disease, that are easily protected against by vaccination but are incurable once contracted and can easily wipe out a flock.

I order vaccination supplies from an online veterinary supply company—Jeffers Livestock—and administer the vaccinations myself. Most vaccines come in a size suitable for vaccinating 1,000 birds, which is not particularly suitable for a backyard flock. I vaccinate my laying chickens for Newcastle disease and infectious bronchitis (IB).

Newcastle disease is a highly contagious viral illness of birds that has been recognized since the 1920s. It manifests in various forms, some of which cause as much as 90% mortality in a flock. Newcastle disease infects and is spread by all manner of birds, and it is endemic throughout Western Europe and North America. Most birds don't experience the levels of mortality and debility that manifest in domestic chickens, though. It is primarily spread by droppings. In plain English, this means that all that is needed for your flock to be wiped out is for a sparrow to poop into your chicken yard while flying over. (As a side note, the virus causes a mild conjunctivitis in humans and is particularly toxic to cancer cells in humans while leaving normal cells practically unharmed. Research into this is ongoing.)

So vaccinating your flock is a good idea. Meanwhile, while the Newcastle vaccine is available on its own, it can also be purchased as a combined vaccine for IB.

IB is caused by a highly contagious coronavirus that mutates rapidly. While the immediate mortality rate from IB tends to be low, it can permanently damage the kidneys and reproductive tracts of chickens, hurts shell pigmentation, and makes the eggs unappetizing. Thus, especially if you visit the backyard flocks of other poultry owners, vaccinating your flock for IB makes sense.

So, now that you've decided to vaccinate your flock, how do you go about doing it? First you have to get the vaccine — which I order from Jeffers Livestock. Trouble is, the teeny-weeny 7 ml (less than two teaspoons) vial contains enough dosage for 1,000 chickens. For those of us with a smaller flock of 20 birds or so, it isn't practical to use the watering directions. So how do you administer the vaccine?

The vaccine comes with directions. If you can't find them, you can get them from the company Web site.

Two methods are of interest. The first is to use an included plastic dropper and administer one (very small) drop of vaccine into either the nostril or the eye of each bird. My birds are pretty tame. They jump up onto my shoulders to keep me company and have no real issue with me picking them up or handling them. So in my case, this method works just fine. I set up a chair in the chicken yard and bring a couple of pieces of bread with me, and as each chicken takes a turn jumping up onto my lap, I gently hold its head still and beak closed and put a drop on one nostril. I then briefly close the other nostril with a finger until the drop gets sucked in, give the chicken a piece of bread, and send it on its way.

But not all chickens are so friendly and cooperative. When I was a kid, we had some chickens who thought they were kamikazes or something, and securing their cooperation in such an endeavor was unlikely. So we vaccinated them through their drinking water.

The question is how do you translate dosage instructions intended for 1,000 birds so they work for a small flock of 10–30 birds? Here's how I do it.

I rehydrate the vaccine in the vial using high-quality bottled water. I shake it thoroughly and then dump it into a 100 ml graduated cylinder. I add water to bring the total volume to 100 ml. Now I know that each milliliter has enough vaccine for 10 birds. I set that aside.

Then I turn my attention to the waterer. I take it apart and clean it thoroughly with hot soapy water, rinse it thoroughly, and then dry it with paper towels. My water at home isn't chlorinated. If you have chlorinated water, do the final rinse with bottled water.

Then, I put 1 gallon of bottled water, 1 teaspoon of powdered milk, and 1 ml of vaccine for every 10 birds into the waterer and stir it up. Then I make sure that for the next 24 hours it is the *only* source of water available for the birds. The next day, I clean out the waterer thoroughly and then fill it up with my normal watering solution plus a vitamin supplement. The vaccines are *live virus* vaccines, and they put some stress on the birds, so I give them the vitamins to help them deal with that.

Speaking of live viruses—I should mention that if you aren't careful while playing with this vaccine, you'll get a mild case of conjunctivitis—also known as "pink eye"—or maybe some cold-like symptoms. Nothing serious though.

While I use this method for the Newcastle vaccine, it will also work for other vaccines that are dosed for larger flocks.

Antibiotics

Sometimes vaccinating chickens makes them sick, and they need medicine. Other times, they will get sick from germs you have brought home on your shoes from visiting someone else who has chickens or even from buying a couple of adult birds and introducing them to the flock—even if you keep them in a separated space for 10 days beforehand, which you should always do.

This is a tough situation. If you are raising birds organically and they need antibiotics and you use

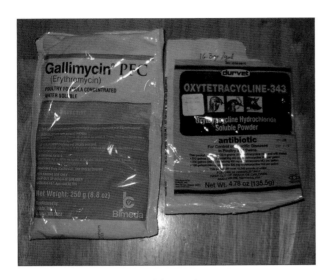

⊗ Antibiotics commonly used for poultry.

while the meat is safe to eat one day following discontinuance of erythromycin, I have no data indicating that the eggs are ever safe to eat again. So laying chickens treated with erythromycin to cure illness should be transitioned into being meat birds and replaced with new layers.

As with vaccines, antibiotics are usually packaged in sizes suitable for much larger flocks, but a bit of math will let you know how much to use. One thing you will definitely need, though, is an accurate scale weighing in grams. Digital scales used to be quite expensive but can now be found for less than $30.

them, the chickens are no longer organic—so you may be stuck destroying the birds.

The most likely reason you would resort to antibiotics with chickens is respiratory illness. These sorts of illnesses aren't all bacterial—some are viral and unaffected by antibiotics. Nevertheless, I have found that most often the respiratory illnesses characterized by wheezing and nasal discharge or sneezing have all responded.

Antibiotics will find their way into the eggs of laying birds, so the eggs should be broken and added to the compost pile during treatment and for a week afterward. The two most common antibiotics used for chickens are variants of tetracycline and erythromycin, both of which are available mail order or right in the feed store without a prescription. A study of tetracycline residues in eggs found that on the second day after finishing treatment, any residues in the eggs were undetectably low.[49] So disposing of the eggs for seven days following treatment is fine. On the other hand,

Food

During the active growing season, birds will provide about half of their own food by foraging if the farmer keeps the size of the flock suitable for the area being foraged, but during the winter and for the first weeks after hatching, they will need to be given commercial feed. (The amount of pasture required per bird depends on the type of vegetation being grown in the area. Start with 300 square feet per bird, and adjust from there.) You can also feed grain and vegetable leftovers—such as bread and pasta—to your chickens. Technically, you can feed them meat as well, but I would avoid the practice because too many diseases are being spread these days by feeding meat to livestock—things like mad cow disease that can spread to humans and is incurable. A small flock of birds will be much less expensive to feed than a house cat, and the feed is readily available at agricultural stores. A number of bird feeders are available commercially, or they can be built by the farmer. Make sure that whatever you use for a feeder, it can be raised or lowered so that its lip

[49] Donahue, D., Hairston, H. (1999) Oxytetracycline transfer into egg yolks and albumen, *Poultry Science* 78 pp. 343–345

is even with the backs of the birds. Building the feeder this way, and never filling it more than half full of feed will significantly reduce the amount of feed, that ends up on the floor since chickens have to raise their heads to swallow.

If birds are used for pest control, a fencing system should be created that allows the birds to forage in and around beds that are sown with cover crops but not in beds growing food crops A small flock of birds will devastate a garden in short order because they like to eat most things that humans eat. They make excellent manure that should be added to the compost pile if gathered. Otherwise, just leave it in the beds containing cover crops to naturally degrade and provide free fertilizer for the next growing season.

Commercial feed comes in many varieties. Both medicated and nonmedicated versions of mash, crumbles, and pellets are available. If you specify it is for laying hens, the clerk at the store will know exactly what you need. The medicated versions aren't typically necessary. You can also buy a mix of cracked corn and rye called "scratch feed." Scratch is about half the price of regular feed but is not, in and of itself, a complete ration— although chickens tend to prefer it over regular feed. All feeds are very attractive to rodents, easily rotted by water, and a lure for grain moths, so they should be kept in metal storage containers with tight-fitting lids.

One winter, I kept a feeder with both scratch and regular feed available in the coop for the birds that were confined while the snow was deep. I also kept bales of alfalfa hay in the coop, covered with a tarp. Because the birds preferred the scratch to the complete ration, they became nutritionally deficient and sought to make up the difference by eating the hay. One of the hens developed

⊗ Containers for keeping feed safe from pests.

an obstruction of her crop this way and had to be euthanized. So I have learned not to provide scratch while the chickens are confined, especially if an edible litter—like hay—is used.

What we do instead, when the chickens must be confined because of bad weather, is provide a daily bunch of greens such as lettuce or kale to supplement their feed. This helps give the yolks a nice color and keeps the chickens from getting bored.

Housing

All birds have similar housing requirements though their habits are a bit different. A coop should be built for the birds with about three square feet of floor space per bird. Technically, as few as two square feet can be adequate for chickens, and ducks require only three square feet each, but the coop should be sized to account for temporary increases in flock size during the spring and summer. For a flock of 20 birds, which is the largest practical flock for a small lot, that means a 100-square-foot coop—a size that can be accommodated in a number of configurations such as

8 × 12, 10 × 10, and so forth. Enough floor space helps to reduce stress on the birds and prevents behavior problems. The most prevalent behavior problem resulting from inadequate living space is chickens pecking each other, which can lead to infections and other problems.

The subject of construction techniques required to build a chicken coop is beyond the scope of a book on farming. McMurray Hatchery (www.mcmurrayhatchery.com) has two suitable chicken house plans including a complete bill of materials for less than $15 each as of this writing. Judy Pangman has also written *Chicken Coops*, a comprehensive book containing 45 illustrated plans for chicken coops to suit every circumstance and budget.

For our chicken coop, I used a product called Star Plates available from Stromberg's Chickens. It allows for building a floor in the shape of a

⊗ Some hen houses are an exercise in geometry, but they don't need to be.

⊗ Nearly completed chicken coop.

pentagon and an extremely strong and secure shelter. It also, per square foot, works out to be less expensive than many other approaches plus allows for a natural draft when used with a small cupola.

No matter which way you'd like to build a coop, I'd like to convey a few aspects of coops that I believe to be important.

First, a coop needs to have a smooth floor, made out of plywood, for example, that is well coated with polyurethane or a similar substance that is impervious to moisture and easily cleaned or disinfected. The floor should be strewn with wood shavings, peat moss, or a similar clean absorbent material that is replaced anytime it becomes excessively damp or dirty in order to prevent infections. Some experts recommend against using hay, but that is precisely what we use without any difficulties as long as we don't store the hay bails in the coop.

Second, any windows should be made out of Plexiglas rather than real glass and preferably located high enough on a wall that the chickens can't get to it easily. That way they won't be tempted to fly into it and break their necks.

Third, even the smallest omnivores, like mice and rats, can cause serious problems in a bird coop, so it is important to construct the coop in a fashion that will exclude even the smallest predators. I learned this lesson the hard way back when I was 12 years old and a rat got into our chicken coop and managed to kill three adolescent birds. The easiest way to achieve this is to build the coop on pilings.

Finally, nests should be provided. These are most easily built onto the walls in such a way that the birds can get into them easily via the roosts and they are up away from the floor. Ducks, being more secretive, prefer a covered nesting box on the floor. Nests should be filled with straw, wood shavings, or peat and kept clean. The farmer should provide half as many nests as there are birds.

Because of the way the noses of birds are designed, birds cannot create suction with their beaks. As a result, they have to raise their heads

⌄ Adequate and comfortable nesting boxes are important.

to swallow. What this means in practical terms is that birds sling water all over the place and make the litter on the floor of the coop wet if the lip of a watering device is too low. If the lip of the watering device is even with the level of the backs of the birds, the mess created will be substantially reduced. It is more important with some birds than others, and particularly important with turkeys, to make sure plenty of water is available anytime they are given feed in order to avoid choking. Water provided should be clean and free of debris, and the container should be designed to keep birds from standing in it or roosting on it. If birds stand in or roost over the water source, they will certainly contaminate it with droppings.

Many books on poultry cover the lighting arrangements needed to maximize growth or egg laying. Light affects the hormonal balance in birds and therefore affects when a bird will molt (lose and replace its feathers), lay eggs, desire mating, and so forth. When birds molt, they temporarily stop laying eggs, which is a big deal on a commercial scale. Likewise, egg production naturally decreases as the amount of available light decreases. All of this can be affected by controlling the amount of light that birds receive and, to a lesser degree, the food supply.

This brings up a fundamental difference in the mind-set of a mini-farmer who is raising birds as compared to a large commercial enterprise. In a large commercial enterprise, the life span of a laying chicken is about 16 months because it has been pushed to its physical limits by that time and has outlived its usefulness in terms of the cost of food and water that it consumes compared to the wholesale value of eggs in a commodity market. Likewise, because it has laid eggs daily without respite since reaching adulthood,

the minerals in its body have become depleted and the quality of the egg shells has declined. So by the time a chicken is 16 months old, it is consigned to the compost heap because it isn't even good for eating.

A mini-farmer can have a different outlook because the birds are multipurpose. The birds serve to consume pests and reduce the costs of gardening, consume leftovers, produce fertilizer, provide amusement with their antics, and lay eggs or provide meat for the table. The economic equation for the mini-farmer is strikingly different, so the treatment of the birds will likewise be different. If birds are allowed to molt when the seasons trigger molting and come in and out of egg production naturally because of seasonal light changes, they are subjected to considerably less stress, and their bodies are able to use dormant periods to recover lost minerals and nutrients. In this way, it is not at all unusual for nonspecialized

⊗ A radiant heater behind the roosts keeps chickens warm in cold winter climates.

bird breeds to live several years with moderate productivity.

One other thing to consider if you live further north is the need for heat in the coop. Where we live, temperatures below zero are not uncommon, and there can be days in a row with temperatures never budging out of the teens. In these conditions, their water can freeze, and they can suffer frostbite. The water is easily dealt with via a simple water fount heater available at agricultural supply stores. For general heating of the coop, mine is insulated using thermal reflective insulation, and I've installed a simple 400W flat-panel radiant heater behind the roosts so the chickens can stay warm at night.

Collecting and Cleaning Eggs

Chickens usually lay midmorning, but there's no predicting it completely. They're chickens, after all, and lay when they are good and ready. Ideally, you should collect the eggs immediately, but this is seldom practical—especially if, like me, you work a regular job. I've never had a problem with freshness simply collecting the eggs when I get home from work and putting them in the refrigerator immediately.

There are a couple of phenomena pertaining to eggs that may become an inconvenience: dirty and broken eggs. Every once in a while, chickens will lay an egg that has a thin shell and breaks while in the nest. Sometimes, they may lay an egg with no shell at all. When these break, they coat any other eggs in the nest with a slime that makes them unmarketable. Obviously, the proverbial ounce of prevention applies in that having enough nesting boxes will reduce the number of eggs coated with slime in any given box. However, chickens tend to "follow the leader" to an extent and have a decided tendency to lay eggs in a nesting box where another egg is already present. So even if you put up one nesting box for each bird, this problem wouldn't be solved completely.

Then, of course, there is the problem presented by the fact that eggs leave the body of a hen through the exact same orifice used for excrement. Meaning that sometimes eggs will have a bit of chicken manure on them. Not usually, but sometimes. In addition, chickens who have been running around outside in the mud on a rainy day will track mud back into the nest and make the eggs dirty.

For minor dirt and manure, just scraping it off with a thumbnail or using a sanding sponge is fine. But for slime and major dirt that won't come off easily, water washing is required.

Water washing can be extremely problematic and yield unsafe eggs if done improperly. When the egg comes out of the hen, it has a special coating that, as long as it is kept dry, protects the

Farm-fresh eggs are easy to sell as they are qualitatively superior to even the best store-bought eggs.

interior of the egg from being contaminated by anything on the shell. But once the shell becomes wet, the semipermeable membrane of the shell can be compromised, and a temperature differential can cause a partial vacuum inside the egg that sucks all of the bacteria on the shell inside—thus creating an egg that is unsafe.

Nevertheless, the techniques and technology for properly water washing an egg are very mature and well understood. Special egg-washing machines exist, but on the scale of a mini-farm, they are so expensive (about $6,000) they don't make sense economically. One alternative that I haven't tried yet is a product called "The Incredible Egg Washer" that sells for less than $120. But let me tell you about the safe and low-cost technique that I use for our small-scale operation.

First, clean your sink and work area thoroughly, and get a roll of paper towels so they are handy. Next, make a sanitizing solution from the hottest tap water by mixing two tablespoons of bleach with one gallon of water. You can multiply this by adding four tablespoons of bleach to two gallons of water, and so on. Put the sanitizer in a cleaned watering can and the eggs in a wire basket. Pour the sanitizing solution over the eggs very generously, making certain to wet all surfaces thoroughly. Wait a couple of minutes, and then use a paper towel that has been dipped in sanitizer to clean the egg. Use a fresh paper towel for each egg. Then, rinse them very thoroughly with sanitizing solution and then set them aside to dry on a wire rack. It's important to let them dry before putting them in egg cartons, because wet eggs tend to stick to egg carton materials.

The Broody Hen

Sooner or later, you are going to run into a hen who is very interested in hatching some eggs. If that is part of your plan—great! She'll sit on any egg, so take some others from adjacent nests that were laid that day, and slide those under her too. If, as in my coop, the standard laying nests are up in the air, make her a new nest that is closer to the ground—6 to 12 inches. That way, once the chicks are hatched, they won't hurt themselves if they fall out of the nest.

Usually, though, when a hen goes broody, you don't want it to happen. The hen will sit on the eggs, keeping them at a high temperature, so that when you collect them a few hours later, they have runny whites and just aren't fresh anymore. Just collecting the eggs out from under her for a while won't work—she'll just keep setting forever. The solution to this problem is a "broody cage."

A broody cage is any cage fashioned with a wire bottom and containing no litter. I've used a small portable rabbit cage for the purpose. If you keep a broody hen in this for 36 to 48 hours, it will break her of the desire to sit on the eggs. It is extremely important that you provide adequate food and water in the cage or you will force her to go into molt.

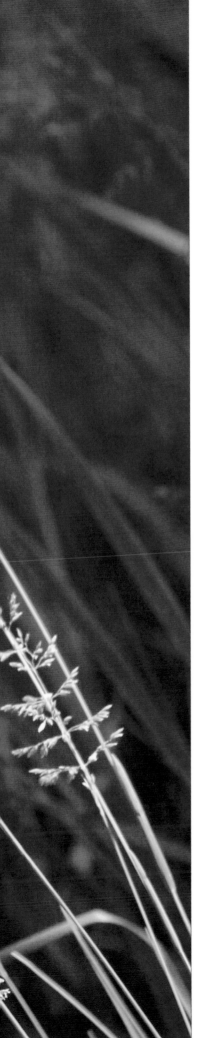

Raising Chickens for Meat

16

A lot of people are squeamish about killing animals of any sort for food. Still others have moral or religious objections to the practice. If you have moral or religious objections, please skip to the next chapter as there is plenty of other information elsewhere in this book to help you raise a healthy diet without meat. If you are merely squeamish, though, this chapter may put you at ease. Be forewarned, though, that this chapter contains graphic pictures of chicken slaughter.

Selecting Chickens

For sheer efficiency, the easiest choice is to order day-old Cornish cross chicks from your local agricultural supply store. These are also known as "broilers." These are bred to grow quickly with lower feed requirements and to pluck easily. These are a sort of hybrid franken-chicken and are simply voracious eating machines. In fact, they eat so much and gain so much weight so fast that they may start dropping dead or breaking their legs from sheer weight anytime after 12 weeks of age.

⊗ Broilers gathered around a waterer.

Another way to obtain chickens for meat is to let a couple of hens stay broody in the spring and raise a handful of chicks to broiler size by fall. Come fall, pick all the new roosters to be meat birds, plus any of the older hens that aren't laying, leaving yourself with a flock around the same size you started with in the spring—about 10 to 20. The meat birds get processed in the fall, vacuum sealed, and frozen. You should take newly hatched chicks and raise them in the brooder, and thenceforth keep them separate from your regular laying birds. Otherwise, your hens will figure out that you've killed them and get spooked, and your rooster will get aggressive.

Housing for Meat Birds

Unlike chicks of other breeds, broilers can usually be removed from the brooder at about four weeks old because they are pretty well feathered, and it's during a warm time of the year. This is good, because otherwise they'd outgrow the brooder. Regular layingbirds raised for meat should be kept in the brooder for six weeks before going outside.

Meat birds are around for only three months of the year, at most, so permanent housing doesn't make as much sense for them as it does with laying hens. What a lot of small farmers use, and we use one too, is a device called a "chicken tractor." A chicken tractor is a portable enclosure that lets the chickens get fresh air and fresh grass. It is moved every day so the chickens don't end up lying around in their own excrement.

There are about a million ways to make a chicken tractor. Just search on the Internet, and you'll find hundreds of designs, many for free. Your choice of design should allow for about four square feet per bird. Many designs are completely enclosed to exclude predators and keep birds from escaping. So far, I've had no real predator problems, and the Cornish crosses that we grow are too heavy to fly, so our chicken tractor is on wheels and has sides made of only three feet of chicken wire.

Feeding Meat Birds

Meat birds should receive a starter/grower from the day they arrive until the week before they are processed. The week before, they should be put on a leaner ration. For this you can use either a finishing feed or ordinary layer crumbles like you give your laying hens. As broilers, particularly, seem to have a nearly insatiable appetite, you should feed them by weight according to the directions on the bag.

⊗ The easiest housing for meat birds is a chicken tractor.

Some breeds of meat birds will forage while in the chicken tractor, but the broiler crosses will mostly just lay around and eat feed. So you shouldn't count on forage providing a lot of their food.

Slaughtering Birds

As a kid, my family raised chickens, and sometimes I got stuck with plucking them, which seemed to take forever and was less than pleasant. But then I got older and wiser and learned of better ways!

Food should be withdrawn from birds destined for slaughter 12 hours before the appointed

⊗ A killing cone. They don't need to be this elaborate.

time, though continuation of water is advisable. This precaution will make sure no food is in the upper digestive tract and thus reduce the possibility of contaminating the meat with digestive contents.

Usually, you should not carry a bird by its feet due to the potential for spinal damage, but for purposes of slaughter it is acceptable if done gently. Catch the bird by its feet and immediately hold it upside down. Swing it a little on its way to the killing cone, and it should settle down. Provide support for its back while carrying if needed. Then insert it head down in the killing cone.

The proper way to slaughter a bird, except for farmers whose religions specify another method, is to cut off the bird's head while the bird is either hanging from its feet or inserted upside down in a funnel-type device called a "killing cone." Use a good, sharp, strong knife for this. Put a leather glove on your weak hand, and grab the bird's head, holding its beak closed. Then, take the knife and cut off the head in one smooth motion. Once the head has been removed, any squawks or twitches observed thereafter are a result of pattern-generating neurons in the spinal cord and *not* conscious volition. I checked with my local veterinarian on this, and he assured me that cutting off the chicken's head is entirely humane. When the head is cut off, the neck will flex all over the place, splattering blood everywhere. I put a piece of Plexiglass in front of the killing cone to avoid getting blood on me. The bird should bleed out in 65 seconds or less, but it doesn't hurt to leave it for a couple of minutes because you don't want to scald a bird if it still has a breathing reflex because it could inhale water while being scalded.

Hanging the bird upside down or using a killing cone is important for two reasons. First,

⊗ A proper knife makes slaughtering easier.

it helps remove the greatest possible amount of blood from the bird's tissues, which presents a more appetizing appearance. Second, it helps keep the bird from struggling and hurting itself.[50] Blood collected from the bird can be added to the compost pile. If a killing cone isn't used, a noose can be used to hang the bird upside down by the feet.

A killing cone, mentioned previously, is a funnel-shaped device with a large hole on the top into which the bird is inserted headfirst. The hole in the bottom is large enough that the bird's head and neck stick out, but nothing else. The entire device is usually about a foot long. Killing cones can be purchased via a number of poultry suppliers, just be sure to order the correct size for the birds being killed. They are simple enough that anyone can make one from sheet metal and rivets, and many people have improvised by cutting the top off of a small traffic cone.

Once the bird has been killed, it needs to be scalded and then plucked. In scalding, the bird is dipped and then moved around in hot water for 60 to 90 seconds to break down the proteins that hold the feathers in place. Commercial processors use rather elaborate multistage arrangements for this process, but a mini-farmer simply needs to have a bucket of water of the correct temperature ready. Most on-farm slaughtering processes for chickens and guineas use what is called a *hard scald* that loosens the feathers and removes the outer layer of skin. For this, the water temperature should be between 138 and 148 degrees.[51] This temperature range is sufficiently important that it should be measured with a thermometer.

For a small operation, the easiest way to get the right temperature is to fill a five-gallon bucket half full of water and insert a thermometer. Slowly add boiling water from a large pot on the stove until the temperature of the water in the bucket is on the high side of the recommended range. Then, once the bird has been killed, grab it by the feet and hold it under the water for 60 to 90 seconds, sloshing it up and down slightly. The timing on this has some room for flexibility, so you can just count. If more than one bird is being processed, keep an eye on the temperature and add boiling water whenever the thermometer drops close to the low side of the recommended temperature range. The water should be replaced every dozen chickens, any time it has been allowed to sit unused for a half hour or more, or any time the water has obviously been contaminated with feces. In the case of broilers, this is usually for every chicken.

[50] Mercia, L. (2000) *Storey's Guide to Raising Poultry*

[51] Fanatico, A. (2003) *Small Scale Poultry Processing*

⊗ The first incarnation of the Markham Farm chicken plucker.

Once the bird has been scalded, the feathers are removed in a process known as plucking. It is easiest to hang the bird by its feet and use both hands to grab the feathers and pull them out. If the bird was killed and scalded correctly, this shouldn't take long, although it *is* messy. The feathers can be added to a compost pile and are an excellent source of nitrogen. A few small "pin feathers" will remain on the bird, and these can be removed by gently pressing with the back side of a butter knife. A few hairs will also remain, and these can be singed off by going very quickly over the carcass with a propane torch. If you process a lot of chickens, you might consider an automated plucker that is easily made at home. The most impressive homemade plucker is the Whizbang Chicken Plucker, designed by Herrick Kimball, and the plans are in his book titled *Anyone Can Build a Tub-Style Chicken Plucker*. I have designed a less expensive table-style chicken plucker and have included complete plans, parts list, and photos in the next chapter.

The bird's entrails should now be removed in a process called evisceration.

1 Loosen the bird's crop, which is between the breast meat and the skin, by following the esophagus down to the crop and loosening it. As you'll note, I wear disposable gloves for processing.

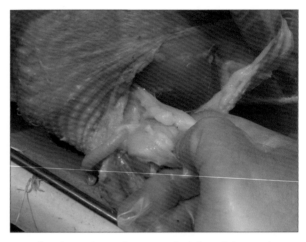

⊗ In this photo, the trachea is on the left and the esophagus is on the right.

2 A sharp knife is used to carefully (so as not to puncture any intestines and contaminate the meat) make an incision from the vent in the skin of the abdomen up to the breast bone. There will likely be a layer of fat there, which you can carefully pull apart by hand.

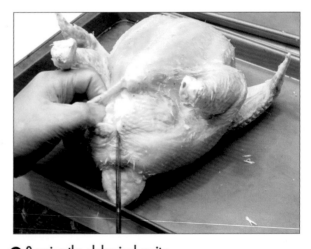

⊗ Opening the abdominal cavity.

3   The viscera are carefully removed by hand. With the breast facing up, just reach your hand into the body cavity as far as you can.

⊗ Reach your hand deeply into the cavity.

4   Gently grab a handful of viscera, and pull it completely out of the body cavity. Then scrape the lungs off the backbone. (They are bright pink.) Some people save the heart, liver, and gizzard. If you do, separate them from the rest of the viscera and refrigerate them immediately.

⊗ You may need to remove a couple of handfuls of entrails.

5   Cut out the vent, being careful not to contaminate the bird with the contents. Use a garden hose to wash out the body cavity afterward.

⊗ Carefully cut out the vent.

6   Turn the bird on its back and cut off the neck. A lot of folks use the neck for making chicken stock, so if you do, it should be refrigerated immediately.

⊗ Put the bird on its back and cut off the neck.

7 Turn the bird right-side up and cut off the oil gland.

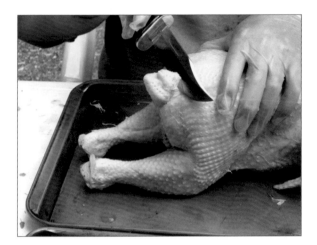

⊘ Don't forget to remove the oil gland.

8 Now, give the chicken a thorough inside and out rinse with the garden hose and put the completed whole chicken in a tub of ice water. Make sure to keep an eye on the ice and keep it cold! I add a tablespoon of bleach (to kill germs) and a cup of salt (to pull residual blood out of the meat) to the water, but neither is strictly necessary. If you can keep the water ice cold for four hours before freezing the bird, it will be more tender than it would be if frozen immediately.

⊘ Monitor the ice water to make sure it remains icy.

Bird blood, feathers, entrails, and other parts can be composted just like anything else, although many books on composting say to avoid it. Many authors counsel to avoid animal tissues in compost because they can be attractive to stray carnivores and rodents and because in a casual compost pile, sufficiently high temperatures to kill human pathogens may not be achieved. But if you make thermophilic compost, the only precautions needed are to make sure that any big parts of the bird are cut up and that the parts are buried in the middle of the pile with plenty of vegetable matter. In this way, the compost itself acts as a biofilter to stop any odors, and the high-carbon vegetable matter, combined with the high-nitrogen bird parts, will form seriously thermophilic compost in short order. Consequently, the nutrients that the birds took from the land are returned to the land in a safe and efficient manner.

17

The Markham Farm Chicken Plucker

If you are processing only 1 or 2 chickens for meat, just plucking by hand is fine. But we usually process 10 to 15 chickens at a time, and under those conditions plucking becomes too time-consuming for efficiency. I had tried the cheap drill attachments with no luck, and building my own tub-style chicken plucker seemed awfully expensive—hundreds of dollars—to make economic sense. We needed something that could be built much less expensively and still do a good job; thus arose our own chicken plucker design that I'll be sharing with you.

Construction

1   Use the two 7-1/2-inch pieces and two 12-inch pieces of 2 × 4 lumber to construct the drum holder as illustrated, using two deck screws for each union. The center of the second cross-piece is 3-1/4 inch from the connected end. Drill 3/16-inch holes at 1-1/8 inches and 4-3/8 inches from the free ends of the 12-inch pieces. When done, paint the piece and let it dry.

Parts List

1	12" long 1/2" diameter steel shaft	Grainger Part # 5JW35
2	½" Pillow block bearings	Grainger Part # 2X897
2	4" sheaves for 1/2" diameter shaft	Grainger Part # 3X909
1	10" spoked sheave for 1/2" diameter shaft	Grainger Part # 3X934
1	4L V-belt, 1/2" × 54"	
1	2" sheave to fit whatever motor you are using	
1	1/4–1/2 hp motor; 1600–1800 RPM	
1	Piece of 4" diameter PVC pipe, cut 6.5" long	
25	Chicken Plucker fingers	Stromberg's Item # FIN
2	7-1/2" pieces of 2 × 4 lumber	
2	12" pieces of 2 × 4 lumber	
1	24" pieces of 2 × 6 lumber	
1	12" × 20" piece of flat wood 1-1/2" thick	
4	1/4" × 2" lag bolts with 1/2" drive heads	
4	1/4" flat washers	
1	4-1/4" T-hinge with screws	
2	4-1/2" lag bolts	
12	2-1/2" deck screws	
1	12" × 10" piece of 1/4" plywood	
Paint		

Additional hardware as needed to mount the motor to the piece of 2 × 6 board.

⊗ Unpainted drum holder.

2 Cut off a piece of 4-inch PVC pipe that is 6-1/2 inches long, and then use a flexible ruler (like the kind you get in the sewing section) to put four longitudinal lines evenly spaced every 3-1/2 inches around the circumference.

3 Mark two of the lines opposite each other at 1-1/4 inch, 2-9/16 inch, 3-7/8 inch, and 5-1/4 inch from one end. Mark the other pair of opposite lines at 1-15/16 inches, 3-1/4 inches and 4-9/16 inches from the same end. Then use a 3/4-inch spade bit to bore holes centered on each mark. After, pull plucker fingers

⊗ Plucker drum marked longitudinally.

⊗ Plucker drum with fingers installed.

until they sit in each hole. This will require some muscle!

4 Complete the drum by inserting the sheaves (with tightening screw facing outboard) into either end of the drum, running the shaft through both sheaves, aligning the outside edge of each sheave with the outside edge of the drum, and then tightening the sheaves to the shaft. Then, secure the sheaves to the drum with epoxy. For this sort of work, I prefer the putty type. Set aside while the epoxy cures.

5 Paint the large board and allow it to dry. Then, insert the steel loop. On the large board, the loop should be 1-1/2 inches from the rear edge and 4-3/4 inches from the right edge. Use pilot holes to keep the steel loops from splitting the boards. Use screws to secure the rectangular end of the T-hinge on the big board with the hinge facing up, the back 8-1/4 inches from the back edge of the board, and the right 1-7/8 inches from the right edge of the board.

6 Paint the 2 × 6 board and allow it to dry. Insert the steel loop centered and

⊗ Completed plucker drum.

⊗ The large board with hinge and hook installed.

1-1/2-inch from the top edge and install mounting hardware for the motor as necessary to position the shaft 13-3/4 inches from the bottom and facing left.

7   Connect the 2 × 6 board to the large board using the T-hinge such that the right edge of the 2 × 6 board is 1-1/4 inches from the right edge of the large board, and then mount the motor to the 2 × 6 board.

8   Attach the drum holder you made in Step 1, holes facing up, to the front of the large board with the left side of the drum holder aligned with the left side of the large board and the rear edge of the drum holder 4-1/2-inch back from the front edge of the large board. Use deck screws drilled in from the bottom of the large board into the long boards of the drum holder.

9   Slide the shafts on either end of the drum into the pillow block bearings, mount the bearings to the drum holder using the 1/4-inch lag bolts and washers, and then loosen the Allen screws in the sheaves so that the shaft is even with the end of the left-hand bearing and projecting a few inches out of the right-hand bearing. Make sure the Allen screws on both bearings are facing left and that the drum is centered and moves freely; then tighten down

⊗ Recycled 2 × 6 board with hook and hardware.

The 2 × 6 board and the large board connected with the T-hinge.

the Allen screws on the bearings and sheaves. Finally, attach the large spoked sheave to the right side of the shaft with the Allen screw facing to the right.

10 Place the entire machine on a stable flat surface with the drum portion hanging off the edge. Run a V-belt between the sheave on the motor and the sheave that rotates the drum. Adjust the sheaves on their respective shafts

until both are in the same plane. Then attach a bungee cord between the two steel loops to keep tension on the belt. Depending on your arrangement, you may need to use an alternative such as steel wire and a turnbuckle for tensioning.

11 Cut a slot suitable for allowing the shaft to pass through the 1/4-inch plywood, and then paint it and allow it to dry. Finally, attach it to the long right arm of the drum holder with short

The plucker drum and bearings mounted on the drum holder.

The drum holder attached to the large board.

⊗ Plucker with belt and tensioner installed.

⊗ Safety shield installed. Keep hands away from the belt and pulleys!

wood screws so that it prevents chicken parts from being caught in the spoked sheave.

About the Motor and Electrical Safety

My first plucker with this design was made using a motor I had picked up at a yard sale for $2, but the design illustrated here features a 1/4 horsepower farm-duty motor I purchased for $110. The motor should be wired according to the directions that came with it, paying close attention to make sure that it is turning clockwise (when viewed from the rear) and properly grounded. The clockwise turning means the chicken feathers will go down toward the ground rather than up into your face during operation.

Because chickens are wet from the scald while being plucked, there is a hazard with water being around electricity. Therefore, it is extremely important that you plug this device into a terminal strip that contains an integral ground-fault circuit interrupter (GFCI). These are not cheap, but they could save your life from an unexpected electrical shock. Don't skip this.

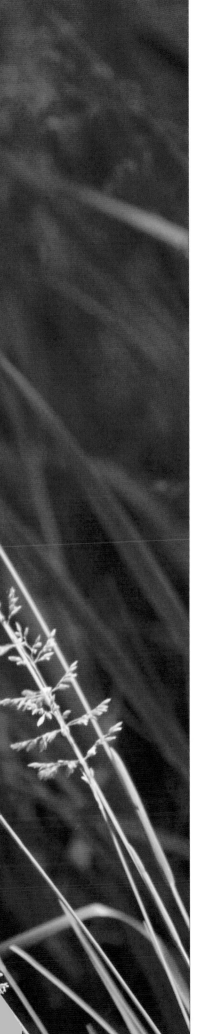

18

Public Domain Thresher Designs

The two main components of the I-Tech rice huller are a hand mill/ flour mill or grain grinder and a rubber-faced disk made from

- a rubber disk,
- a steel washer for mounting the rubber disk on the hand mill, and
- cyanoacrylate glue ("super glue" or "krazy glue") to attach the rubber disk onto the steel washer.

The stationary disk (A) is removed and replaced by a rubber-faced disk (B). Turning the auger handle (C) presses rice grains between the rubber-faced disk (B) and rotating disk (D), and then they are rolled out. The soft rubber disk allows the hulls to be removed with minimal damage to the rice kernels. Natural (gum) rubber is used for the rubber disk because it has better abrasion resistance than synthetic rubber. (The "Corona" hand mill is available from R&R Mill Co., 45 West First North Street, Smithfield, UT 84335, USA.)

Short-grain rice can be hulled at a rate of 200 g/min. The percentage of rice hulled varies from 75% to 99% depending on the rice cultivars, the spacing between the stationary rubber disk and the rotating abrasive disk, and the uniformity of spacing between the disks. A tin-plated steel

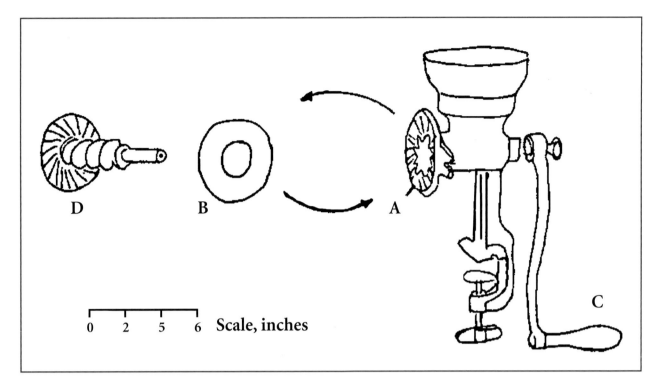

0   2   5   6   **Scale, inches**

D   B   A

C

❂ Standard grain grinder modified to husk rice and spelt.

burr disk may produce a black gum residue when hulling rice, until the tin is worn off. No black residue was found when using a cast iron disk or stone disk.

The grain huller also hulls millet (*Panicum miliaceum*), sesame (*Sesamum indicum*), and spelt wheat (*Triticum spelta*) as well as removes saponins from quinoa (*Chenopodium quinoa*). To "wet" hull sesame, soak the seeds in 1% (w: v) lye (sodium hydroxide) solution for 10 seconds to 5 minutes, then rinse with water and 1% solution of acetic acid (Shamanthaka Sastry et al., *J. Am. Oil Chem. Soc.* 46:592A, 1969; Moharram et al., *Lebensmit. Wissen. Tech.* 14:137, 1981). A steel burr disk is preferred for wet hulling sesame, while a stone disk is preferred for hulling spelt wheat.

A hand-operated rice huller has a (A) stationary disk, (B) rubber disk, (C) handle, and (D)

rotating disk with auger. Remove the stationary disk and replace with the rubber-faced disk.

In the United States, the C.S. Bell model 60 (cost: $325) and the Corona hand mill (cost: $40) represent two ends of the spectrum of hand mill quality. For serious hulling, the C.S. Bell is the better choice. This mill weighs 54 pounds, its auger shaft is supported by two bronze bearings with oilers, the grinding disks self-aligns and the mill can be motorized. The bronze bearing with oilers allow the shaft to rotate at 300 rpm without heating up (C.S. Bell, PO Box 291 Tiffin, OH 44883, phone 419-448-0791).

The Corona hand mill weighs 14 pounds, it has no bearings, the grinding disks do not self-align, and the mill cannot be motorized (R&R Mill Co., 45 West First North, Smithfield, UT 84335, phone 801-563-3333).

Conversion of a Leaf Shredder/Wood Chipper into a Grain Thresher

This invention was declared public domain August 1994, a gift to humanity.

A portable, engine-driven thresher can be made by modifying a leaf shredder/wood chipper or a hammer mill. Small shredders/chippers use five to eight horsepower gas engines that rotate at 2,800 or 3,600 revolutions per minute (rpm). The modification requires

- converting the free-swinging hammers into rasp bars,
- reducing the rotational speed of the hammers (250 to 1,000 rpm on a 12-inch diameter hammer arms), and
- altering the discharge port to allow smaller, threshed material to pass through a 3/8 to 3/4 inch screen while retaining larger materials.
- (Optional) If electricity is accessible, the gas engine can be replaced with a 1/2- to 3/4-horsepower capacitor start electric motor (1,725 rpm).

Materials: A five horsepower, 2,800 rpm "Roto-Hoe model 500" leaf shredder/wood chipper is used (see picture following the text). Additional parts include

4 2-inch C clamps (A),

6 5/8 × 3-inch bolts (B),

6 1/8 × 1-inch cotter pins (C),

1 5/8-inch inside diameter × 18-inch drip irrigation tubing or garden hose (D) as spacers between hammers, and

1 8 × 10-inch sheet metal or cardboard (E) to block the slotted portion of the leaf shredder/wood chipper exit port.

Modification: The Roto-Hoe shredder has six sets of three free-swinging hammers (F). Convert the six sets of hammers into six rasp bars as follows: Cut the 5/8-inch tubing (D) in segments to fit between the free-swinging hammers (F). Tie the free-swinging hammers (F) together by inserting the 5/8-inch bolt (B) into the hole of the first hammer, followed by a segment of tubing (D) as a spacer, then another hammer, followed by a second segment of tubing, followed by the third hammer. Drill a 5/32-inch hole on the threaded portion of the bolt that protrudes from the third hammer. Reassemble the bolt, hammers, and spacers together and lock the bolt in place with the cotter pin (C) installed in the 5/32-inch hole. This assembly constitutes a rasp bar. Repeat the above procedure and tie together the remaining five sets of free-swinging hammers. Manually rotate the rasp bars and check for clearance between the rasp bars and the walls of the threshing chamber. If there is insufficient clearance, adjust the bolt position, grind the bolt head, or cut the bolt length to obtain the necessary clearance between the rasp bars and the walls.

The Roto-Hoe shredder exit port consists of a slotted section and a 3/4-inch diameter punched-hole screen. Use the sheet metal or cardboard (E) and C clamps (A) to block the slotted portion of the exit port (G). The threshed grain exits through the 3/4-inch holes.

Start the engine and spin the rasp bars. Again, check for clearance between the rasp bars and the walls of the threshing chamber. If there is a knocking sound, grind the bolt down to obtain the necessary clearance.

Operation: Start the engine and spin the rasp bars. Dried plant materials with vines, stems, and leaves are fed in batches through the hopper. After

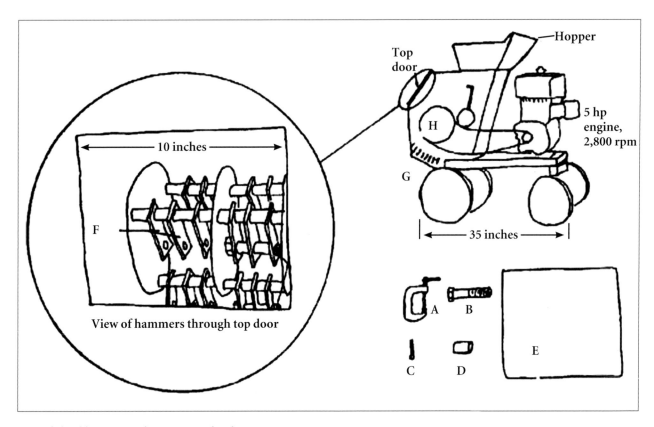

Labels within figure: Hopper, Top door, 5 hp engine, 2,800 rpm, H, G, 10 inches, F, 35 inches, A, B, C, D, E

View of hammers through top door

⊗ Leaf shredder converted into a grain thresher.

threshing for one to three seconds, open the top door to eject the longer vines, stems, and leaves that have not been chopped up. Seeds and small bits of plant material exit through the punched holes at the bottom. The mixture of seeds and plant material must be separated after threshing.

The 3/4-inch diameter holes in the exit port are suitable for larger seeds (e.g., beans) and seeds with loosely attached husks (e.g., wheat, bok choy, and amaranth). Small seeds and seeds with tight husk or pods (e.g., barley, clover, and radish) require smaller diameter exit holes to retain the larger unthreshed materials while passing the smaller threshed grains. This can be achieved by attaching a screen with smaller openings under the 3/4 inch diameter punched holes.

Larger seeds crack easier than smaller seeds. Reduce the rasp bar speed to decrease the percentage of cracked seeds. Use a larger pulley (H) and/or reduce the engine speed to achieve the desire rasp bar speed:

250–400 rpm for beans and large seeds
400–800 rpm coriander, radish, sunflower
600–1400 rpm wheat, oats, barley, rice, and small seeds

Typical threshing rates (pounds of seeds per hour):

Amaranth 66
Bok choy 22 to 30
Oats 94
Pinto bean 117
Soy bean 81 to 127

19

Preserving the Harvest

Since the purpose of a mini-farm is to meet a substantial portion of your food needs, you should store your food so that it is available over the course of the year. The four methods of food preservation that I use and will be explaining in this chapter are canning, freezing, dehydrating, and root cellaring. These methods have all been practiced for decades in the United States and can be undertaken with confidence. Each method has its strengths and weaknesses, which is why they are all covered. Advanced techniques that I won't be explaining in this chapter include cheese making, wine making, and meat curing.

Canning

Perhaps the most intimidating form of food preservation for the uninitiated is canning. Stories are everywhere about people dying from botulism because of improperly canned foods, so some people conclude that canning is an art like making fugu (the poisonous Japanese blowfish) in that the slightest mishap will render canned foods unfit. Fortunately, these impressions are not accurate. Modern canning methods are the result of decades of research and can be followed by anybody with a sixth-grade education. (Yes, I knew somebody personally with a sixth-grade education who canned safely.) Those few cases of poorly canned goods resulting in botulism poisoning in the modern era stem from people who do not follow the most basic directions on how to can.

Current standards for home canning come from research by the USDA that is continually updated. Most of the standards haven't changed for decades, because the research methods are quite thorough. The USDA researchers deliberately introduce viable heat-resistant bacteria spores into foods in home canning jars and then use temperature sensors inside the jars as they are canned. After canning, the cans are kept at the precise temperature necessary for best bacterial growth for several months and then opened in a sterile environment and tested for presence of the bacteria or any other spoilage.

The USDA standards published around World War I allowed for up to 2% spoilage, but the standards published since that time require 0% spoilage. This means that foods canned at home using current USDA guidelines are completely safe. Actually, the times and temperatures provided by the USDA also contain a safety factor. This means that if experimenters achieved 0% spoilage at 237 degrees for 11 minutes, the standards specify 240 degrees for 15 minutes. Times and temperatures are always rounded *up*, never down.

There are two methods of canning: boiling water bath and steam pressure. The choice of method depends on the level of acidity of the food being canned. This is because the length of time that spoilage organisms will survive at a given temperature is longer in foods that are *less* acidic. So less acidic foods get canned using the steam pressure method that produces a temperature of 240 degrees; more acidic foods get canned in a boiling water bath that produces temperatures of 212 degrees. The length of time specified for canning is based on how long it takes the heat to fully penetrate a particular food in a particular-sized jar. The standards are written for half-pint, pint, and quart jars. If a mixture (such as stew) is being canned, then the canning time and temperature for the entire mixture is based on that of the ingredient that requires the most time. By using the correct method, container, and processing time, you can be assured of the safety of your canned food.

Home Canning Jars

Jars for home canning are available at Walmart and many hardware and grocery stores, although their availability is seasonal. These jars are heavy walled and specifically designed to withstand the rigors of temperature, pressure, and vacuum created by home canning. Forget the old-style (though attractive) jars with rubber gaskets and wire closures since they are no longer recommended by the USDA. Today's standards specify two-piece caps that include a reusable metal ring called a "band" and a flat nonreusable lid that has a sealing compound around its outer edge. The bands can be used until they have warped or rusted, but the lids must be thrown away once they have been used and bought new.

Home canning jars are expensive—about $7/dozen at the time of writing. So figure a bit over $0.50 apiece. However, their durability easily justifies their cost—home canning jars will last decades. By the time a jar has seen use for 20 seasons, its cost has dropped to $0.02. Once the jars and bands are purchased (new jars usually come with bands), you just need to buy new lids for each use—which are usually less than $0.10 each. There are a handful of brands of home canning jars available, and on the basis of my own experience, I recommend Ball and Kerr, which are both manufactured in the United States by Jarden Corporation. I especially recommend Ball lids, because their underside is coated with a compound that keeps the food from coming into contact with the metal of the lid. This helps food stay fresher longer, and they cost the same as noncoated lids.

My stepmother often used glass jars from spaghetti sauce, mayonnaise, and similar products as long as the bands and lids fit and the rims were free from nicks or imperfections that would prevent a good seal. The good news is that she saved money. The bad news is that sometimes these jars would break and create a mess and lose the food. Most authorities counsel against using these one-trip glass jars because they aren't properly tempered, and their higher risk of breakage could cause injury and loss of valuable food. For these reasons, I recommend using jars specifically designed for home canning. If economy is a big consideration, then it is worthwhile to visit yard sales and flea markets where you can buy inexpensive, properly designed jars for home canning.

Foods and Canning Methods

As I mentioned earlier, the type of canning method required depends on how acidic the food is. Acidic foods (with a pH of less than 4.6) need only a water bath canning method while less acidic foods (with a pH greater than 4.6) require steam pressure canning. Unfortunately, the combination of time and temperature in a pressure canner can render some foods less nutritious and other foods unappetizing. Broccoli is a good example in that it requires such an extensive period of pressure canning to be safe that the results aren't worth eating. Broccoli is much better preserved through either freezing or pickling. The goal, then, is to use the method that preserves the maximum nutrition and palatability while maintaining a good margin of safety. So if I don't list a canning method for a vegetable (Table 19, page 198), it is because I have determined that it is better preserved using some other method.

An age-old method for canning foods that cannot be safely canned otherwise is to raise the acidity of the food by either fermenting it or adding vinegar. Sauerkraut is a great example because cabbage is not suitable for either canning or freezing in its fresh state, but if acidified through lactic acid fermentation (and thereby becoming sauerkraut), it can be canned in a boiling water bath while retaining its most important health benefits. (Technically, with great care, you can freeze grated cabbage, but your results may vary.) Pickles are made either by fermenting vegetables in a brine (which raises their acidity through the production of lactic acid) and/or by adding vinegar. These methods create a sufficiently acidic product so that only a brief period in a water bath canner is required.

Boiling water bath canning is suitable for all fruits, jams, jellies, preserves, and pickles. Tomatoes are right at the margin of pH 4.6, so they can be safely canned in a boiling water bath if a known amount of citric acid (or commercial bottled lemon juice) is added. The correct amount is one tablespoon of lemon juice or 1/4 teaspoon of citric acid per pint. Vinegar can be used instead, at the rate of two tablespoons per pint, but it can cause off-flavors. The only time I would recommend vinegar is in salsa. The acidity (or, rather, the *taste* of the acidity) can be offset by adding two tablespoons of sugar for every tablespoon of lemon juice, which won't interfere with the canning process. While few people choose to can figs (usually they are dehydrated instead), it is worth noting that they are right on the border line of acidity as well and should have lemon juice added in the same proportion as tomatoes if they are being canned. Everything else—vegetables, meats, seafood, and poultry—*must* be canned in a steam pressure canner.

Boiling water canners are pretty much maintenance free. Just wash them like any other pot, and you are done. Pressure canners, on the other hand, require some minimal maintenance. The the accuracy of the dial gage on top of the canner should be checked annually by your Cooperative Extension Service. If it is inaccurate, send it to the manufacturer for recalibration. When the canner is not in use, store it with the lid turned upside down on top of the body. Never immerse the lid or dial gage in water! Instead, clean them with a damp cloth and mild detergent if needed. Clean any vent holes with a pipe cleaner. The rubber seal should be removed and cleaned with a damp cloth after each use. Some manufacturers recommend that the gasket be given a light coat of vegetable oil, and some don't—so be certain to follow the manufacturer's directions. If you follow manufacturer's directions in using your pressure canner, it won't explode, as was sometimes the case years ago. Modern canners have a number of built-in safety features that our grandmothers' models lacked, and aside from deliberately defeating those safety mechanisms, an explosion is practically impossible.

Foods to be canned are packed into hot glass jars using either the fresh-pack or the hot-pack method. The methods are pretty much self-explanatory from their names: Fresh-packed foods are put into the jars fresh and then hot liquid, brine, or syrup is added, and hot-packed foods are put into jars after having been heated to boiling. In some cases, either method can be used. Once packed, the jar is filled with liquid (brine, broth, syrup, pickling juice, etc. depending on the recipe) up to within 1/4 to 1 inch from the top of the jar. This space is called headspace and is needed to accommodate the expansion of the food in the jar as it is heated and allow for a good vacuum seal.

Using a Boiling Water Canner

Boiling water canners come with a wire rack that holds the jars so that they won't be sitting on the bottom of the canner or bumping into each other and breaking. Using a rack ensures that water of the same temperature surrounds the jars on all sides so that heating is even and therefore the best results are obtained.

Jars need to be sterilized for canning. My method is a little different from that in most books, but it works quite well, and I've never had a jar spoil.

1. Fill the canner halfway with the hottest water from the tap.
2. Put the jars you plan to use in the rack, without any lids.
3. Submerge the rack and jars in the canner, adding enough tap water to completely fill

all the jars and stand 1-1/2 inches above the tops of the jars.

4. Put on the lid and bring water to a vigorous boil, then adjust the heat to obtain a steady rolling boil.

5. Meanwhile, put a smaller pot on the stove without water, uncovered, but apply no heat. Put the lids (but not the bands) in this pot, making sure that the sealing compound is facing up.

6. Remove the jars from the canner one at a time using a jar lifter, and empty the boiling water in them into the smaller pot until it is nearly full and set them aside on a dish towel. (Once the smaller pot is full, empty the water in the remaining jars into the sink.) Keep the lids in the standing boiling water at this point—additional heating of the lids is not required.

7. Lift up the rack in the canner so that it is supported by the sides of the canner.

8. Put the product into the jars (a special canning funnel is helpful for this), allowing for proper headspace, get the lids out of the hot water in the smaller pot one at a time using tongs, and place them on the jars, then secure with a screw band tightened only finger-tight. (If you tighten it any more than that, the jar will break when you heat it in the canner.)

9. Put the filled jars in the wire rack, and submerge them in the water in the canner.

10. Turn up the heat on the burner a bit if needed to maintain a steady rolling boil. Start the timer once that boil has been achieved and put the lid on the canner.

11. Once the appropriate time has elapsed, remove the jars and place them on a dish towel at least 2 inches from each other on all sides and allow to sit undisturbed for at least 12 hours.

12. If additional product (more than one canner load) is being processed, pour the water back into the canner from the smaller pot, put clean jars in, and add any needed water to completely fill and submerge with 1-1/2 inches of water on top of the jars, then repeat the process starting at Step 4.

Using a Pressure Canner

Each pressure canner is a little different, so read the manufacturer's directions and employ those in preference to mine if there is a contradiction. Pressure canners don't rely on completely submerging the jars. Instead, they rely on surrounding the jars with superheated steam at 240 degrees. They also come with a rack, but instead of being made of wire to hold jars securely in place like with a boiling water canner, it is a simple aluminum plate with holes in it. Put it in the canner so that the holes are facing up. When using a pressure canner, I don't sterilize the jars before use. Instead, I just make sure they are extremely clean, and I keep them in a large pot of near-boiling water at a simmer. You can also wash them in a dishwasher and keep them hot with the dishwasher's heating element.

1. Put the rack in the canner and put three inches of very hot tap water into the bottom.

2. Put already-filled and lidded jars on the rack using a jar lifter, leaving some space between the jars.

3. Put the lid on the canner, but leave off the weighted gage, turn up the heat until steam

starts coming out of the port where you would put the weighted gage, and let the steam exhaust for 10 minutes.

4. Put the weighted gage on the port and keep the heat adjusted for a steady rocking motion of the gage. Start timing from when the steady rocking motion starts.

5. Once the time is up, turn off the heat and let the canner sit until the dial gage reads zero or when no steam escapes when the weighted gage is nudged. Wait an additional 2 minutes just to be sure.

6. Remove the cover and then remove the jars with a jar lifter and put them on a towel, leaving 2 inches between them on all sides.

7. Leave the jars undisturbed for 24 hours.

Fruits

Practically any fruit can be canned, and all except figs are sufficiently acidic that they can be canned without additives. (Figs require the addition of one teaspoon of lemon juice per pint.) Fruit should be in peak condition, free from obvious blemishes or rot, and well washed. To be sufficiently heated during the canning process, fruits that are larger than one inch should be cut up so that no single piece is larger than a one inch cube. Pits and stones of large-seeded fruit should be removed, and the fruit should be treated in an antioxidant solution, particularly once it has been cut to prevent discoloration. Antioxidant solutions can be bought commercially, or you can make your own by mixing 3/4 cup of bottled lemon juice with a gallon of water.

Fruits are usually canned in sugar syrups because the sugar helps the fruit keep its color, shape, and flavor, although the sugar isn't strictly necessary to prevent bacterial spoilage. If you prefer, can the fruits by using plain water rather than a syrup. I don't recommend the use of artificial sweeteners in syrup because saccharine turns bitter from canning and aspartame loses its sweetness. (If you have ever bought a diet soda and thought that it tasted a bit like dirt, that means that the product was stored in an area of high temperature and the artificial sweetener was damaged.) A "very light" syrup uses two tablespoons of sugar per cup of water, a "light" syrup uses four tablespoons per cup of water and a "medium" syrup uses seven tablespoons per cup of water.

To fresh-pack fruits, add them to the jars and then pour simmering syrup (or water) into the jar until it is filled up to within 1/4 inch of the rim. Put the lids and screw bands on the jars finger-tight, and completely submerge in a boiling water canner for the specified time for that particular fruit. Then remove the jars from the canner and leave them to cool for at least 12 hours. Hot-packed fruits are handled pretty much the same except that the fruit is mixed with the syrup and brought to a light boil, and then fruit and syrup are added to the jar together.

Applesauce

Home-canned applesauce was a favorite of mine as a kid—I'd open up a couple of homemade biscuits on my plate, heap a generous quantity of applesauce on top, and dig in. Applesauce canned at home is simple, delicious, rich, and flavorful—nothing like the homogenized products available at the grocery store. Naturally, the same process used for applesauce can also be used for pears, quinces, and other fruits. Feel free to experiment!

Here is my recipe and procedure for semichunky applesauce. Yield: 22–26 pints

Semichunky Applesauce

- 1 bushel of at least two types of apples, one type being rather sweet
- a bag of white and/or brown sugar (the actual amount added depends on your taste and the apples selected)
- cinnamon to taste
- allspice to taste
- nutmeg to taste
- lemon if desired

Procedure

- Wash 3/4 of the apples and remove stems, cut up into 1-inch chunks, including the core and peels, and put into a very large pot with about 1-inch of water in the bottom. (You can buy a simple contraption for a few bucks that cores and cuts apples into segments in just one motion—I recommend it highly!) Dip in an antioxidant solution once cut.
- Cook until all of the chunks are soft throughout. Start off on high heat and then lower to medium-high.
- Run the cooked apples through a strainer to remove the skins and seeds and put them back in the pot. (You can do this hot if you are careful.) I use a Villaware V200 food strainer because I could get it for less than $50 and it came with the right screen for my two favorite foods—applesauce and spaghetti sauce. There are a number of strainers on the market—including the classic Squeezo strainer—that will also work fine.
- Peel and core the remaining apples, cut up into small chunks, and add them to the pot

as well. (I have a "Back to Basics" Peel-Away apple peeler that peels, cores, and slices quickly in a single operation. It costs less than $20 at a cooking store.)

- Continue cooking on medium-high until the newly added chunks are soft.
- Add sugar, lemon, and spices to taste. You will probably need less than 1/4 cup of sugar per pint if you used some sweet apples.
- Reduce heat to a simmer to keep the sauce hot while canning.
- Pour the sauce into freshly washed pint or quart canning jars, leaving 1/2 inch of headspace.
- Put on the lids and bands finger-tight.
- Completely submerge jars in boiling water in a boiling water canner for 15 minutes for pints or 20 minutes for quarts.
- Allow the jars to cool in a draft-free place for at least 12 hours before removing the bands, labeling, and storing in a cool dry place for up to two years.
- Enjoy!

Jellies

Jellies are made from fruit juice and sugar, and use heat and sugar for their preservation. The distinctive consistency of jelly comes from an interaction between the acids in the fruit, the pectin it contains, the sugar, and heat. Many fruits contain enough natural acid and pectin to make jelly without having to add anything but sugar. These include sour apples, crab apples, sour cane fruits, cranberries, gooseberries, grapes, and currants. Some fruits are slightly deficient in acid, pectin, or both and will require a small amount of added lemon juice, pectin, or both. These include ripe apples, ripe blackberries, wine grapes, cherries, and elderberries. Finally, some fruits simply won't make jelly without adding a significant quantity of lemon juice and/or pectin. These include strawberries, apricots, plums, pears, blueberries, and raspberries.

Because sugar plays an important role in the preservation of jellies, the amount called for in a recipe shouldn't be reduced. It also plays an important role in making the product gel, so using too little sugar can result in a syrup instead of a jelly.

The juice used to make jelly can be extracted in a number of ways. If you use a juice machine, use it only for fruits that would require added pectin anyway, such as berries, plums, and pears. This is because a juice machine won't properly extract the pectin from high-pectin fruits. The traditional way of extracting the juice is to clean and cut up the whole fruit (it is important to leave the peels on because pectin is concentrated near the peel) and put it in a flat-bottom pot on the stove with added water. For soft fruits, use just enough water to prevent scorching, but with hard fruits like pears you might need as much as a cup of water per pound of fruit. The fruit is cooked over medium heat until soft and then poured through a jelly bag. If you want a crystal-clear product (which I don't personally care about but many folks find aesthetically important), it is important not to squeeze the jelly bag but instead let the juice come through naturally and slowly. You should get about one cup of juice per pound of fruit. Jelly bags in various sizes can be purchased from cooking stores and over the Internet. If you use a juice machine, you should still strain the resulting juice through a jelly bag. If you can't find jelly bags, you can use a double-layer of cheesecloth lining a colander instead.

Once the juice has been extracted, it is combined with sugar and other ingredients (e.g., lemon juice and/or pectin depending on the recipe) and boiled on the stove until it reaches a temperature of 220 degrees as measured with a candy thermometer. The boiling point of pure water is 212 degrees, but that boiling point is raised when other substances such as sugar are added to the water. As water evaporates and the proportion of sugar in the water increases, the boiling point will slowly increase. If you live in the mountains, subtract 2 degrees for every 1,000 feet you live above sea level. So if you live at 3,000 feet, subtract 6 degrees—so boil the mixture only until it reaches 214 degrees. This is because the higher you are above sea level, the more easily water will evaporate because of lower air pressure.

Once the required temperature has been reached, fill sterilized jars with the hot mixture up to 1/4 inch from the top, put the two-piece caps on the jars finger-tight, and process in a boiling water canner for five minutes for half-pint or pint size. There are all sorts of jelly recipes on the Internet, but here are two of my favorites.

Strawberry Rhubarb Jelly
- 3 pints of strawberries
- 1-1/2 lbs of rhubarb stalks
- 6 cups of sugar
- 3/4 cup of liquid pectin

Pulverize and then liquefy the strawberries and rhubarb in a blender. Using either a jelly bag or two layers of cheesecloth, gently squeeze out 3-1/2 cups of juice and put it in a saucepan, mixing with the sugar, and then bring to a rolling boil. Add the pectin and allow to boil vigorously for *one minute only*, remove from heat, and immediately pour into hot sterile jars, leaving 1/4 inch of headspace. Process five minutes in a boiling water canner. Yield: 5 half-pints.

Apple Jelly
- 5 lbs apples
- 5 whole cloves
- 1/2 tsp cinnamon
- 8 cups water
- 8 cups sugar

Wash the apples and cut them in quarters, and put them in a covered casserole pan with the eight cups of water and spices. Put in the oven at 225 degrees overnight. In the morning, strain through cheesecloth or a jelly bag and collect the liquid. Add it to the cooking pot one cup at a time, simultaneously adding one cup of sugar for every cup of liquid. Heat to a rolling boil, stirring constantly, and check with a candy thermometer until it is boiling at 220 degrees. Immediately pour into hot sterilized pint or half-pint jars, tighten the lids finger-tight, and process for five minutes in a boiling water canner. Yield: 8 half-pints.

*

The same techniques covered in the recipes above can be used successfully with other fruits. For fruits high in natural pectin and acid, use the second recipe as a guide, and use the first recipe as a guide for fruits lacking pectin. For fruits that lack both pectin and acidity, use the first recipe as a guide but add 1-1/2 tsp of lemon juice per cup of liquid. Jams are made the same way except the entire fruit is pulverized and used, rather than just the juice.

Brined Pickles and Kraut

Pickling preserves food by raising its level of acidity. It is used for foods that are not naturally acidic enough to be safely canned using a boiling water method. The two methods most widely used are lactic acid fermentation in brine, and infusing with vinegar.

Brine fermentation is most often used with cucumbers to make kosher-style dill pickles, but it is also used to make sauerkraut. Many other vegetables—like collard greens—can also be processed this way, but since I've never tried it myself, I can't guarantee the results will be tasty! There are three very important aspects of doing brine fermentation. First, keep everything clean. Second, use only plain salt with no additives whatsoever, or all sorts of cloudiness and discolorations will result. (Regular salt contains anticaking agents that will make the brine cloudy as well as iodine that will inhibit proper fermentation. Use canning salt!) Finally, pay close attention to the correct procedure, or your pickles will be soft and possibly even slimy.

Brine fermentation can take several weeks. It is also temperature sensitive and works best at temperatures ranging from 55 to 75 degrees. Before starting brined pickles, make sure you have both the time and the space to leave the containers undisturbed for a while. You should only use glass, nonchipped enamel, or food-grade plastic containers for fermentation. Under no circumstances should you consider using a metallic container because the product will become contaminated and possibly even poisonous. Don't use old-fashioned wooden barrels because sterilizing them is practically impossible. Start off with well-cleaned containers and well-washed produce.

Brined Dill Pickles
- 5 lbs of 3- to 4-inch pickling cucumbers
- 3 heaping Tbsp whole pickling spice
- 8 heads of fresh dill (1/3 of a bunch)

- 3/4 cup white (distilled) vinegar
- 1/2 cup pickling salt
- 5 pints (10 cups) of clean pure water

The proportions of salt, vinegar, and water in this recipe are not approximations—measure them exactly! You can double or quadruple the recipe if you keep the proportions the same for a larger batch of pickles. Put half of the pickling spices and a light layer of dill in the bottom of a clean food-grade plastic pail or pickling crock. Put in the cucumbers. Mix the remaining dill and spices with the salt, vinegar, and water and pour over the cucumbers. If the amount of liquid isn't enough to come about two inches above the cucumbers, make more liquid from water, salt, and vinegar according to the same proportions. Take a clean plate and place it on top of the cucumbers so they are held completely under the brine. The plate may need to be weighted down with a second plate. Cover the container loosely with plastic wrap covered with a clean towel held on with a couple of bungee cords tied together around the container like a big rubber band. Try to keep at room temperature—certainly no warmer than 72 degrees and no cooler than 60 degrees.

Uncover and check the pickles for scum once a day. Use a clean spoon to scoop off any scum, then put the towel back on. This should be the only time the pickles are uncovered. After three weeks, check the pickles by removing one from the container, cutting it lengthwise, and tasting it. If it is translucent and tastes like a good dill pickle, you are ready to can the pickles. If not, wait another week and try again.

Once the pickles are ready, remove them from the brine and pack into cleaned and cooled glass jars with a couple of heads of dill added to each jar. Take the brine, pour it into a large saucepan, and bring it to a boil, then pour it over the pickles in the jars, leaving 1/4-inch headspace. If you run out of brine, make additional brine from 4 pints of water, 1/4 cup of salt and 2 cups of vinegar raised to boiling. (Again, proportions are exact rather than approximate—use measuring cups!)

Put the lids on finger-tight, and process 10 minutes for pints or 15 minutes for quarts in a boiling water canner. Yield: 10 pints.

Sauerkraut
- Cabbage
- Canning/pickling salt

Any sort of cabbage can be used for this recipe, but larger heads tend to be sweeter. Remove any damaged outer leaves, quarter the heads, and remove the hard cores, then weigh the cabbage on a kitchen scale. Weighing the cabbage is important because the weight determines the amount of salt to use—3 Tbsp of salt per 5 pounds of cabbage. Shred the cabbage into slices of about 1/8 inch thickness, and using clean hands thoroughly mix the cabbage with the salt. Put the mixture into a five-gallon food-grade plastic container a little at a time and use a clean potato masher to mash the mixture until enough juice has been squeezed out of the cabbage that at least one or two inches of juice are above the cabbage by the time all the cabbage has been added.

Fill and seal a noncolored food-grade plastic bag with a mixture of 6 Tbsp salt and one gallon of water, and put this on the cabbage to weigh it down and keep it completely submerged, then cover the top of the container with plastic wrap. Keep the container at room temperature, and in four weeks, your sauerkraut will be ready. Just like with the brined pickles above, check daily for scum and remove any that you find. Once the kraut is ready, pour it in a large pot (or a portion of it at a time depending on the relative size of your pot) and heat while stirring to 190 degrees as indicated by a candy thermometer. Do NOT let it boil. Pack into clean canning jars and add brine to leave 1/4 inch of headspace, and process in a boiling water canner for 15 minutes for pints or 20 minutes for quarts. Yield: depends on how much cabbage you use.

Quick Process Pickles

Quick process pickles rely on vinegar for their acidity rather than fermentation, so they are faster and easier to make. (And you needn't worry about scum!) The vinegar used to make pickles lends its own character to the pickles, so be cautious about using flavored vinegars such as red wine, cider, or balsamic vinegar unless specifically required in a recipe. When the type of vinegar isn't mentioned in a recipe, use white distilled vinegar. The preservation process relies on a certain specific amount of acid, so always use vinegar that is 5% acidity.

Bread and Butter Pickles
* 4 lbs cucumbers, washed but not peeled
* 3 thinly sliced medium onions
* 1/3 cup of canning salt
* 4 cups distilled vinegar
* 3 cups sugar
* 2 Tbsp mustard seed
* 1 Tbsp + 1 tsp celery seed
* 1-1/2 tsp turmeric
* 2 tsp whole black pepper

Slice the cucumbers 1/4-inch thick and the onions as thinly as practical. Combine all of the ingredients except the cucumbers and onions in a large sauce pot and bring to a simmer (not a boil!). Add the cucumber and onion slices, and bring to a very light boil before turning down the heat to low. Pack the slices into jars and then fill with pickling liquid to 1/4 inch headspace, and put the lids on the jars finger-tight.

For the most crisp pickles, pasteurize by placing the jars in water deep enough to be at least 1 inch over the top of the jar lids that is kept at 180–185 degrees (check with a candy thermometer) for 30 minutes. Alternately, you can process in boiling water for 10 minutes for either pints or quarts. Allow to sit six weeks before using for the development of full flavor. Yield: 4 pints.

Vegetables

Vegetables (other than tomatoes) are not acidic enough to be canned using the boiling water method. Instead, they must be processed in a pressure canner for a fairly long period of time. The process is essentially the same for all vegetables, the only difference being in the processing time. For larger vegetables, cut into pieces so that there is at least one dimension less than 1/2-inch thick, bring pieces to a boil in water (to which 1/2 tsp of salt per quart can optionally be added), pour hot into clean jars allowing the right amount of head space, put on the caps finger-tight, and process for the time specified in Table 19. You might consider using a little sliver (1/2-inch × 1-inch) of kombu kelp instead of salt. Kelp enhances the flavor of canned vegetables because of the natural glutamaic acid that it contains.

Generally, the pressure canning methods employed with vegetables destroy a good portion of the vitamin C, so I recommend freezing instead. Regardless, the macronutrient and mineral values of vegetables remain intact after canning, so it is worthwhile if you don't have a freezer or reliable electric service.

Meat

Meat is usually better vacuum sealed and frozen, but where the electrical supply is unreliable or too expensive, canning meat is a viable alternative. Because canning times and temperatures for meats are significant, most vitamins that can be destroyed by heat, especially vitamin C, are destroyed in the process. On the other hand, both the protein and mineral value is unaffected, so as long as you have plenty of vegetables in your diet, canned meat isn't a problem.

While the USDA says that putting raw meat into jars and then processing it is safe, it is my opinion that the flavor suffers. So I recommend that all meats first be soaked for an hour in a brine made with 1 Tbsp salt to a gallon of water and then at least lightly browned in a little vegetable oil until rare and then packing into the jars. Once the meat is packed into the jars, the jars should be filled with boiling water, meat broth, or tomato juice to leave the amount of headspace described in Table 19. Most people prefer 1/2 tsp of salt added per pint, but this is optional. Put on the lids finger-tight, and process for the appropriate length of time. You can season meats before canning them, but avoid sage because the prolonged high temperatures can cause bitterness. Also, any meat broth you use *shouldn't contain flour, corn starch, or any other thickening agent* because under pressure canning conditions, thickening agents congeal and make it impossible to get all

of the air properly evacuated from the cans, and the risk of spoilage is increased.

Soups, Stews, and Other Mixtures

When canning anything that is a mixture of more than one ingredient, the time and headspace requirements from Table 19 that are the longest and largest for any of the ingredients apply. So if, for example, a mixture of carrots and peas were being canned, the processing time and headspace requirements for peas would be used since those are the greatest. The same warning about thickening agents regarding meats applies to stews as well.

Buffalo Stew
- 4 lbs buffalo stew meat cut into 1-inch cubes
- 12 medium red potatoes cut into 1/2 inch cubes
- 5 medium yellow onions, diced
- 2 lbs of carrots sliced 1/4-inch thick
- 2 stalks celery
- 1 Tbsp cooking oil
- 1 tsp salt
- 1/2 tsp ground black pepper
- 1 tsp thyme
- 1 clove garlic
- 3 quarts water

Get the three quarts of water boiling in a large saucepan and brown the stew meat in oil in the bottom of another large saucepan. Add all of the spices and vegetables to the meat, stir thoroughly, cover, and allow to cook down for five minutes. Then pour in the three quarts of boiling water slowly and carefully, and bring everything to a boil. Put into jars leaving 1 inch of headspace, and process in a pressure canner for 75 minutes for pints or 90 minutes for quarts. Yield: 9 pints.

Freezing

Like canning, freezing has its pros and cons. In its favor is that it is easier and quicker to freeze vegetables and meats than it is to pressure can them, and the resulting product is usually closer to fresh in terms of quality. Some things, like broccoli, are just plain inedible when canned but perfectly fine when frozen. The downside is that when freezing an appreciable amount of food, a large freezer is required—which isn't cheap. Figure at least $300 for a new one at current market price. Also a consideration is the ongoing ever-increasing cost of electricity. And, if you are in an area prone to long electrical outages, you could lose the entire contents of your freezer if you don't maintain a backup power supply of some sort. So you'll have to weigh the advantages and disadvantages. We have a reliable electric supply and not a lot of spare time at my house, so we do a lot of freezing.

I used to freeze in regular freezer bags from the grocery store or wrap things in freezer paper. No more! Now, the only method I use, and the only method I recommend, is vacuum sealing. Vacuum sealing consistently yields a superior product that keeps up to five times longer, so it is what I'll describe.

Getting a Sealer

I got my first vacuum sealer at a Boy Scouts yard sale, complete with instructions and a bunch of bags, for $3. Evidently, people often purchase sealers thinking they will be handy and use them once or twice, and then they end up in the yard sale bin. It may not be practical to wait around for a sealer to show up at a yard sale while harvest season comes and goes—but it never hurts to look.

There is another big reason why these sealers end up in the yard sale bin: the price of bags. The name-brand bags at the store that carry the same name as the sealer you buy will cost over $0.50 each. You don't have to do a lot of math to see that spending that much on just the bag to store a product (like broccoli) that you could buy frozen at the store for $0.99 isn't a winning proposition. I'll give you some solutions to that problem in the next section.

There are two suitable sealers on the market in various configurations available at department stores—the Seal-a-Meal and the FoodSaver. I've found both to be adequate, though you will find the FoodSaver a bit more expensive. I prefer the Seal-a-Meal since its design allows it to work better with a wide variety of bags. These are light-duty home-use units. They work fine for the amount of freezing that I do for the carbohydrates and vegetables for a family of three because we tend to freeze in relatively small batches of 10 or fewer packages at a time. Heavy-duty commercial units are available—but you should hold off on these until you see if the less expensive home-use units will meet your needs. Certainly they will work fine as you ramp up for the first couple of years.

Bags

As mentioned earlier, the name-brand bags for sealers are expensive—sometimes even more than $0.50 apiece. Luckily, you can get around this problem a number of ways. First, keep an eye out for the sealers and bags at yard sales. Second, use plastic rolls instead of premade bags because by cutting them to size for what you are freezing, you will use a lot less and save money. Finally, you can buy bags and rolls from brands other than those made by the manufacturer of your sealer. Two sources come to mind. First, a number of manufacturers make less expensive bags and/or rolls including Black and Decker, FoodFresh Vacstrip, and Magic Vac. These usually cost less than half of what the other bags do. Second, check the Internet. There are eBay stores dedicated strictly to vacuum sealers that offer good deals and also Web sites dedicated entirely to getting good prices on bags, such as vacuum-sealer-bags.com. With these resources in hand, you will see the superior properties of vacuum sealing become financially viable.

The Freezing Process

Freezing is a six-part process that requires harvesting, blanching, cooling, drying, sealing, and freezing. First, since no form of food preservation can actually improve the quality of food, harvest as close to freezing time as possible, and thoroughly clean the produce. Hose it off with the garden hose outside first, then put it in a big bucket to soak that contains two tablespoons of salt per gallon of water to draw out any insects. Then cut it up as needed, rinse out the salt, and weigh it into portions using a kitchen scale. For vegetables, figure 4 ounces per person. So for a family of four, you'll want your bagged portions to be about 16 ounces, or 12 ounces for a family of three.

⊘ Weighing produce for consistent portions helps with menu planning.

Next comes blanching. Blanching serves to inhibit the enzymes that destroy the quality of food in storage. There are two common methods—placing the produce in boiling water for a period of time, or steaming it for a slightly longer period of time. Both methods work, but I recommend steaming because it preserves more of the vitamin content of the food. The blanching time varies depending on what is being frozen (see Table 18).

When the allotted blanching time has passed, the produce should be dumped into a bucket of ice water so that it is cooled down immediately. (I slip a metal colander into the bucket first so that it holds the produce and makes it easy to retrieve.)

Leave the produce in the ice water for the same amount of time as it was being blanched, then take it out and put it between a couple of

⊗ This steam blancher is just one of many steamers available.

⊗ Cooling down the produce in ice water after blanching.

Table 18: **Blanching Times**

Produce	Water Blanch	Steam Blanch
Artichoke, globe	7–10 min	Not recommended
Artichoke, Jerusalem (chunks)	5 min	7 min
Asparagus spears	3 min	4 min
Beans, lima, butter, edamame	3 min	5 min
Beans, string	4 min	6 min
Beet roots, sliced 1/4"	12 min	Not recommended
Broccoli	4 min	4 min
Brussels sprouts	4 min	6 min
Cabbage, shredded	2 min	3 min
Carrots	3 min	5 min
Corn (on the cob)	10 min	Not recommended
Corn (whole kernel)	5 min	7 min
Greens of all sorts	3 min	5 min
Parsnips, sliced	2 min	3 min
Peas, shelled of all sorts	2 min	3 min
Peppers	3 min	4 min
Potatoes, sliced/cubed	5 min	7 min
Turnips, diced	3 min	4 min

superclean, dry, and fluffy towels to pat dry. You have to do this when vacuum sealing otherwise the large water content gets in the way of making a good seal.

Once the produce has been dried, it is placed into bags and sealed. After the bags have been sealed, put them into the freezer in various locations so that they will freeze more quickly. Come back and rearrange them in 24 hours.

For some vegetables, particularly potatoes, and Jerusalem artichokes, discoloration can be a problem. This is easily solved by adding one tablespoon of citric acid or two tablespoons of lemon juice per gallon of water to the ice water being used to cool the vegetables after blanching.

Meats and fruits aren't handled the same way as vegetables. Usually, meats are frozen raw, though I find that they freeze better if first soaked in a light brine (one tablespoon salt/gallon) to draw out any blood and then patted dry. The reason for drawing out the blood is so it doesn't interfere with vacuum sealing. Another way to accomplish the same thing (which I do with ground meats)

⊗ Sealing with a vacuum sealer preserves freshness longer.

⊗ Drying the produce with freshly cleaned towels before bagging.

is put the meat in a regular zipper bag and put it in the freezer overnight, then remove it from the zipper bag and immediately seal it in a vacuum bag—the frozen juices then won't interfere with sealing. With wild game such as squirrel or deer, I recommend soaking for an hour in a light brine, as that removes some of the "gaminess" from the meat.

Fruit is best frozen in a sugar syrup like used when canning. Once the sugar is dissolved in the water, you can add 1/4 teaspoon of vitamin C or 2 teaspoons of lemon juice per pint of syrup to prevent darkening. Slice or dice the fruit and put it in a can or freeze jar or suitable plastic container and then cover the fruit with syrup, leaving one inch of headspace to allow for expansion in the freezer.

Dehydrating

Drying food is one of the oldest methods of food preservation. By removing most of the moisture from foods, enzymatic action and microbial growth are retarded, and the food will keep for a long time. Food loses more nutritional value from drying than from freezing, and dehydrated foods will seldom reconstitute with water to look like appetizing fresh produce. But even at that, dehydrated products make a conveniently stored, tasty, and healthy addition to soups, stews, and sauces. When my daughter was little, I used to powder mixed dehydrated vegetables in a blender and stir that powder into her spaghetti sauce so she'd get a mix of vegetables without knowing it. She also loves dehydrated apple rings as a snack, and other dehydrated fruits make a great addition to oatmeal in the morning.

Just like vacuum sealers, dehydrators run the gamut from inexpensive units available at department stores costing less than $50 all the way to commercial-sized behemoths. I recommend starting with a small model that includes a fan and thermostat since that will be easy and trouble free. You can always switch to a more expensive commercial or even homemade unit later. (Dehydrators lend themselves easily to homemade solutions, and literally dozens of free designs—including solar designs—are available on the Internet just by doing a Web search that includes the terms "homemade" and "dehydrator.") You can use a dehydrator for fruits, vegetables, and meats, though the process for the three is somewhat different.

Vegetables destined for the dehydrator need to be cut in slices no more than 1/4 inch thick and blanched just as though they were going to be frozen. This helps them dehydrate better and keep longer. Fruits should also be sliced no more than 1/4-inch thick and then dipped in a solution containing one tablespoon lemon juice per quart of water before being put in the dehydrator. Fruit shouldn't be blanched. Every dehydrator is different in terms of its drying characteristics, so use the drying times and temperatures recommended in the literature that comes with your particular model.

Meats, especially ground meat and poultry, are problematic because dehydrating is not the same thing as cooking, and the temperature seldom gets high enough to ensure pathogen destruction. This becomes an issue because bacterial contamination of these meats is common, so failure to thoroughly cook them can result in serious illness or even death. There are some jerky mixes available at department stores that are specifically formulated to deal with potential contamination of ground meats through the use of nitrites. If you choose to use one of these mixes, follow the directions precisely! Outside of this exception, I don't recommend making jerky or dried meat from either ground meats or poultry. Other meats—like beef steak/roast, venison, buffalo, and so forth—are perfectly fine.

Most jerky recipes are for raw meat. In recent years, a number of universities have done studies and concluded that the practice can no longer be considered safe and that meat for jerky should be precooked in a boiling marinade. With the foregoing in mind, then, here is my general-purpose jerky recipe.

Brett's General-Purpose Jerky
- Start with prefrozen and partially thawed beef, buffalo, moose, venison, and so on. Trim

away any visible fat and slice meat into uniform 1/4-inch-thick slices across the grain.

- Create marinade in a saucepan by combining 2-1/4 cups of water, 3/4 cup teriyaki soy sauce, 1/2 tsp of liquid smoke, and a dash of Tabasco sauce. Raise to a gentle rolling boil.

- Putting only a few strips of meat in at a time, boil a few strips in the marinade until uniformly gray then remove from the marinade with tongs and place on the drying rack of the dehydrator. Repeat this process until all of the meat strips have been used.

- Dry according to manufacturer's directions, or at a temperature of 140 to 150 degrees for six or more hours.

- Test to see if the jerky is done by taking a piece off the dehydrator, letting it cool to room temperature, then bending it. If it cracks but doesn't break, it is done.

Root Cellaring

Root cellaring is one of the best methods of preserving certain foods, including onions, cabbage, potatoes, carrots, parsnips, and apples, among others. The key to success at cold storage is establishing conditions conducive to long storage life, and these conditions include darkness, certain temperatures, and particular ranges of humidity.

Many things can be preserved via root cellaring for some small period of time ranging from days to a couple of weeks, while others can be preserved for times ranging from several weeks to several months. Invariably, food that can be stored only for a short time is better preserved via some other method. This includes all brassicas except late cabbage, asparagus, beans, sweet corn, cucumbers, summer squash, lettuce, tomatoes, eggplant, spinach, melons, and peas.

Other foods, though, can be preserved in a root cellar for extended periods assuming proper temperatures and humidity are maintained. Unfortunately, these aren't the same for all crops, but thankfully we don't have to be too fine-grained in our specification because, in general, crops that do well in a root cellar fall into broad categories.

Everything but onions and garlic will do well with humidity ranging from 85% to 95%. Onions and garlic require humidity ranging from 50% to 75%. All fruits store best at temperatures as close to 32 degrees F as possible, and almost all vegetables as well, except for late potatoes, which do best at 35 degrees F to 40 degrees F.

So, in general, cold storage requires an environment that is humid, dark, and close to 32 degrees F without going under. The real question becomes how to create and maintain such an environment in homes that were not designed with root cellars.

If you have a cellar of any sort, a portion of it can be turned into a root cellar simply be walling off a corner, insulating the walls thoroughly, providing some sturdy shelves up off the floor, and installing some ventilation that will allow cool air to enter near the floor (PVC pipe is good for this) and warm air to exit near the ceiling. You'll want a thermometer so you can keep an eye on the temperature and shut off or limit ventilation if it starts to sink too low. (This may or may not be a problem depending on where you live.) If humidity is insufficient, you can add a humidifier.

Most produce should be placed in open-weave baskets and kept up off the floor and shouldn't be piled deeply as the pressure from the weight of produce on the lower layers could cause premature rotting. Fruits should be stored only one layer deep and, if possible, individually wrapped in tissue and not touching other fruit. Carrots and parsnips should have the tops snapped off and then be buried in dampened clean sand in a box sitting on the floor.

If you don't have a basement, you could bury a drum in the ground or build an external root cellar. For more details on how to build root cellars, check out the book *Root Cellaring* by Mike and Nancy Bubel.

Table 19: **Canning Times and Methods**

Food	Packing Method	Head-space	Canning Method	Time for Pints	Time for Quarts
Apples (sliced)	Hot packed	1/2"	Boiling water	20 min	25 min
Applesauce	Hot packed	1/2"	Boiling water	15 min	20 min
Asparagus	Hot packed	1"	Pressure (10 lbs)	30 min	40 min
Beans (dry)	Hot packed	1"	Pressure (10 lbs)	75 min	90 min
Beans (shelled lima)	Hot packed	1"	Pressure (10 lbs)	40 min	50 min
Beans (snap)	Hot packed	1"	Pressure (10 lbs)	20 min	25 min
Beef, lamb, pork, venison, and bear (strips, cubes, ground, or chopped)	Hot packed	1"	Pressure (10 lbs)	75 min	90 min
Beets (sliced)	Hot packed	1"	Pressure (10 lbs)	30 min	35 min
Berries (all types)	Either	1/2"	Boiling water	10 min	15 min
Carrots (sliced)	Hot packed	1"	Pressure (10 lbs)	25 min	30 min
Cherries	Fresh packed	1/2"	Boiling water	20 min	25 min
Cherries	Hot packed	1/2"	Boiling water	10 min	15 min
Corn	Hot packed	1"	Pressure (10 lbs)	55 min	85 min
Fish	Fresh packed	1"	Pressure (10 lbs)	100 min	Don't use quarts
Fruit purees	Hot packed	1/4"	Boiling water	15 min	20 min
Greens, spinach, chard, kale, collards	Hot packed	1"	Pressure (10 lbs)	70 min	90 min
Jams and jellies	Hot packed	1/4"	Boiling water	5 min	Don't use quarts
Meat stock (any nonseafood meat with seasoning)	Hot packed	1"	Pressure (10 lbs)	20 min	25 min
Peaches, pears, plums, and nectarines	Fresh packed	1/2"	Boiling water	25 min	30 min
Peaches, pears, plums, and nectarines	Hot packed	1/2"	Boiling water	20 min	25 min
Peas (shelled)	Hot packed	1"	Pressure (10 lbs)	40 min	40 min

Food	Packing Method	Head-space	Canning Method	Time for Pints	Time for Quarts
Peppers (hot/sweet)	Hot packed	1"	Pressure (10 lbs)	35 min	Don't use quarts
Pickles (fermented)	Fresh packed	1/2"	Boiling water	10 min	15 min
Pickles (quick process)	Hot or fresh	1/4"	Boiling water	10 min	15 min
Potatoes (1/2" cubes)	Hot packed	1"	Pressure (10 lbs)	35 min	40 min
Poultry, rabbit, or squirrel with bones	Hot packed	1-1/2"	Pressure (10 lbs)	65 min	75 min
Poultry, rabbit, or squirrel without bones	Hot packed	1-1/2"	Pressure (10 lbs)	75 min	90 min
Pumpkins and squash (pureed)	Hot packed	1"	Pressure (10 lbs)	55 min	90 min
Rhubarb	Hot packed	1/2"	Boiling water	10 min	10 min
Sweet potatoes (cubed)	Hot packed	1"	Pressure (10 lbs)	65 min	90 min
Tomatoes (acidified)	Fresh packed	1/4"	Boiling water	40 min	50 min
Tomatoes (acidified)	Hot packed	1/4"	Boiling water	35 min	45 min

20

Selling Your Produce

The mini-farm gains its first economic advantage through growing enough food to reduce family food bills. During the first two years of mini-farming, it is likely that the family will use all that can be produced. But in the third and subsequent years, it is quite possible to both reduce food bills and sell enough food to replace a job when the two economic aspects are added together. Growing enough food to reduce food bills is easy, but the idea of selling produce looks like a bear at first glance. And, certainly, it *is* a bear if you anticipate trying to persuade the local branch of an international conglomerate supermarket chain to buy your products. It is unlikely to work, and even if it did, it would be a bad idea because you'd be positioning yourself in competition with global corporations using massive economies of scale and below market rate labor, so you wouldn't make any money.

It is important to understand that just as there are areas in which a mini-farm is at a disadvantage compared to agribusiness, mini-farms have notable strengths that provide a competitive edge as well.

The hottest agricultural niche right now is organic produce. The organic label has caught on to such an extent that even major department stores are offering it. The problem is that along with this positive interest in chemical-free produce, major corporations have gotten into the act and have started to squeeze the small farmers out of the market.

But all is not lost. Large-scale agribusiness organics suffer from many of the same problems as conventional produce—especially problems associated with shipping long distance, picking produce before it ripens, and selecting varieties for shipping characteristics rather than flavor. This is where the small farmer has an insurmountable edge over the competition, because the small farmer can specialize in varieties selected for taste and provide naturally ripened produce that hasn't lost its nutrient content from sitting in a warehouse for two weeks.

Locally grown organic heirloom vegetables and herbs are extremely attractive to locally owned superettes, convenience stores, restaurants, and natural food stores, not to mention the neighbors!

There are other advantages that come from the fact that mini-farms operate on a small scale. A mini-farmer can talk to the owner of a local health food store or restaurant and strike a deal to grow specific crops. A large warehouse can't do that. The mini-farmer can also grow labor-intensive crops that resist automation and where the attention of the farmer can net a superior product. In addition, specialty crops can be selected. Specialty crops, like purple potatoes or exotic lettuces, make no sense at a large agribusiness scale but will find a ready market through farm stands, local stores, and restaurants. The "Biggest Little Farm in America" uses this approach to earn $238,000 on just 1/2 acre of land.[52] Considering all of this, it is no surprise that the number of small farms is increasing at a rate of 2% per year and is likely to continue increasing at that pace for as long as the next 20 years![53]

Sales to stores would, of course, be at wholesale rather than retail price. This cuts the profit margin but has the advantage of a ready market. Restaurants and neighbors—through delivery to the restaurant or setting up a farm stand—represent retail pricing. The downside is that getting business from restaurants can be difficult, and farm stand sales are uncertain, but the benefit in terms of higher profit margin merits consideration.

Folks who are likely to consider mini-farming may have difficulty seeing themselves as salespeople, but selling your produce is very different from other sorts of sales. First, you are selling something you have created with your own hands and in which you have pride. Second, you are selling something of incomparable quality. Finally, instead of trying to create an artificial need, you are selling something that everybody needs already. As a result, it is something that can be approached with a sense of personal integrity in the spirit of a truly mutually beneficial transaction.

Approaching a local restaurant owner or the proprietor of a small health food store is not difficult because you already have something that these folks want: superior vegetables from a local supplier. There is marketing and public relations value in using vegetables from a local source, and local produce has superior taste and nutritional quality because long-distance shipping is avoided. The key is simply to present a proposal that eliminates risk on the part of the owner while advancing mutual benefits.

---

[52] Macher, R. (1999) *Making Your Small Farm Profitable*

[53] Ibid

The largest risks for the local restaurant and health food store are lacking supply when it is needed and purchasing goods that either cannot be sold or would hurt their reputation. This latter concern is allayed by providing samples and consistently delivering the highest-quality goods. The first concern requires a little thought.

As a single small farm, a mini-farm doesn't have the scale to protect against crop losses, freak hail storms, and the like. In spite of the best intentions, a mini-farmer really can't promise unfailing supply. Likewise, a restaurant or store of even small size would sell far more produce than a mini-farm could supply in the best of seasons. The solution is to make it clear to the customers that the intent is to provide no more than 20%

of their needs, so their current relationships with larger suppliers remain intact. In this way, you will be able to sell all that you can produce, and your customer has no risks. This straightforward technique works extremely well.[54]

Organic and Certified Naturally Grown

Organic produce grown without chemical insecticides, fungicides, or fertilizers commands a premium price about 40% higher than conventional produce. It therefore stands to reason that organic production should be strongly

---

[54] Bartholomew, M. (1985) *Ca$h from Square Foot Gardening*

considered simply from a marketing perspective, not to mention for the health aspects.

The use of the term *organic* to refer to food products is regulated by federal law under the National Organic Program. The gist is that if the gross income from produce is less than $5,000 annually, a farmer can use the term to refer to products as long as they are truly grown using the standards of the program. If the gross income is greater than $5,000, then significant fees apply for certification, and a great deal of paperwork is required. The fees are generally on a sliding scale—meaning "the more you make, the more they take."

A mini-farm is likely to start out making less than $5,000 in gross sales yearly, so using organic labeling from the beginning is perfectly feasible; once that threshold is crossed, the funds for certification can be considered a cost of doing business. Even at that, it pays to shop around for a USDA-accredited certification agency whose fees don't gobble up all the profits! Many state departments of agriculture are accredited by the USDA, and this is the least expensive route.

An alternative to the expense of the National Organic Program is Certified Naturally Grown, a voluntary program that follows the same guidelines but has no associated fees. Certified Naturally Grown is oriented toward small local producers and features rigorous inspections offset by streamlined paperwork requirements. My own farm has been Certified Naturally Grown.

Taxes and Accounting

It should go without saying, but I'll say it anyway because it is important: Keep all of your paperwork, receipts, and so forth in order, and file your taxes properly on time. It is possible that by following the rules, you actually make minimal money after accounting for expenses, but it all must be properly accounted for or you'll ultimately have an unfortunate encounter with the IRS. There are a number of special deductions and rules applicable to farmers, and the IRS has a Web site dedicated to explaining these.

Outside of tax matters, careful accounting is important to your bottom line. As a small business, you need to know what you should be growing because it earns you a profit and what you should stop growing because it is losing you money. The only way to do this is to keep track of your income and expenses down to a crop-by-crop basis.

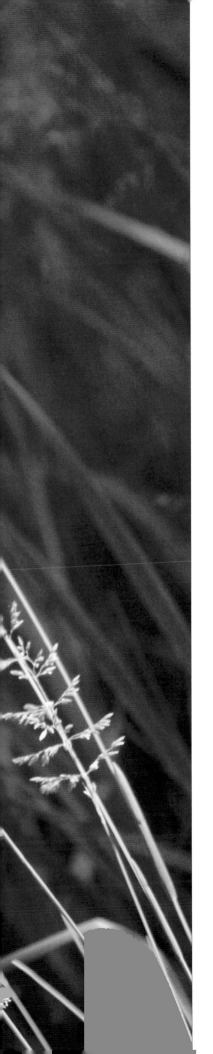

21

Putting It All Together

Especially if you are new to gardening or farming, the preceding chapters may seem to contain an overwhelming amount of information about a million things that you have to keep track of all at once in a delicately orchestrated dance: crop rotations, cover cropping, insect and disease prevention, seed starting, planting dates, and so forth. In a sense, it *is* finely choreographed, but there is a way to deal with all of this so that everything falls in place: Start small.

The easiest way to get the hang of all this while gaining some benefit and keeping expenses in line is to start a small garden composed of only three 4-foot × 25-foot raised beds—a mere 300 square feet. Within that space, all of the techniques described in this book can be practiced and fine-tuned to the individual circumstance, and minor mistakes are easily corrected. Also, and I am not kidding, by using intensive agricultural methods, you will easily grow more vegetables in 300 square feet than most people do in gardens seven times the size. Your problem won't be with gardening—it will be with storing everything it produces!

To give you an idea, in one 4-foot × 14-foot bed from April through September, my family harvested 22 pounds of broccoli, 8 pounds of cauliflower, 16 pounds of cabbage, 90 pounds of tomatoes, 23 pounds of pole beans, 40 pounds of cucumbers, and 15 pounds of potatoes, not to mention onions, beets, carrots, spinach, and Swiss chard in prodigious quantities. That is just from 56 square feet—so imagine what you can do with 300 square feet!

The point here is to start at a small and easily managed level while you get the hang of things and then expand from there. Expand as you gain confidence and ultimately start a small commercial enterprise as well.

The Garden Year

I count the garden year as beginning in fall, and I believe that you should as well. Fall is when all the activity from the prior season draws to a close with all of the garden refuse and leaves finding their way into the compost pile and cover crops being planted for the winter. Because things are somewhat rushed in the spring, fall is the best time to dig new beds and expand the space in use.

Through early winter in the northern United States there isn't really much to do except plan the garden and look through seed catalogs while staying warm. Now is the time to decide what you will grow and order the seeds. If you wait until spring to do this, you will be too late since many plants—like onion seedlings—need to be started in late winter to be ready to plant in the spring. Chilly fall and winter evenings are likewise a good time to separate out and prepare your own seeds from the prior season's harvest.

By the time late winter arrives, it is time to start seedlings for onions, leeks, chives, and many herbs. Shortly thereafter, the cole crops get started along with annual flowers. Then come the tomatoes and peppers. Around this same time, the onion and cole crops are being planted out, followed shortly by seeds for spinach and lettuce. Soon, carrots, beets, peas, turnips, and parsnips get planted. After the last frost date, the tomatoes, peppers, corn, and beans get planted, followed by squash. About the time the tomatoes are planted out, it is time to start seedlings for the fall planting of broccoli. And you will be harvesting the long-growing winter cover crops like winter wheat and vetch for the grain and to put on the compost pile.

You get the idea: Gardening doesn't start on the last-frost date. Instead, it starts in the fall! If you start in the fall and follow the timing charts in this book, you will most definitely collect a tremendous amount of food even if you start small.

Help around the Corner

For a variety of reasons—lifestyle, economics, philosophy, and you name it—small farms are springing up all over. Many of these new farmers are first-generation farmers, and they have already encountered a lot of what you will be experiencing. Unlike other industries in which everybody jealously guards trade secrets, farmers come together to help each other out. As a result, there are many initiatives filled with people ready and waiting with advice and wisdom that would otherwise require a PhD to obtain.

Such resources can be found on the Internet via a simple keyword search and via links from Cooperative Extension Service Web sites. Here in

New Hampshire, there are a number of farming organizations—including one sponsored by the state—intended specifically for beginning farmers! Similar groups exist all across the country.

Speaking of the Cooperative Extension Service, every state has at least one so-called land grant university. These universities were originally established under the Morrill Acts of 1862 and 1890 with primary missions to teach agriculture, classical studies, mechanical arts, and military tactics. The Hatch Act of 1887 established agricultural experiment stations at these universities to advance the state of agricultural science, and the Smith-Lever Act of 1914 established the Cooperative Extension Service to disseminate the data gained at the experiment stations. As a result, there is a branch of the Cooperative Extension Service associated with a land-grant university in every state; many of these services have branch offices in every county within a state.

The Cooperative Extension Service can provide, either in person or via publications or Web sites, a wide array of information. The available information ranges all the way from how to safely can foods at home to the specific varieties of apple trees that will grow best in your area. The amount of research and information available via the USDA, various state departments of agriculture, and Cooperative Extension Services is impressive and represents a valuable resource.

State governments also have their own agriculture departments under various names. These departments often have research grants available. Some do organic certification far less expensively than private organizations; many administer a plethora of programs designed to enhance the progress of agricultural endeavors in their respective states. They also, of course, publish a lot of regulations, which also should be examined, particularly regarding handling of livestock, creation of value-added products in the kitchen, sale of seeds, and so forth.

A number of private, semiprivate, and quasi-governmental agencies have a lot of information available as well. Baker Creek Heirloom Seeds has a bulletin board where people help each other with ideas and advice. The National Sustainable Agriculture Information Service offers a number of informative workshops and symposiums. Ecology Action offers self-teaching modules by mail order. Regional organic growers associations also hold workshops and annual events for information and networking.

So there are a lot of places to turn for help and advice—most of them at minimal or no expense. Millions of dollars are spent every year to establish the infrastructure that will help make you successful, so it makes sense to take advantage of it all.

The Final Analysis

Starting a mini-farm can provide you with the safest and most nutritious food available while saving more on the food budget year after year. The superior nutrition combined with outdoor exercise will make everyone healthier, and the economic benefits of selling excess production can enable any number of personal or family goals.

This book is a tour of everything you need to know to get started, but don't stop here! Go to the bibliography for a list of other recommended books. Knowledge is power in that it increases your odds of success in any endeavor.

From the Markham family to yours, we wish you all the best!

Bibliography

Ashworth, S. *Seed to seed*

Bartholomew, M. *Ca$h from square foot gardening*

Bartholomew, M. *Square foot gardening*

Bradley, F. *Rodale's garden answers*

Bubel, N. *The new seed starters handbook*

Campbell, S. *Let it rot!*

Coleman, E. *Four season harvest* and *The new organic grower*

Deppe, C. *Breed your own vegetable varieties*

Ellis, B.; Bradley, F. *The organic gardener's handbook of natural insect and disease control*

Gooch, B. *The ultimate guide to squirrel hunting*

Grounds, R. *The natural garden*

Jeavons, J. *How to grow more vegetables*

Jenkins, J. *The humanure handbook*

Johnson, J.; Johnson, M. *Successful small game hunting: Rediscovering our hunting heritage*

Kains, M. *Five acres and independence*

Macher, R. *Making your small farm profitable*

Mercer, L. *Storey's guide to raising poultry*

Pangman, J. *Chicken coops*

Richey, D. *The ultimate guide to deer hunting*

Schwenke, K. *Successful small scale farming*

Index of Tables

Alphabetical Index

Notes